A Dragger Across the West

By Craig Fox

Reality is THE MAKER'S TOOL

Dedicated To Those That Help…

To the memory of Lucy the Wonderdog:
fetcher extraordinaire, and devoted companion
through multiple treks, major journeys,
adventures and homes.

Edited by John Milbert
CFox1957@gmail.com

Table of Contents

Forward

When I first met Craig Fox, he'd just come into the Grande Ronde valley, in northeast Oregon, on foot. Not that unusual if he'd only been hitchhiking on I-84, but having done so overland from Colorado in the company of two burros and a dog made him immediately intriguing.

Being by nature and inclination unwilling to adopt the social herd mentality myself, we developed a friendship based on a mutual love of the outdoors, and a lack of the material acquisitiveness that seems to dominate most people's lives. We'd both rather hike big mountain timber than try to build a bigger IRA or 401K.

A true anachronism, Craig struggles to live within, without really accepting, modern western cultural expectations. He's one of the rare few individuals who truly is content with "enough". For many years, he's lived in what the vast majority of people would consider substandard housing, at considerably below the poverty level. He buys only the most durable and functional outdoor clothing, which he repairs until it simply is no longer possible. Every three years, he buys eight new heavy duty T-shirts, a major wardrobe overhaul. Designer labels and logos are conspicuous by their absence. Food is simple, the same multi-grain gruel every day, with a few fresh vegetables from some generous person's garden in season, daily popcorn, and on rare occasion, a piece of meat.

Contrast this with a unique artistic talent, coupled with a deep need for live music, and the inner conflicts simmer. He can't tolerate enforced routine, and a time-clock embodies all that frustrates him most. How can he market his artwork and dance to live music if he can't generate the income needed to live in an urban environment? There, he is verily a stranger in a strange land.

When he first told me he was going to write this book, I was skeptical. He'd need to have access to a computer, learn to operate it, and, least likely of all, discipline himself to the routine and huge time commitment required. I didn't expect it to happen. When he found a computer with a word processing program and, with considerable effort got it to operate properly, I still wasn't convinced. I couldn't imagine him spending the hours indoors, even in winter.

Craig set up a folding card table as his writing desk, with a cast-off folding chair, in a combination living/sleeping area, all the windows and doors covered with thrift-store blankets to keep out the arctic winds, and one ceramic heater to heat the entire house.

I went out to visit him after a week, expecting to find him dejected, defeated, with perhaps a page of ramblings. When he willingly allowed me to read what he'd done so far, three things became evident: he really was going to write this book, it was going to be good, and he needed someone who knew him well enough to edit it so that others reading it would fully understand what he was saying. I volunteered. He accepted.

I didn't try to edit what Craig wrote; I simply rearranged some of it to make Craig's speech mannerisms more easily understood to readers, especially as he described his personal trials. A few grammar and syntax alterations, a little more adjective variety, and some pruning here and there completed it. Any punctuation crimes committed are mine.

What really sets Craig and his book apart, and which will become increasingly apparent as you read each page, is that he is consistently honest, not only with others, but with himself, about himself.

You are about to embark on a journey unique in our time and culture. Really, multiple journeys: in time, in vast landscapes, and in the heart. Prepare to find yourself becoming deeply immersed in "Burro Magic".

John Milbert

Chapter 1:
The Turning Tide

I knew the next stage of the trip was actually going to happen when ... quite magically ... I found the exact kind of dog that I was looking for: a two-year-old, or older, female Heeler.

I was leaving, within the month, to begin the challenging adventure of walking with a couple of large pack-burros from Northwestern Colorado to somewhere in Oregon. The very sociable burros were great companions to have along on an extended journey, but I also loved the true friendship that a dog could bring, so I urgently wanted to find one before this leg of the trip began. The difficulties of such a long journey meant that I couldn't deal with the goofiness of a young puppy, or any disabilities that might hinder an elderly dog. The biggest requirement I had for a dog was that it couldn't go chasing off after something, or wanders away on its own. My canine companion would have to want to stick right with me at all times.

I'd learned, in the past, with a couple of other dogs I'd owned, that female Heelers were the perfect fit for my kind of traveling. A Heeler is an Australian cattle dog, so named because of the way they nip at the heels of the cattle they are herding. Small to medium-sized dogs, they are highly pack-oriented, smart, and consider staying with their person "the most important job on earth."

I'd already checked at the Steamboat Springs animal shelter, but found nothing close to my exacting doggy-description. I called about a dog that was posted on the local feed store's bulletin board. We met at a town park.

The dog was only part Heeler, which could be OK, but, as we stood in the park, he wandered off to check out some other nearby people. Not a good sign. Also, it wasn't female. I was very partial to females, because of their steadier temperaments, so I passed on that dog. Another factor took him out of contention. They wanted seventy dollars! At the moment, I had fifty dollars to my name.

Money and I hadn't mixed much for decades. I lived on about $3,500 a year for much of that time. That was far below the poverty level. Compared to my usual cash flow, the poverty level was wealth. During the months leading up to the journey, I was so completely unable to generate money, even by my less-than-meager standards, that I'd become convinced I was supposed to go on the upcoming adventure dirt poor. Walking with a pair of burros to Oregon by myself, and then finding a place for us to live (I'd never been there, and didn't know any one) was difficult enough. I'd been in a bit of a panic, thinking that I needed more money for such a huge endeavor. The script was obviously being written differently, so I relaxed a bit and accepted the challenge. I was more than qualified to walk burros across the landscape. I was one of the most experienced. Apparently, it would be "better sport" for me to do it totally broke.

I'd been on major burro pack trips ten other summers. Most of the journeys had been about ninety days long; a few were shorter. Two other years, I took trips that were only ten and fifteen days long. They didn't count, because I'd settled on the standard of "forty days in the wilderness" to be considered a real journey. One of my adventures was exactly forty days long, perfectly fitting "the standard."

It was during that particular forty-days-in-the-wilderness that I had the inspiration to take my burro-packing to another level. I was sitting against a boulder, on a tiny island, in the midst of a cascading mountain stream, surrounded by an amazing flower garden, churning water, and mountain panoramas far into the distance. A sapphire-blue lake lay sparkling below me. I was in a particularly euphoric mood when I had the vision of taking my burro packing on the road. During the preceding summers, I'd just been going out on loops and returning home. This new vision was to keep moving west, finding new places to live as we went. The goal of the adventure was to reach Oregon. I didn't have any concrete reason why that was the goal. It just felt like the thing WE should do. I considered the burros to be the other parts of "we", since they were as much a part of making the journey as I was.

The burros really seemed to enjoy being in the mountains on pack trips. Burros are quite smart, and they were very stimulated by all the different sights, sounds, and smells. With all they had to figure out and do on pack trips, it had to be a more fulfilling life for them than just hanging out in a pasture waiting for some hay. Also, we were usually in places with very good grazing, especially in the high mountains where grand meadows could literally spread for miles. They seemed particularly fascinated with the expansive views that we encountered, and often stubbornly insisted on stopping to gaze a while at the spectacular panoramas.

I'd been living for nearly ten years in the tiny northern New Mexico town of Tres Piedras, Spanish for "Three Rocks". Fewer than 300 people lived in the area, and it was thirty miles to the next town. I was caretaker of a fantastic 500 acre piece of property, which held one of the ancient rock formations for which the town was named.

They were beautifully sculpted and covered with gnarled, Bonsai-esque trees growing out of the cracks. A tiny flower grew nowhere else in the world, but upon these three great stone monuments. I spent many days joyously roaming around on the weather-polished old rocks. It was like having my own park, and I might have happily stayed there for the rest of my life. I loved living in Tres Piedras, and in many ways those were some of the best years of my life. But the inspiration to go on my mission, "wandering the west with burros", was so powerful that ... I just had to go.

I had very good friends in the area, and leaving them became the most brutal part of going on the journey. I understood why most people don't leave their family, friends and familiar surroundings. Humans are herd animals, so it's abnormal to take off alone. It's hard to leave the comfort of the group, and go out into "uncharted waters". People seek a safe, stable home; probably, most people who move to other places do so because they are forced to leave. Often, I felt how crazy I was to go out adventuring, particularly because, so many times I found myself treading on such thin ice. My greatest comfort in moments of doubt and fear was my understanding that it was the right thing for me to be doing. I'd experienced so many amazingly magical moments on previous sojourns that it seemed obvious: The Maker wanted me walking burros. I had a wonderful mental image of myself wandering around with burros. It seemed that my good attitude and belief in supernatural support allowed miracles to happen.

The summer after I had my inspiration to walk to Oregon, I got it together to leave my longtime home in northern New Mexico. Some good friends, who were instrumental in making my years at Tres Piedras wonderful, trailered us over to where we could best start our long, long journey. The good-byes were almost too hard.

We started our walk to Oregon on the Continental Divide Trail at the New Mexico/Colorado border. The trail went north up through the spectacular South San Juan Wilderness, then turned west, through some of the most rugged country in all of Colorado: the Wimenuche Wilderness. The difficult, nearly 100 mile long section of trail was mostly above tree line, much of the way 12,000 feet or higher. There were places along the way where the only things in view for immense distances were soaring wild peaks. Gorgeous meadows, awesome jagged mountains. I was truly in love with being in those heavenly places.

Near the town of Silverton, Colorado, the Continental Divide trail turned north, so we left that trail there, and headed west into the Four Corners area. We descended the high mountains towards the town of Cortez, Colorado, where I found a great place to live with someone who became a very dear friend. My plan for the next summer was to walk across the deserts of southern Utah, then cross the desolation of central Nevada into Oregon.

That winter in Cortez, I drove out into the nearby expanses of Utah, to check out next year's prospective burro packing route. I found the beautiful sculptured red-rock landscape too dry, with much too little grazing, to allow us to travel across it. Also, having just spent a summer in heavenly high mountains, I knew my heart would be more satisfied if I took a roundabout route to Oregon, by first heading north up through the awesome grandeur of the Colorado mountains.

We did a relatively short, two month adventure in the rugged spires of the Silverton area that next summer. Silverton was the scene of enormously rich silver mines in days not-so-long-past. I took great joy in scrambling around the old mining ruins, amazed by the things the old-timers had built; searching the tailing piles for interesting rocks and, hopefully, a little of what they had been seeking. I was in awe of the old-timers for enduring the brutal work and living conditions during their quest to obtain the hidden treasures of the area. Even in mid-summer, the high-country weather was extremely harsh. Most afternoons, violent hail and lightning storms would engulf the mountains. Lightning was a real and active threat in the higher reaches of the Colorado peaks. You sure didn't want to be caught out in an exposed high place when one of those monstrous, ferocious storms came rolling in. It could be a truly terrifying experience: lightning striking too close, deafening thunder all around. There are no atheists in a high altitude lightning storm.

We got a trailer ride back to Cortez for that winter. It was such a good place for us to live, and I lived with a truly good friend. I worked in the kitchen at the hospital/nursing home, filling in when full-time workers had a day off. Most of the time I cooked; though many days, I washed dishes. Washing dishes had been my "road game" for years, because, if I was willing to do it, I could usually find work. Dishwashing was also much less stressful than the mental mayhem that went with so many other kitchen jobs. If I had to have a job, and could find nothing else to do, dishwashing was my usual choice. As long as I didn't do it too long at a stretch, I could survive it. If I stayed at any job too long, I'd eventually go crazy. There was something about the enforced routine that became intolerable after a period of time.

A regular job was akin to slavery, so I'd escape at any opportunity. I worked to make money for my immediate needs. Since I had absolutely no career ambitions, a menial job was my best option. It required nothing more than showing up and following routine.

The first day I had to wash dishes at the hospital in Cortez, I was feeling very sorry for myself. Once again, I was going to have to do the dirty, menial task. Part of the job was clearing tables in the nursing home dining room. Disgruntled, I entered the room, backing through the door to pull in the dirty dish cart. When I turned around, my life was immediately changed in a most beneficial, though painful way. I found myself in a room full of very old, severely sick and disabled people; some literally in the last days of their lives; being among those who really had reason to complain put my trivial whining in its place. Washing dishes was a blessing compared to what those people were going through. I realized how fortunate I really was to be fit and healthy. I was also confronted with the fact that, at some point, life does end, so I'd better get on with living. Being among those who had nothing but pain, with death the only light at the end of the tunnel, helped me appreciate what I did have. That experience convinced me even more that following my love of wandering with burros was right for me.

The following summer, we got a trailer ride back to the area where we'd finished the previous year's pack trip, and headed north through the West Elk, Raggeds, Maroon Bells and Flat Tops Wilderness areas. This was some of the most beautiful country in Colorado. One of the high points on the trail, aptly named "Oh Be Joyful Pass", summed up that summer's mood. Robin's-egg-blue-sky days, with towering mountain spires, stretching to the horizon; entire mountainsides blanketed with flowers bordered the trails, with water abounding in deliciously clear streams. Following the babbling streamlets up to their source to drink the icy nectar straight from the mountainside was a favorite delight: "Actualized Heaven" ... to sit amidst such scenes, to really experience those moments, as often as possible, was my goal. It was only real while it was happening. Memories were just faint and faded shadows compared to the actual experience.

That summer's stroll north ended with our arrival in the swanky ski resort town of Steamboat Springs. Steamboat was in a very pretty valley, surrounded by rounded aspen-covered mountains, different from the sharp-rugged mountains and conifers common to the rest of Colorado. It was a pretty area, and I had some great times there, but for me much of Steamboat was tainted by something which I detest: extravagant mansions.

I hate any kind of waste. The ridiculously oversized structures had far more space than anyone needed for any practical reason. What I saw was an enormous waste of resources. All of the extravagance was just a display of selfish greed, vulgar at best. I realized, (in my better moments) that it wasn't individuals I despised, as much as their herd's philosophy. The dominant culture promotes selfish over-consumption. I believe greed is the cancer of humanity. I thought of the energy wasted on these black-holes, used only a few days a year, but devouring resources nonstop. What real good might have been done with all of those precious resources!

Luckily, the skiing, snowboarding, and general good times of a resort area attracted a fair number of crazies, so I did have some good friends and experiences during my time living there. One of the things that I liked most was all of the live music regularly played in the bars and clubs. I'd loved dancing to live music for many decades, so I saw as many of the good bands as I could.

The journey to Oregon stalled in Steamboat for four years. I lived most of the time on a beautiful piece of property owned by an eccentric artist. Each of the first three summers that I lived there, I spent three months up in the mountains. I had the joy of bringing a dear friend on good parts of each of those trips. It was great to have someone along who had the same love of nature's beauty. We simply went to a new wilderness area and stayed there the entire summer. The three trips were taken in the Zirkel, Flat Tops and High Uintas Wilderness areas. I was very self-indulgent, spending all of those summers seeking out moments of bliss in the astounding beauty and solitude of the high mountains. I was intoxicated with doing exactly what I wanted to do, exactly where I wanted to do it. Being surrounded by the majesty of the mountains, always having that beauty entering the eyes was PURE medicine.

We usually camped just below tree-line, in the big spruce forests, where we could get some protection from the winds and rain. Outside in all kinds of weather, many times in open exposed places, made me feel that trees were true friends, very comforting in harsh weather, an island in the storm. My favorite activity in those high paradises was taking day hikes, off-trail, all around the area in which we were camped. From the high reaches of the forests, access to the tundra above timberline was easy.

These bare, open areas offered some of the best walking. Forests, with underbrush, fallen trees and limbs made walking around off-trail more difficult. We moved on when the desire to explore other places arose, usually after about four or five days in each delectable spot. We traveled without a definite plan, following the natural flow of events, and the desire to go or to stay. I enjoyed about as much actual freedom, during those idyllic outings, as I could ever have hoped to attain.

The really high country of Colorado had only about three months available for burro packing, between the spring thaw and the first fall snows. We were lucky if we could reach the high country above 10,000 feet before the 4th of July. The snows usually started again in early September. If it didn't snow by the 15th of September, winter was overdue. We'd usually stay through a few snows before giving up the high ground in fall. I was always a bit leery at that time of year, and camped only in places where we had a down-mountain trail, so that we could better escape a big snowstorm. We could have real trouble if a big storm dropped several feet of snow, and we were camped where we had to go over a high pass to get out of the wilderness. We could deal with lesser storms. If we waited for a couple of days, the snow would usually melt off that early in the autumn.

On the pack trip in the High Uintas in Utah, tragedy ended my trips for over a year. One of my burros was killed. I went to work full-time in a cabinet shop, which nearly killed me. I had a great boss, and the other workers were friends, but after a year of straight work, my wheels completely came off. Like every other time that I'd worked full-time, I just went completely mad with anger and frustration. I felt powerless in the regular world. Something deep inside just wouldn't allow me to live that kind of life, no matter how hard I tried.

Call it "The Caged Wild Beast Syndrome." How could I not want to escape? The woods had always been my sanctuary away from the social scrutiny that I, the eccentric, found so crushing, so limiting. The woods represented FREEDOM.

The traits which made a regular job and a normal life so confining, fitted me perfectly for going out alone on adventures. Cruising with critters through the great wide-opens of the American West matched my abilities and wants to a tee. Most people would consider wandering isolated mountains and deserts alone, for months at a time, as dangerous and scary. It was completely the opposite for me. I feared town life. When I escaped town, and reached the trailhead to begin a pack trip, I heaved a huge sigh of relief, "Survived another one". During all those months on pack trips, I never feared being harmed. I felt very safe and totally "At Home" in the Out-Out. Whenever a journey neared its end, I felt a growing dread. Soon, I'd have to leave the magic of the mountains and go back down, where I'd have such a hard time surviving. If winters weren't so cold and snowy, I never would've gone back "down below". I didn't hate people. I was just so pathetic at doing what I had to do to make it in the "real world", and life on the trail was such Heaven. Basically, I was a throwback to a more aboriginal type of person; not by training, but just by my nature.

The cabinet shop job ended in early winter, when work dried up for a while. This was good for me, because the vibration of the power equipment had started to bother my right hand, which I'd broken years before falling on ice. When I broke that hand, I discovered a talent I hadn't previously known about.

With my right hand in a cast, I was playing around, trying to sign my name with my left hand. I found that I could fluently write backward, mirror writing, with my left hand! It was as if I had been doing it my whole life. When the cast came off, I discovered that I could write right handed forward, and left handed backward at the same time! I took it a step beyond, and found that I could also draw mirror images, using both hands at once!

While it was certainly an interesting discovery, I'd never spent time or energy pursuing it further, until my second winter at Steamboat Springs, when I broke my left knee skiing. While I was healing, I finally had time to just sit there and experiment with acrylic paints. I was successful enough at it right away to sell some art work, but not enough to make ends meet. Breaking bones twice led me to discover and then develop the quirky talent which confirmed my abnormality.

The slowdown at the cabinet shop, combined with access to top-rate tools and advice, gave me the chance to make some beautiful frames for my art. Some I made with molded alder, but my favorites were those I made from walnut scraps that otherwise would have been wasted. I took thin, leftover strips and, after many steps and a small piece of my thumb, had a good stack of high quality frames.

After the cabinet shop job ended, the rest of the winter turned into a psychological nightmare. I came as close to going completely mad as I'd ever been. Anger, frustration, a sense of futility, about myself and everything else, nearly overwhelmed me.

My "sins" grew from my inability to make money and from being much too self-absorbed. My other frustration was with the culture in which I found myself. Since childhood I'd followed politics, and didn't care for most of what I'd seen. It was extremely upsetting. My insanity became complete enough for me to consider running for public office, or walking for public office, as the case might be. Maybe I'd run for Congress in a rural district, where I could walk around with the burros and meet people. I considered both major political parties equally corrupt, but the rules required picking one of the established brands. Since the Democrats had a donkey as their symbol, my choice was obvious. I wasn't pachyderm packing.

One of my main platforms would be to put lie detectors on people in power, since one old saying is certainly true in all cultures, in all times, "power corrupts". To ever have honest people running things, something like putting lie-detectors on them would have to occur. Walking around with the burros, as I campaigned for public office, would at least allow me to vent my frustrations, instead of just having my anger churn away inside. Running for public office was about the craziest idea I had ever had, and betrayed how insane I was at the time. I was the most unlikely person to go into politics, the ultimate outsider. If I entered the hostile world of politics, I'd be ripped to shreds. All my years of other-than-normal activity, had left a lot of skeletons in my closet. I would be unelectable. Even worse, it would be a full-time job.

I knew that the only thing that could cure my boiling brain was a pack trip, but not just another summer tour. I needed to get on with the journey to Oregon. I had a real urge to try to get there in just one summer. The town of Bend, in the central part of the state, held an appeal. I had driven through there twenty years before, and remembered it as a quaint little town, in a good location for my preferences. Bend had mountains nearby, and not much rain, being on the dry side of the Cascade Mountains. The other side of the Cascade's, had wetter weather than I thought I would like. As a destination, Bend, 1000 miles away, gave me a tangible target. The real plan was just to get to Oregon, and keep walking until someone offered us the RIGHT place to live. Such plans had worked in the past. I assumed that the future would work out similarly.

My chronic Steamboat Springs lousy "luck" ended one morning at the local coffee shop. A friend since my first days in town called out from across the room, "Did you see the ad in the paper about the free dog?" He read the ad aloud, "Three year old female Heeler, free to good home". He laughed at the good home part, since I was about to become homeless when I began the journey to Oregon.

Immediately, I called, got directions to the house, and sped over there as quickly as I dared. The prospect of finding such an important piece of the complex puzzle I was trying to put together was extremely exciting. A married couple was breaking up, and the dog didn't fit in with either of their new lives. They showed me to the small fenced-in backyard where they kept the dog. She was beautiful, white, shaded almost black by leopard-like spots, with soft reddish fur on her legs and head. She was extremely hyper, which I didn't really like in a dog, but I was immediately convinced that she was the right dog for me, since she so exactly fit the rest of my desired-doggy-description. I decided to overlook what turned out to be a temporary flaw, and accepted her immediately. When I told the owner that I'd soon be walking to Oregon, she thought the dog would love it.

I was a great human for the right dog. Not only would we be constant companions, but the sights, sounds, and smells for a dog to explore while on an extensive trek, made my new partner about as lucky as a dog could be. "Lucky", that would be a good name for her, though I eventually named her Lucy. I was very excited when we drove back to town; not only did I have a great new companion, but I also felt that the tide had finally turned in my favor. It was so amazing to find the exact dog I was seeking in such a small town. That was the miracle which told me, unquestionably, that the walk to Oregon would happen.

I still had plenty to figure out during the month before the trip started. We had to leave sometime in the middle of May. If we left earlier than that, the grasses for the burros wouldn't be grown yet. If we left later, we'd run out of time to make it to Oregon. Also, the first stretch of the trip was relatively arid. I wanted to be through that part before the real summer heat started.

The other major consideration was that, during the previous year, I'd gotten two new burros to replace the one I'd tragically lost. I couldn't handle three burros by myself, with two of them being rookies, on a trip that would be largely along the side of the road. Burros don't always follow directly behind each other. The back burro could be in the middle of the road, without me having an easy way to shoo it off the road when a car was coming. I decided to bring along someone to help.

I found a man in his mid-20s, who wanted to go with me on the adventure. We trained with the burros for a couple of weeks, and it seemed that it would be great to have him along, but right about the time I got Lucy-dog, he backed out on me. I'd told him not to worry about money, because it was beyond expectation how well the world treats someone on adventure. He said that the prospects of going on such a huge journey without any money were too much of a gamble for him. It would have been fun to share the experience of a true adventure with a competent, fun person, but it was probably best that he backed out. I was so set in my ways, and my own rhythm, that it was best for me to go alone. I was so accustomed to doing things my way, being the boss without having to consult anyone. One of the greatest joys through the years of burro packing by me was that I didn’t have to compromise or come to agreement on what to do. Sole authority over what I could control gave me complete freedom.

The old-timers, who originally came across on the Oregon Trail, used to choose a leader with complete authority, who ran the wagon trains like a military operation. There were times on such a journey when conditions were very harsh, but the train still had to keep moving. Democracy would have been disastrous. On our journey, my companion would've had to listen to me, and do what I told him to do, since I was the one with all of the experience, burros, and equipment. I would have been a commander more than a partner. I could be very intense, and my manner was not always gracious. At some point in the long journey, we would likely have had a falling-out.

Better that he backed out early, rather than in the middle of the expedition, when it would've been harder to figure out an alternative plan. I'd also probably get more help from people I met along the way, since most people would consider making the trip alone to be harder. I knew I could do it by myself. So, after being upset for part of the day, when he told me he wasn't coming along, I quickly recovered my attitude and got on with preparing for the trip.

Chapter 2
In the Beginning

When I was 7 years old, I moved with my family from Wisconsin to Connecticut. Someone asked me how I felt about the move. I replied that it would be fine with me, as long as there were woods. At about the same time, I realized that my main profession would be philosophy: Reality Construction.

As departure time drew closer, the thought of walking the burros to Oregon ... by myself ... grew more intimidating. Actuality was much more daunting than planning. This trip would be similar, in many ways, to my first burro adventure, so my mantra became, "If I could do that first trip then, I can make this walk to Oregon now". My first trip had really set the bar high, as to what level of difficulty, danger, and outright foolishness I was willing to tackle on adventure. I was absolutely clueless, which was one of the main reasons I was able to complete that trip. If I'd known what I was getting into, I would've never considered trying such a foolhardy venture. Had I understood how many things that had to go exactly right, and the whole mountain of things that mustn't go wrong, I would have been overwhelmed, and surely failed.

Being too foolish to be afraid can come in handy; especially if that's nearly all you have working in your favor.

I'd been a poker degenerate during the 1980s, in the Nevada casinos. While it was wonderful living on the north end of amazingly beautiful Lake Tahoe, I eventually totally bottomed out there. On a bus trip from Taos, New Mexico back to Lake Tahoe, with ten dollars to my name, I realized I needed a change. The bus passed near Moab, Utah. I'd visited Moab briefly a couple of times before, and had really liked the area, with its wildly sculpted red-rock cliffs and canyons. I could leave the bus in the middle of the trip, for up to a month, and complete the journey later, without any penalty. I decided to stop in Moab, and see if it might be a good place for me to live.

The bus had a long, nighttime layover in Denver, before heading to Moab. The seats in the bus terminal were too hard, and the lights too bright, for me to sleep. As I sat there, bored, a scruffy, bearded man sat down next to me and began to talk. He told me that his life was working with horses, mules, and burros. He'd had all kinds of adventures with them, mostly with horses and mules. Burros were a bit small for his liking. Listening to him was like meeting someone out of the century past. He'd even handmade the satchel he was carrying. Having nothing better to do, I sat there and listened to his stories of many years of working with the sometimes difficult animals. During the hour-long conversation, he told me many do's and don'ts of working with pack animals. "Once you've led them in a certain order, always keep them in that order or you'll have trouble. Better to work with the animals when it's cool. If it's really hot, everyone gets cranky and potentially troublesome." He poured out knowledge to me. It was an introductory class on working with pack animals. BURRO MAGIC had already begun.

The next afternoon, I left the bus at Crescent Junction, about thirty miles north of Moab. Crescent Junction was a diner and a couple of other buildings in an otherwise stark, desolate landscape. I hitchhiked down the secondary road to Moab. A trucker picked me up, and deposited me on the roadside, just before crossing the Colorado River near Moab, so I could better see the magnificent view as I walked across the bridge. Here, the mighty, roiling Colorado River is squeezed between 400 foot high, red-rock cliffs. A breathtaking place, to be sure. The red-rock formations were sculpted into all kinds of intriguing shapes. Arches and Canyon Lands national parks were close by.

It was getting late in the day, and I needed a place to camp. There were many wonderful camping places all along the shore, upstream from the bridge. I didn't know about those camping areas, so I took what began to look like the wrong route. I walked the last mile or so into Moab, on through town, and continued south along the highway. My backpack was painfully heavy. Instead of being packed light for backpacking, I was lugging extras for generalized travel. This section of road was fairly built up with houses and businesses, not good for camping at all, and it was starting to get dark. At this point I came upon a youth hostel.

Usually, I would never have considered spending the night in such opulence, particularly when I had camping gear, but I felt very drawn to the place. When I learned that a spot in the bunkroom would cost me seven dollars, I swallowed hard. That would leave me with three dollars to my name, and I was a long way from home. Despite my poverty, I did the unbelievable, and paid out most of my net worth for a place to stay the night. It turned out to be one of the best decisions of my life.

That evening, while I sat in the hostel's common room, eating and watching TV, an older man paused at the door to look around. Our eyes met, and we each nodded a greeting before he headed up the stairs. The next morning, I went out early for a short walk around the area. On the way back, I saw him walking toward me on the same side of the road. When we came up to each other, we both stopped to talk. He looked at my feet and stated that I needed new shoes. I had to agree, since my only footwear was a beat up pair of sandals, held together with multiple wrappings of duct tape. I told him that my last pair of shoes had died weeks before. He asked what I was doing in the area; I told him I wanted to hike into the La Salle Mountains for a few days, via a back road that left from that side of town. He laughed, and said I'd die of thirst going that way, but, if I wished, I could ride to his home in Castle Valley. From there, he'd drive me as high up the road on that side of the mountains as he could. It was still early spring, and before too high up, we'd find snow. I quickly accepted his offer, got my gear from the Hostel, and met him at the supermarket.

Due to poor eyesight, he had no driver's license, so his truck was hidden near the river, outside of town. We walked a couple of miles to his old truck, and drove fifteen amazing miles up the road, following the winding Colorado River through the astoundingly beautiful red-rock canyon. He lived several miles off the main canyon in Castle Valley; a deep, wide side-canyon that led to the La Salle mountains. He had a few acres on the valley floor, where he'd built a small, very rustic cabin, and a horse corral.

We were sitting on the front porch, drinking coffee, when he made a startling offer. He had two burros at his daughter's place, on the other side of Utah. If I'd go there, and walk the burros back the 250 miles to Castle Valley … he would give me one of them.

I'd taken several backpacking trips before, but never with large animals. I'd never even ridden a horse. All I'd ever done with an equine was feed one apples over a fence. Now, someone was suggesting I walk across a major chunk of central Utah with a couple of burros, with one of the low-cost beasts as my only reward. It immediately sounded like the most fantastic idea I'd ever heard. I'd always been a walker, and loved animals. Camping was my favorite activity. With hardly a moment-of-thought ... I agreed. I'd go back to Lake Tahoe to settle some business, and return in two to three weeks to begin the wild adventure.

The next morning, he drove me into the La Salle Mountains, until we hit snow, and dropped me off in an aspen grove. I thanked him for all of the help he'd already given me, and for his amazing offer. I stayed on the mountainside for a couple of days, hiking around the area as well as I could with my shoddy footwear. The forest was good, but I was drawn back down into the magnificent Colorado River canyon. When I'd been in Moab, I'd bought what food I could with my last three dollars, to supplement the little bit I already had, but that was gone. I recycled some aluminum cans I found along the road, to buy enough food for the several days I stayed in the canyon.

Back at Lake Tahoe, I scurried around trying to sell anything I could. I'd been bottomed out for so long that there wasn't much to sell. I only raised enough to buy a pair of old-style canvas basketball shoes. I left "Pokerville" with eleven dollars, a backpack, and my tail firmly between my legs. A long-time poker buddy, "Ol' Joe", drove me to the Reno Airport. When I offered him my last eleven dollars, to pay somewhat for the huge favor of driving me all the way to Reno, he said he thought I'd need it more than he would.

Fortunately, my parents had given me a round trip ticket to a family reunion and paid all expenses. Instead of returning to Lake Tahoe, I exchanged the return trip for a bus ticket to Moab. The reunion was excellent. My sister, her young son, and newborn daughter were there, so all four living generations of the family got together. I didn't tell anyone about my financial situation. Leaving the gambling world of Nevada sounded good to my parents. I didn't give them many details about the proposed burro pack trip, since I didn't have much of a plan, or knowledge of what I was about to do.

On the way to Moab, I had some good luck when I got off the bus in Laughlin, Nevada. I ran into someone I'd known for many years in the poker business. She put me into a low-stakes poker game, where I won forty-five dollars. She declined her traditional half of the winnings, and gave it all to me: boost HUGE.

Back in Moab, I didn't go directly to my benefactor. Instead, I took up residence in a cave, high above the Colorado River. I walled up the front, under a large overhang, with some small rocks, leaving just enough of an opening to crawl through. The ancient Native Americans, who'd lived nearby, a thousand years before, built similar structures, so my cave was quite appropriate to the surroundings. The really outstanding feature of the site was that it was in the upper layers of the cliffs forming the Colorado River canyon. In front of the cave was a thirty foot wide, steep sloping ledge that ended in a 400 foot cliff straight down to the river.
The beautifully sculptured red-rock formations of Arches National Park were directly across the deep, narrow canyon from my cave.

The spectacular landscape stretched for miles. I didn't particularly trust all the tons of rock hanging above me in the cave, so I spent most of my time outside on the ledge, using the cave for storage. There was a juniper tree on the slope about twelve feet away from the rock face. I hung my sleeping hammock between the tree and a metal bolt jammed securely into a crack in the rock face. It was a spectacular and somewhat nervy place to camp, since I was a bit height-shy.

I explored the amazing other-worldly rock formations during the ten days before going on the crazy burro-enterprise, and did some more successful aluminum prospecting to buy food. During one walk, in the rocky maze, I found a freshly overturned jeep, with no one in sight. Next to the wrecked vehicle was a broken-off car-compass. I pried the little round compass out of its holder and put it in my pack. I felt a little guilty, stealing the compass, but I felt that I really needed the direction finder for the walk across Utah.

The night before I left on the great adventure, I walked several miles to Moab and went "out on the town." Going down a narrow hallway to the men's room, I brushed up against a young man. He howled in pain, and said he'd been injured in a jeep rollover. I learned that it amazingly was the same jeep I'd come across, and told him about my theft of his compass. He just waved it off. It was the least of his worries.

The man who owned the burros bought us bus tickets to his daughter's home, in the tiny town of Vernon, Utah. We arrived just as the day was ending, and immediately went out to see the burros. I'd only seen burros once before, in the old west town of Oatman, Arizona.

There, tourists buy little bags of peanuts to feed the "wild" burros, which were really tame peanut-hogs. "Billy", was equally tame that evening. He would become one of the most important beings in my life. The other burro was 100 yards out in the pasture, so we'd meet him in the morning.

The conversation that evening was interesting, to say the least. Most of the family believed that I should first practice in some nearby hills, to see if I had any chance of succeeding on a longer journey. My benefactor thought otherwise; declaring that going on a practice trek wouldn't get me any closer to the finish, and that I should start straight out for Moab. Following his advice led to my success. If I'd gone on a practice run first, I would have learned how nearly impossible the journey was. The advantage that my total ignorance gave me would have been lost if I'd understood what would actually happen. Had I known, I would have been fearful, hesitant, and probably not have taken the journey at all, particularly as unprepared as I was. Fortunately, ignoring any kind of rational thought, I decided to begin the long, improbable journey the following day.

My lack of equipment was as profound as my lack of knowledge and experience. I didn't have a tent. All I had for protection from the elements was a nylon rain poncho I could wrap around my hammock. Later, I found a sturdy piece of plastic sheeting on the side of the road. The only warm clothes I had were a wool city-overcoat, and a fleece vest with a broken zipper, kept closed with a shoe lace run through holes in front. I had to pull it over my head to get it on and off.

A couple of sweatshirts, t-shirts, socks, underwear, two baseball caps, a wide brimmed grass hat, and one pair of jeans made up my wardrobe. A sleeping bag, thin foam sleeping pad, one small cooking pot, some utensils, a wok, a small backpacking stove with two fuel bottles, two water containers, and a backpack were all I owned. The burros had one set of panniers, a saddle, two halters, a saddle pad, a few lengths of rope, and a bucket.

Early the next morning, the two burros were tied to the front gate, waiting to be loaded. Since I had so little gear and only one set of panniers, Billy would carry all of the gear, which was still hardly anything. The other burro, "Broguey", was shorter, and much older. He would get away with having no load to carry for awhile. Both of the burros had very agreeable dispositions, and waited calmly as we prepared to leave. It took just a few minutes to load Billy-burro with my meager pile of gear, and tie Broguey to Billy's saddle. The family had all left for work, so, without any fanfare … I took Billy's lead rope and … we began THE JOURNEY.

My benefactor walked with us for a mile or so, until we reached the first fork in the road. He had to hitch north to the town of Tooele, where he would catch a bus back to Moab. My road headed to the southeast, also to Moab, but over a much different route. He wished me luck, I thanked him for all he'd given me, and we parted ways. I was on my own. It was an astounding, memorable moment in my life. When I looked out over the sagebrush plain, toward some low juniper covered hills, I realized that I was actually walking two burros across Utah.

I wish someone had been secretly filming the whole thing. Because of my ignorance, it was a complete comedy routine. Some of the best grazing in the otherwise parched area was right along paved highways. Road surfaces shed all of the rain onto the area right along the road, effectively irrigating a relatively green swath in an otherwise brown world. Keeping the burros fed was good, but made huge difficulties in another way. It was mid-May, and the spring grasses were just up. It was the juiciest grass of the year, and after a winter of old dry-hay, the burros were hot after it. Every time we paused to rest along the way, the burros would want to munch the greenery. When it was time to start again, the burros would refuse to budge from the fresh eats. I assumed the classic human-pulling-the-stubborn-burro pose. Countless times, with the burro planted firmly in place, I pulled on the lead rope, and leaned at a forty-five degree angle to maximize my pull on the rope, futilely attempting to get the stubborn beasts to move. One of the most frustrating aspects of the situation was that the burros were very sensitive to emotions. If I got angry, they'd be spooked, and even more difficult to move.

I received much timely help and good cheer from people all along the way, and quickly realized what a magic experience walking burros across the landscape was for me. At one particularly hard moment, I was even encouraged to keep going by an ant. I was under a tree having a snack, resting during the very difficult day, when I observed a tiny little ant trying to pull a crumb of my food back to its nest. The chunk of food was nearly too big for the small ant to move, but it just kept trying … and trying … and trying. I watched it struggle with its oversized load for a time; before understanding, and continuing on with my own oversized load … walking across Utah with a couple of burros.

For the first 125 miles, I pretty much pulled the burros along every step of the way. After that, they got more used to what we were doing, and we reached an agreement and rhythm that somehow worked. The roadside had many aluminum cans. I stopped frequently along the way, and harvested cans. While I collected, the burros had a few minutes to graze, before we continued on our way. They liked this arrangement. Consequently, they began to walk along more agreeably.

Early in the trip, we stopped at a roadside rest area that had fifty-five gallon drums as garbage cans. Each drum was lined with two very thick sturdy plastic garbage bags. I took one clean bag from four different cans, doubled the bags, and lashed the two resulting double bags together along the upper edges with some baling wire I'd found. These were "canniers", since they carried the aluminum cans I picked up along the roadside. I could make some money doing this, and also clean up the rural roads we traveled, so I didn't feel guilty about stealing the plastic bags from the rest area. I hung the canniers over Broguey's back, and stomped the cans flat with my foot to maximize the number I could fit into the canniers. I sold the cans by the pound when we got into a town (making maybe five dollars), and bought more rice and lentils, the cheapest food I could find. I really starved on that first trip, my meager diet didn't have enough fat, and my pot was too small to cook as much as I needed.

My attitude was so extraordinarily good that I just dealt with whatever difficulty I was having. Along with God's good graces, (a good card to hold), all I had on my first trip was my positive attitude, faith, and extreme determination to pull it off, no matter how hard it was.

Completing the journey required keeping an eye on the big picture, and ignoring the harshness of some of the immediate moments. Despite all the hardships, I knew before I'd gone very far that I'd be going on more burro trips. Walking with burros just turned out to be the perfect thing for me to do. The way all of the many needed elements flowed so effortlessly together assured me that we would succeed. After a month of struggles beyond any I had ever imagined, we arrived in Castle Valley, victorious. My benefactor rewarded me not only with Billy, the best burro; he also gave me an old horse named Lady, so that I could continue my adventures.

After a month-long break to recover from the "happy ordeal", we continued into the high mountains of Colorado. I was very fortunate to have the horse and burro, instead of two burros, when we got to the mountains. At that time, I wouldn't have been able to get the stubborn, untrained burros up over the rugged high mountain trails. The horse followed along whenever I wanted to move, unlike the burros who moved when they were inclined. My canvas sneakers were worn all the way through the soles by the time I reached the higher terrain. I lined them with cardboard to protect my socks. I finally replaced them with real hiking boots, when I got a five-day dishwashing job in Lake City, Colorado. We hiked all the way to the Taos area, in northern New Mexico.

That first trip was so wonderfully magical. It gave me confidence in my ability to go out and succeed at such an improbable feat. Even more important, all the perfectly timed miracles that we needed, and received, to make such a nearly impossible journey, proved to me that The Maker wanted me walking burros.

His good graces on the burro trip surely didn't have anything to do with me being a fine, upstanding individual. I'd just spent close to a decade being a narcissistic jerk in Pokerville. That first trip felt as if angels followed us up the road, tossing us miracles when we needed them; not because I was good and righteous and therefore deserving, but rather as if WHAT I was doing was just SO amusing. "Hey Gabriel, Check out this guy!" My slapstick ignorance and the near impossibility of the task made miracles necessary. If we were to continue on our way, we had to be showered with good fortune, or the entertainment would be over. Apparently, one way to find favor is to give God a chuckle. The heavenly help confirmed my belief in a purposefully created universe. Faith in that philosophy gave me courage to continue.

Soon after arriving in New Mexico, I sold the horse, and got another burro. The horse moved easier than the burros, but I really loved burros and wanted to keep working with them. One New Mexico winter, my burro buddy Billy died. The vet told me he died from a heart problem. Even though I'd only known him for a couple of years, it was extremely brutal to have him die. Billy had helped me so much to have a better life and he was such a good and gentle being. Billy-burro will forever be in my heart. New burros to replace Billy and the horse came from the sprawling Philmont Boy Scout ranch. Philmont is where boy scouts come from all over the world, for the ultimate retreat and camping experience.

They raised burros there, and sold the females when they were six months old, for the extraordinary, cheap, price of forty dollars apiece. A long-time buddy gave me two burros named Fanny and Beanie as birthday/Christmas presents. It was great fun to get the animals young, so that I could train them the way I wanted, and have them grow up with me.

Soon, I was very attached to both of them. Fanny was a total character, the wild one, with a mind of her own. Beanie was always much more placid than her rambunctious buddy. I'd heard that, with horses, you want to be their boss. For me, it was better to be their friend, and get them to like going on walks with me. This method required more patience and effort but, in the long run, it made the pack trips much more enjoyable. The burros became like big, loving dogs with me, and we enjoyed traveling the high wild places.

Ten years of traveling had taken us to northern Colorado, ready to move on. The trip to Oregon was going to be a lot different than my last seven wanderings. Those had all been high mountain adventures, following rough, isolated trails in National Forests, much of it designated wilderness. Except for not camping too close to water in Wilderness, I was free to be anywhere I wished. Some years, I didn't see cars for nearly the whole summer.

Walking to Oregon would be entirely different. Much of the time, we'd walk alongside highways and, for most of the way; we'd be surrounded by private land. Finding suitable campsites would be much more difficult. Re-supplying on the road would at least be easier than in the forest. Re-supply in the mountains was always one of the biggest challenges. The burros could only carry about forty days worth of food at a time, so, in the middle of summer, I either had to come down and meet someone with supplies, or cache them ahead of time.

I was a functionalist in nearly every way. I didn't care about the appearance of my clothes, only that they were warm, dry, and comfortable. This helped a lot on pack trips, since my clothes got so worn and dirty. I wore my clothes until they were rags, even though it was a very unfashionable thing to do.

Fashion (a herd concept) was a non-issue, since I wasn't really a part of the herd in which I found myself. It weirded me out that the culture was so obsessed with "THE look." Judging people because of their appearance and that of their possessions seemed as foolish as could be. By my mid-twenties, I'd decided to ignore the whole thing, and just always wear my normal jeans, t-shirt, sweatshirt, or my nylon camping gear, whatever the occasion. I was always different, since I was very young. I've had long time friends turn to me in exasperation and exclaim, "Do you always have to do it differently?"

Function also ruled my food choices. I believed that eating was meant to fuel and grow the body, not just entertainment. This was a major advantage on the trail. I could eat the same bland meal over and over, without caring. My main diet for close to twenty years had been a multi-grain and bean gruel. Quinoa, millet, buckwheat, rice, lentils, mung beans, and a float of olive oil were the main ingredients. In town, I would also cook up some onions, cabbage, collard-greens, kale, chard, cauliflower or broccoli to add to it, depending on what was good and/or available. After about ten years of experimentation, town gruel actually became quite tasty. The basic camp gruel was pretty austere. I also ate plenty of popcorn, nuts, and pasta (with olive oil or in the gruel). Occasionally, when I felt like it, I ate meat as a supplement.

While walking to Oregon we'd only pass through small towns with ordinary grocery stores which usually only carry rice and lentils. This made my gruel sparse, and much less nutritious. Health food stores were the only places to get the other ingredients.

I was surely going to have to expand my usual food list on the trip to Oregon. I knew from experience, that many people would offer me food along the way. In order to not seem ungrateful to those trying to help me, and to fill out my dietary needs, I decided to accept all gifts. My money situation also made accepting food gifts a necessity. I'd been on the skinny side all my life, but, just prior to the Oregon walk, because of my poverty and dysfunctional life, I'd become downright emaciated. This was a real concern, because on nearly all of my previous adventures, I'd lost a lot of weight. I couldn't afford to get any skinnier if I expected to make it all the way to Oregon. I'd need all the calories I could get, all along the way, to be successful.

Luckily, I had nearly all the gear I needed. Through the years, I'd acquired or made the gear required for the extensive journeys. I made my panniers out of sturdy, waterproof vinyl-coated polyester, so that my gear would stay dry without having to cover the load with a tarp. I attached everything with nylon straps and quick-release, easy-adjust, plastic buckles, instead of leather straps and ropes. I wanted the best, most efficient equipment I could get, instead of trying to be historically authentic. I wasn't trying to recreate some bygone days, but attempting to do the deed, as best I could. Walking with burros was difficult enough. I tried to make it as easy as possible with all of the modern materials that were available. In Nylon, I trusted.

My major need for the trip was rubber boots for the burros. Burros have tougher hooves than horses, so they usually don't need horseshoes. I'd tried using horseshoes in the past, running into problems when they fell off mid-trip.

Once, in the middle of the Wimenuche Wilderness area, a burro lost shoes on front and back, and was starting to limp. Even if we weren't in the wilderness, it was still a long way to any kind of town. I was worried enough to get on my knees and pray for help for my burro.

We had to get off the mountainside anyway, so the next morning we went down into the breathtaking meadow, at Wimenuche Pass. It was miles long and about a mile wide, right between huge peaks. I was admiring the magnificent scenery, when a horseman, riding fast, galloped into the scene. I saw him from a least a half mile out, and watched intently as horse and rider flung themselves across the tall-grass meadow. He pulled up when he got to us, and asked how we were doing. He'd been high on the mountainside making a cell-phone call to his girlfriend, and he was late for cooking a meal at the outfitter's camp where he worked. I told him about the lost horseshoes. He laughed, "That's no problem, I'm a farrier, and we even have an anvil at camp." I had spare shoes for the burro, so the answer to my prayer for my burro-girl was only a mile or two down the trail. What an amazing occurrence in the middle of nowhere!

I was invited to stay a day, and partake in their meals. The outfitter's client was just one man, so it was an ultra-expensive bow hunt, with his own fulltime guide and the cook/animal handler to help him. The high-rolling city-dweller was probably in culture shock, far out in the midst of a huge wilderness with only the outfitters and me, the wandering mountain man, for dining companions. Later, my helper admitted that he'd had trouble with the law. All I knew was that he was literally a saving-angel on that trip.

The rubber boots I wanted for the walk to Oregon would protect the burros' hooves from getting too worn down. We'd be traveling on hard surfaced roads for much of the trip, and the rubber boots would give the burros more cushion and grip than metal shoes. The boots slip over their hooves, and protect the insides of their hooves from bruises better than regular horseshoes. The drawback was that they could fall off and get lost, and a set of them cost $160. Along with the boots, I also needed a three week supply of food, and a trailer ride to where I wanted to start the adventure.

It was relatively built up around Steamboat Springs, so I wanted to start about seventy miles to the west, near the town of Craig, Colorado. This was wide-open sagebrush country, with a few low hills. It would be a better place to start, away from the traffic, particularly since one of the burros was a rookie. The new burro, Libby, short for Liberty, was born on the 4th of July. She'd done some packing with her previous owner, who'd done an excellent job of socializing her to humans. I knew she'd be a good burro for me when he said that she acted like a big dog with him.

The other new burro, Jubilee, while being friendly toward humans, was an intolerable "ass" toward my older burro, Beanie. The young brat constantly kicked at Beanie, and drove her away from the burro group. Beanie was seventeen years old by this time. After all of my adventures with her, and all she'd done for me, I was very attached to her. Beanie had never bitten or kicked in all the years we'd been together. Being mean to Beanie definitely put the new burro on my shit list. I wanted to keep her if I could, but when my walking partner dropped out, I had to get rid of a burro. The choice was easy.

I tried to sell her, but when I didn't get any takers in the short time I had, I called up the first person I'd met in Steamboat, and offered him the burro for free. I'd first met him when he pulled up in his car and said that he used to have a burro that looked just like Beanie. I camped at his place for several days, until I found a place to live. Now, he agreed to take the burro, and even gave me $200, although I'd asked for nothing. This was a huge boost to me at that moment. I finally got a few small fencing jobs in the month before the journey, giving me enough money for the last basic things I needed.

By far, the most difficult part of starting an adventure was reaching the trail head. The last ten days before leaving were a complete frenzy, physically and mentally. As great as the adventure sounded at first, as the day approached, the reality of such a journey, weighed heavily on my mind. I understood how important this venture was to my future, so I had to ride out my anxiety. Fear wasn't a reason to not go. I kept reminding myself of my success on past burro trips, particularly on my first trip, which was much more difficult than walking to Oregon. I recalled the many magic moments that had gotten us through seemingly impossible situations in the past.

During the first half of my first trip, we walked across the San Rafael Swell in central Utah. It took five days to cross the parched desolation. I was starving, without proper equipment or money for the food I really needed. All the way across the desert, I dreamed of a bag of tortilla chips and a candy bar. I was haunted by the vision of pancakes, coffee and a slice of pie at the upcoming Crescent Junction café. We escaped the desolation at Green River, Utah, and camped near the river, across from a truck stop on I-80.

I had thirty-six cents to my name, so I couldn't buy the long-awaited chips and candy bar. True hunger is torture; starvation in the midst of plenty. The cure for my pain was only a thin piece of paper or plastic away, but I couldn't stop the torture. I didn't have the proper pieces of paper. The punishment seemed too extreme for the crime. I wandered around the convenience store trying to figure out what I could buy. The only thing I found was some penny candy. I bought two individually wrapped Bazooka bubble gums at five cents apiece, just to have something.

That night in my sleeping bag, I opened the wrapper, popped the gum into my mouth, and read the important part of the gum's comic strip, the fortune, "A miracle will happen today." I hopefully concluded that, since this day was almost over, the fortune would apply to the following day.

The next morning, I packed up and crossed the road to the truck stop. I tied the burros to a light-post in the middle of the parking lot, and entered the store. I asked the cashier if she knew where to sell the aluminum cans I'd picked up crossing the desert. She told me where someone lived who collected cans, and told me how to take a shortcut through the back parking lots, past a motel, to the can buyer.

Cutting behind the motel, we encountered a blind couple being led to a car by a sighted couple. They came over to us, took pictures, and petted the burros. The sighted man was from Texas, and said that when he traveled south of the border, it was customary, if you took a picture of someone, to give them money.

He handed me two dollars! I was so excited that I turned directly around, and headed back to the store. On the way, I found a quarter on the ground! I had $ 2.52, enough to buy the chips and candy bar, and still have my two cents worth! As I bought the chips and candy bar, the lady at the cash register offered to buy my five dollars worth of cans. Now, I even had enough money to buy the meal-of-my-dreams at the upcoming café!!

My last task before leaving for Oregon was to pack my gear. I'd done it so often that it was relatively easy. Owning little more than what I took on pack trips made choosing what to bring even easier. I stowed the things that I wasn't bringing in my old car. The car was such a wreck that it would have been scarier to drive it to Oregon than to walk there with the burros. The owner of the cabinet shop where I'd worked graciously let me park the car on his property until I could come back and do something with it.

Even though all of my possessions, not counting animals, would fit in the back of a pickup truck, one of my biggest problems was always what to do with the meager pile of stuff that I wasn't bringing along, but wanted to keep. I kept my most valuable pictures, writings, and a very few other things, in my good buddy's basement in Cortez, Colorado. My paintings were entrusted to another true friend in the Steamboat area.

To walk to Oregon, I had to be CRAZY enough to try, but PRACTICAL enough to succeed. Walking across the landscape gets very real, very quickly. Part of burro packing was a philosophy test. My extremely optimistic outlook while burro packing, theoretically made a favorable outcome likely. I believed that experience was affected by expectations. The team that believes it's a loser doesn't win the championship. It's like a pastry bag where the shape of the ooze is determined by the shape of the nozzle. Differently shaped nozzles produce different results. The same applies to humans. The different "shapes" of human beliefs bring different results. Beliefs are the software of the human-computer. Software determines output. I had two entirely different sets of expectations for two worlds: Burro Packing and Town Life, and correspondingly different results in each world. Burro Packing World was magical, therefore, I floated. Town World was survival, thus, I floundered. The awe in how magically events flowed in Burro World was part of its reward. A good test of a path's rightness was whether events flowed easily together or not.

It helped that I'd so fallen apart in Steamboat Springs, because I didn't really feel I had the choice to stay. This made it easier to move on from what was really a very good place. I believed remaining would have been a complete disaster. The bridge had been burned. As a drowning person sees the shore as life, I yearned to begin the burro trip to save my own life.

Chapter 3
Following My Bliss
May 21 - May 31

May 21, 2006.

The day of reckoning finally arrived. I couldn't finish packing my gear and cleaning my room until that morning. I was in a panic of activity right up to departure time. I was only ready to go twenty minutes before the trailer was scheduled to arrive. Just enough time to say a quick goodbye to my immediate neighbors, who could barely comprehend that I was actually going on this crazy adventure.

All of my possessions for the multi-month walk to Oregon: two sets of panniers, saddle pads, pack saddles loaded with gear, and my back pack, made a small pile beside the driveway. The burros were tied and ready in some nearby trees. My friend who had found Lucy-dog in the paper was on hand to see us off. He was very much into photography, and wanted to get some pictures of the event.

Our ride arrived exactly at the scheduled time. I probably could have found someone in the neighborhood with a truck and a trailer to take us out to the starting point, but because I wanted so much to get on with the trip, without a hitch, I'd hired a professional. She had a big shiny new truck, and the horse trailer was even equipped with video cameras, so that we could watch the burros from the cab. We were leaving town in style, even though I was destitute. It took just a few moments to load the willing burros and toss my meager pile of gear into the truck. Final goodbyes … and, in a flash … we were gone.

The drive through Steamboat and the countryside beyond was surreal. I'd been so extremely excited, for so long, and now the big day, my own Super Bowl, had finally arrived. Our destination was the Lay Valley Bison Ranch, seventeen miles west of the town of Craig. I'd met the owner of the buffalo ranch on car drives, when I stopped to buy buffalo meat. He'd also given me a trailer ride to the High Uintas mountains for a pack trip I'd taken a couple of years before. He wasn't home when we arrived, so I just piled my gear at the front gate, near where it seemed I might be able to camp, and put the burros in a corral. The driver wished me luck, and left us there.

Northwestern Colorado was very rural. The buffalo ranch lay in the tiny town of Lay, which had no commercial district. The town was just a loose cluster of dwellings in a shallow valley, amongst low sagebrush covered hills. A few juniper trees pocked the surrounding hillsides, in an otherwise barren landscape. The wind was blowing strongly and, despite the rather austere surroundings, I was feeling very good about walking to
Oregon. The hardest part was over: reaching the starting point. The rancher soon arrived, and showed me where to set up camp.

I was exhausted from the all of the pre-trip tension. The frenzy of getting to the jumping-off-place had been so great, that I decided to take the first day off. I wanted to calm down some before starting. It was also important that I be able to find things when I needed them, so I wanted to repack my gear before we began. The panniers alone had sixteen different compartments and pockets into which to organize items such as the first-aid kit, spare parts, tools, hats and gloves, etc.

Remembering where everything belonged was a bit challenging. Fortunately, having familiar equipment gave me confidence that I could arrange all of the gear in an intelligent manner.

Besides getting everything in its right place, I also had to balance the weight among the panniers by rearranging my food containers. I had a good supply of food, so the burros would carry about 100 pounds apiece. My large burros could handle that much weight, or more, if we went slowly, particularly in the beginning. I muddled through it, moving items around until I felt that everything was where it should be.

I could face nearly any weather, from searing desert heat, to high mountain snow. I packed multiple layers of clothing that could all be put on at once, to stay warm. Almost all of my clothing was made of synthetic materials, since the major concern was keeping dry. Wet cotton takes forever to dry. I had nylon pants of varying thickness, fleece jackets for warmth, and breathable waterproof nylon raingear. The only cotton items were some t-shirts, underwear, socks, and sweatpants and sweatshirt for sleep.

I packed most of my food in large soda bottles. A relatively new soda bottle was nearly unbreakable and leak-proof, a perfect container for the high-contact sport of burro packing. Burros could pound against obstructions pretty hard along the way. The strong containers kept vital, and potentially messy, cooking oil from leaking into the gear. I'd once packed the precious liquid in its original container, much to my dismay.

Soda bottles also kept at bay the most cunning and destructive wild beast roaming the forests: the relentless and ruthless chipmunk. A campsite where no one else had ever camped would be safe from chipmunks for a few days, as they studied their quarry. But soon the daring intruders would breach the tent and start pillaging the gear. A frequently used campsite usually meant that the chipmunks were already wise to humans, and were ready to plunder without delay. The cute little creatures liked having us around. Peanuts, roasted and salted in the shell were one of my favorite foods. I didn't have a good protective container for them, so chipmunks continually breached security and had a festival, leaving behind a pile of empty shells. I usually spilled at least some of my daily popcorn, and had a rule that if food hit the ground, it was someone else's. I didn't want to be too stingy with the other creatures of the woods.

I had a special treat that first afternoon at the buffalo ranch, when two men arrived to check out the possibility of buying bison for their own operations. We went out into the field with the main herd. The rancher threw out some special food cubes and called them in with a hoot. He'd been raising bison for twenty years, and they knew snack time. We watched in amazement from the top of the flatbed truck as the huge-headed beasts vied for the much-prized food cubes. None of the bulls had been castrated, and there was also a full contingent of cows and calves, so it was essentially a wild herd of buffalo. The enormous bulls commanded attention, pushing and shoving each other, jousting for the coveted cubes. The relatively small youngsters played and bounced about. It was a great thrill to be so close to the mighty beasts. Buffalo were just so hugely wild and robust, compared to the familiar, half-dazed domesticated cattle. I admired the rancher for succeeding at bison ranching by himself, before most people thought it was possible to raise the huge wild beasts on a ranch. I had buffalo meat for supper the next night.

May 23.

I thanked the rancher, for his generosity, and loaded up the burros. I paused to look around and take in the moment: Ready to walk to Oregon with two pack burros, a dog, a three week supply of food, and ninety-five dollars to my name. What a high moment, the adventure was actually starting! I tied Beanie to the metal ring on the back of Libby's packsaddle, took up Libby's lead rope, ... and we were WALKING TO OREGON!!!

We could have headed straight west down the main highway, Route 40. The two-lane, sixty-five mile per hour highway was relatively untraveled. With vehicles moving at such speeds, it could be a disaster if my animals got loose and onto the road. With two untried rookies, young Libby and Lucy, that didn't seem the best way to start. We had another option: a barely-traveled, gravel side-road. The rural route would be much safer, with sparse, much slower traffic, and more enjoyable. The only drawback to the side-route was that it started in a southerly direction; a longer road to Oregon. A successful start was more important than the shortest route, so I opted to start on the longer side-road.

We crossed the pavement and headed south up the rural gravel road. I'd packed burros enough to feel very familiar and at home from the very first steps of the journey. Our way passed through the green irrigated fields of the valley bottom for a mile, before starting up a low sagebrush covered ridge. Fortunately, it was cloudy and cool. We weren't acclimated yet to the heat that accompanies the arid high-desert sunshine.

We were all relatively out of shape, since I'd been too busy to train during the months before leaving on the trip. We paused on the uphill grade every fifty yards or so to rest. Start, stop, start, stop. A pace of many pauses was the usual burro-rhythm uphill. I looked at things in small increments. My goal was just to climb the first little hill.

Lucy was excited at being out in the open, and ran wildly through the sagebrush along the side of the road. She bounced joyously about, until she yelped, and sheepishly came to me with part of a prickly pear cactus stuck on her nose. I pulled off the barbed sticker. She had a lot to learn. I felt a great "Bubble-of-Joy" ... thrilled that we were heading off on this wonderful adventure. From the ridge-top, I could see ahead, down into the wide, shallow Yampa River valley. Beyond, stretched long vistas of rolling hills and distant peaks with snow and tall trees. The Yampa was the major river in the area; draining the melting snow of the Rocky Mountains into the mighty Green River to the west. The scene, behind the gentle rolling sagebrush covered terrain, was etched in my mind. I was full of adrenalin from the excitement of the moment.

The Yampa River seemed like a good place to camp, and a far enough goal for our first day on the road. We made the seven miles to the river easily, but I was tired enough to be glad to stop. I found a good place to camp on a green swath of grass, with a couple of small trees, right on the shore of the wide, slow moving river.

Most of the land along the river was private ranchland, but I was able to find this little slice of public land to camp on, because I had a BLM, "Surface Management Status" map.

The detailed topography map not only showed all of the roads and land features, but also land ownership: private, BLM, state, Indian Reservation, etc. by different colors. They were my favorite maps for this kind of traveling, because of all the information and details they provided. Being able to find a desirable riverside location amidst private property was a huge asset.

Yay!!! ... A successful first day; even though we'd gone straight south, and weren't any closer to Oregon. It was SO exciting to have the first day safely under my belt. I plunked down the gear, and made camp right next to the rolling river, all muddy and swollen with the spring runoff. I was a bit concerned that the river might rise higher and flood us out, since my camp was only about ten inches above water level. The hills near the river were very dry and austere, but all along the hundred-yard-wide river was a green oasis of thick brush and an occasional cottonwood tree. I was not only joyful to be on my adventure, but also to be in such a beautiful spot.

It was fairly windy in such an open area, consequently, to avoid having my tent blown down on the first day of the trip; I just spread out a tarp and set up camp on it. The weather was clear, with no chance of rain, and the bugs weren't out for the year yet, so I really didn't need the tent. WOW, was I ever feeling good to be on the road! I had no fear or apprehension about my situation. I was HOME.

Our camp beside the rolling river was a perfect place to ease into trip attitude. We were all: max tired, even after just one, seven mile day so, in classic burro slow-start, we took the next two days off from walking.

Years earlier in my burro packing career, I'd learned about the ultra-slow-start. My only goal for the first ten days of the trip was to still be going on the eleventh day. A slow start gave us time to get used to the rigors of the demanding adventure. I figured we wouldn't really hit stride until at least forty days into our trek. If I'd been in a hurry, I wouldn't be walking burros. It was startling to realize that the distance a person could easily and comfortably travel in an hour by car, would take us a week of hard toil and, possibly, very real danger. The contrast was amazing. I considered car travel a miracle.

The speed and ease with which a person could travel by air was other-worldly compared to a cross-country walk with animals. Complaints about being delayed a couple of hours on a flight across the entire continent were laughable next to the delays and hardships I faced. It was astounding to realize that only one hundred twenty years earlier, taking pack animals on a long journey would have been an ordinary thing to do. Now, it was like something out of the stone-age.

I worked at reacquainting myself with camp life, which was much harder than town existence. Everything took a little longer and required a bit more effort; getting the water, starting the cooking stove, etc. Just living at true ground level took up a lot more energy; getting up and down from the ground, and bending over to pick up things. There is a reason for chairs and tables, one quickly learns, when doing without. Life outside and on the way was so different from sedentary town existence. The two activities were like separate dreams. I couldn't imagine being in town while on a pack trip, and vice versa. It was good for me that burro packing was so different from town world, where my performance bordered on the pathetic.

I grazed the burros by driving sixteen-inch long, three-quarter-inch thick, steel stakes into the ground and attaching ropes of different lengths, with clips on both ends. This way I could easily adjust the length, by clipping together different lengths of rope. Through years of camping in so many different situations, I had developed a strategy for grazing an area and would carefully choose my tactics for each location to best utilize the crucial resource. One of the most important things was to leave the best patch of grazing near the camp until the morning of departure, so that you still had prime grazing when you really wanted the animals fully fed.

I needed a flat, unobstructed grassy area for this type of grazing, and when hunting for campsites, finding decent grazing was usually the hardest piece of the puzzle. Another way to graze an animal was with hobbles, tying the front legs loosely together, so the burros could only hop around. This was easier as far as time was concerned, because one didn't have to keep moving the grazing stake. But hobbled burros can still roam, getting lost or somewhere you don't want them, on a road or in the camp.

The burros were experts with the ropes. Their mild disposition kept them from getting tangled and panicky. They could even roll on their backs without getting tangled on a short, ten foot rope, if the spot was flat enough. Staking them out on the side of a hill could cause tangling problems. The stakes were the most important item. The rope swiveled around the stakes, so they could happily graze for hours without tangling; tying an animal to a tree quickly caused problems. They'd go around the tree, until they had no grazing room, and they'd damage the tree.

The biggest problem with tying animals to a tree was that trees were hardly ever where you wanted them, alone in a flat meadow. I used a hatchet to drive the stout steel stakes into the ground. To pull the stakes, I had to pound them with the hatchet from several directions, till they loosened enough to pull. Any obstructions, such as bushes, rocks, or loose sticks would cause the rope to tangle.

There usually wasn't a suitable place to bring the burros to water, because of mud, rocks, brush or steep terrain. I almost always carried water to the burros and gave it to them in a five gallon bucket. Finding and carrying the heavy liquid to the burros and to camp was a constant activity, and part of the exercise program. I had two five-gallon buckets, and five two-and-a-half-gallon neoprene water-sacks for transporting and storing water. Two of the sacks were for filtered drinking water. The other three were used to carry unfiltered water when steep terrain or brush made using the buckets too difficult. If the water source was shallow, I used a plastic scoop, made from the bottom of a juice bottle to dip water.

Burros are very much herd animals. Consequently, they always stayed together. If you had one, you had the other. In safe areas, I only staked one of the burros, leaving the other loose to wander. If the free burro roamed too far, or out of sight, the tied burro called her buddy back with a loud, mournful bray. They both loved being the "Free Bird", because they could explore the area, and find the finest fare.

During the second wonderful day by the river, Libby, who was free, started rummaging in my gear. When I shooed her away, Lucy joined in, and got soundly kicked in the chest. She yelped in pain, but luckily turned out to be o.k. She still had a lot to learn. Burros are very good kickers. Farriers had told me that burros were more dangerous than horses, because they were better at side-kicking than a horse. They liked to charge a dog head-on, trying to stomp it with front hooves, or even bite it with their powerful jaws. Burros will often go out of their way to tangle with a canine. Sometimes, burros are kept with bands of sheep as guards against coyotes.

The riverside was a fantastic place to begin the trip. The lush underbrush along the river made a natural refuge for many types of wildlife. Bird laughter dominated the mornings. I saw ducks, geese, great blue herons, hawks, and bald eagles, along with smaller birds who made their homes in the wonderful green oasis by the river. Besides the birds, I saw many deer along the banks, and watched one swim across the wide, swollen river. A good sized snake came swimming down with the current of the river, looking to come ashore just below my campsite. I ran along the shore after the snake, for a better look, but my activity kept it from coming ashore until it was farther down river. It wasn't a rattler.

The midday sun was very hot. Fortunately, we had some small trees for shade. I sat by the river, leisurely watching the parade of dead branches riding the high spring runoff. The river never got much higher, and then dropped several inches. It was a treat to take the time to just sit there and soak up the scene. The joyous start really solidified my positive attitude about walking to Oregon.

I realized that wandering was a major part of my life, and that being fearful about it was foolish. A successful adventure depended on my attitude. This had been proven to me on my first burro adventure, when a positive attitude was about all that I had, other than God's good graces. I'd reached a higher level. Now, I was really ready to walk to Oregon. During the last evening along the river, a bald eagle landed on a nearby dead tree and surveyed the scene.

May 26.

The gravel road went westerly along the Yampa River, before heading uphill onto a dry plateau. It was a clear day, and SO HOT in the direct sunlight. shine in the arid high desert air is intense, heating the ground more than the air, making it feel much hotter than the actual air temperature; in the same way, being in shade and wind felt much cooler than the temperature indicated. Temperatures would drop 35-40 degrees during the nights, making sleep easy, and the first part of each day relatively cool.

Our gravel road joined Highway 40 a couple miles outside the little town of Maybell. We walked along the right shoulder of the paved highway, in the same direction as traffic. Beanie, the rear burro, tended to walk to the right of the lead burro so, if we walked on the left side of the road, Beanie would be out in the traffic. I also preferred to walk in the same direction as the traffic, because seeing fast moving vehicles, particularly big trucks, coming right at us: was extremely disturbing. I tied a large piece of orange cloth on the back of Beanie's packsaddle, and I wore an orange vest to make it easier for passing drivers to see us.

Soon, a car pulled over, and a man and his daughter got out to chat. They'd passed us and found the sight of a man leading pack burros too intriguing to pass by; so they turned back to hear our story. They couldn't believe we were walking to Oregon, many miles and months away. L.A. city dwellers, they were driving across the country on side roads just for the adventure. They were happy that their road choice had given them a chance to meet someone doing something so unique.

Maybell's business district was only a country store, with a couple of gas pumps in front. We passed it and a throng of people in the nearby town park, enjoying the annual Memorial Day dog-agility trials. We passed the last houses, went another half-mile, and found a camp spot right beside the highway. There was good green grass between the road and a fenced alfalfa field; great grazing for the burros, and water running in a ditch next to the field. A row of trees between camp and the highway made it comfortable. The trees gave me some privacy and protection from the blowing wind. I wanted to stay close to town, so that I could easily go see the dog trials and get drinking water. We'd walked seven miles and, at least this time, gotten closer to Oregon.

I set the burros out to graze, and Lucy and I walked back to the park to watch the show. People came from all over the west to participate with their dogs. The town park took up an entire block and was a perfect place for such an event. Participants had their RVs set up under the sprawling cottonwood trees bordering the park. The entire perimeter of the park was camps. Since they all had several dogs, it was a lively scene.

The trials obstacle course, with jumps, tunnels, teeter-totters and poles, was set up in the center grassy area of the park. Knocking down a pole on a jump, or some other mistake running through the course, added penalty time. The dog who completed the course fastest, with the fewest mistakes, won. The courses were changed frequently to make it more difficult for dog and owner. Trainers got their dogs through the course with hand and voice signals. A wide variety of dogs and people participated. It took a lot of training to teach the dogs how to do well. Some people were serious about the results, while others were doing it for the joy of working with their dogs and the camaraderie of fellow dog lovers. The dogs, of course, loved to play, and excitedly ran through the course at their owner's directions. It was a joy for me to watch and be witness to the fun.

Again, staying with the ultra-slow-start, and having the opportunity to watch the dog trials, we took the next day off from traveling. Folks at the competition had seen us arrive in town, and they were extra friendly to us. They gave me a large plate of food at a group meal in the evening and were very kind to Lucy and me. The good food, instead of my usual austere diet was a real boost. I was even able to shower in the park facilities.

Another thing that made our stay in Maybell extra special, was befriending the seventy-something-year-old farmer, who owned the alfalfa field next to our camp. He came out several times a day to move the irrigation water to different sections of his bright green field.

His family had homesteaded the area in 1910, and Maybell became a town in 1911. His pioneer ancestors had arrived walking their herd of cows from the rail line to the north, down to the town. The fit old man told me of his life as a farmer. He reminisced about the old-days; how they only left the farm maybe twice a year, and how things had changed so much with paved highways and fast cars.

The short stay in Maybell boosted my confidence, not only because everyone at the dog trials was so friendly and helpful, but because the rancher was so happy to see us. It confirmed my belief that we'd not only be welcomed, but assisted on the journey ahead.

May 28.

Just past Maybell, there was a fork in the road. Highway 40 continued straight west into Utah, south of the High Uintas mountain chain. If we were crossing Nevada to reach Oregon, we would have taken that route. I had other plans, so we headed northwest on the smaller, less traveled, Rt. 318, a paved road without a shoulder. The lack of a shoulder made it more dangerous, since we'd often be out in the traveled lanes. But traffic was light and the road straight enough that people in cars were able to see us as they approached, which made walking down the highway not so much of a panic.

A cluster of houses, called Sunbeam, was six miles up the road. Sunbeam, without a commercial district, was in a shallow valley created by the meandering Yampa River.

The valley bottom near the river was green with irrigation, surrounded by dry, brown sagebrush hills. Our route, beyond the green valley, led into desert desolation. We needed to stay somewhere in Sunbeam for water, grazing, and shelter from the wind. We camped in the middle of town, on an abandoned strip of land created when the highway through town had been shifted fifty yards to one side. It was odd, camping on the side of the road, in the open, right in the middle of town, but it worked.

Again, we took the next day off, staying with the slow start. We hid from the persistent wind behind a thick wall of sagebrush growing along the road. The burros grazed along the side of the highway, relaxing. I learned from some locals where to find water, at an old homestead on the side of Cross Mountain, in the upcoming dry stretch.

May 30.

We traveled a couple of miles out of the green valley and into the arid hills, before we moved onto the gravel of County Road 10. This route, though a bit longer, roughly paralleled Rt. 318. I wanted to travel on side roads as much as was practical. This isolated road would do the trick. The gravel strip crossed a long sagebrush plain and, in the hours that we walked across it, only a few vehicles came by. From several miles away, we sighted the green spot that was the old homestead.

While Cross Mountain wasn't a huge peak, the long, steep, rocky uplift stood out dramatically in the otherwise rolling terrain. The homestead was a mile off the road.

When we found faint signs of an old road leading to the green oasis, we followed it. A bright green meadow, 100 yards wide and a quarter mile long, covered a gentle slope. An aspen grove climbing the hill betrayed the location of a little stream. Several big bushes where the slope changed from mild to steep gave me a protected flat spot for my tent.
We'd walked a fairly long eleven miles and, with the ideal camping spot, it didn't take long to decide to spend a day at the excellent oasis. It would be our fifth day of vacation in the nine days since we'd started, right about on schedule.

It wasn't entirely a day of leisure, since I did some laundry and repairs. I heated wash water in my largest pot, over my camp stove, storing the hot water in a closed five gallon bucket, until I had enough to churn my dirty clothes. I rinsed them in buckets with cold water from the stream, and hung them on nearby dead brush to dry in the sun.

Life on the trail was hard on gear; hence sewing was a steady occupation. A sewing awl was the perfect tool for trail repairs. The light, portable tool was a wooden handle holding an extra-stout needle and thread. What made it so special was that it made a back stitch, creating a much stronger seam than a regular needle and thread could. Typically, I needed to sew through many layers of thick nylon straps and heavy synthetic fabrics, and the wooden handle allowed me to push through all of those layers. The hole in the needle was wide enough to be threaded with fifty pound test, braided Dacron fishing line. The beloved tool worked well on boots, equipment repairs, or frequent zipper replacements. I sewed the new zipper onto the original for a quick, easy, and still quite acceptable fix.

Years of ultra-poverty had taught me the much-needed skills of clothing and equipment repair. I wore my clothes to rags, repaired them, and wore them again; only giving up on an item when no further repairs would keep it functional. Trail clothes got trashed by the rough use and everyday dirt encountered while crossing the landscape with a couple of burros. Anyone with a strong need to be clean would have had a difficult time dealing with the dirtiness of such an adventure. Fortunately, I was a natural slob; so having a legitimate excuse to be filthy was just another bonus of walking burros.

I had a wonderful day at the old homestead. The green spot was alive with butterflies and birds. Lucy and I hiked up the steep mountainside, following the small babbling stream to its source. Whenever possible, I took my drinking water directly from cold clear springs. I only used springs that flowed from some sort of pipe. I avoided springs that slowly seeped out into a wide spot before collecting into a stream. Officially, it wasn't advised that people drink out of springs. Bacteria were apparently in almost all water, but I'd been drinking from springs for years without any adverse effects. I'd probably become immune to most of what might make me sick in the mountain waters.

When a drinking-water spring wasn't available, I purified water with a small, portable water filter. If the water was too cloudy, the filter would clog quickly. I'd fill a five gallon bucket with water and let it sit undisturbed for several hours, before filtering, to settle out as much debris as possible. I didn't like filtering water, because it required a lot of tedious pumping, especially over a period of months. I searched constantly for good springs, and would walk up to a mile for the precious fluid.

I used two high quality neoprene sacks to carry water. Two-inch-wide nylon straps, attached to the sacks, slung over each shoulder, made it relatively easy to carry forty pounds of water back to camp over the rough, steep terrain. Water that was going to be boiled for hot drinks and gruel was just camp-water; whatever was immediately available, even if it was really ugly. Many times, I boiled drinking water, particularly if it was too muddy to filter. "In Boiling We Trust" was one of my mottos for sure. I kept a bucket of camp-water near the tent for convenience. The spring source, on the side of Cross Mountain, flowed well enough to use as drinking water.

I sat on a rock ledge, near the spring, and took in the VASTNESS of the wide open rolling, sagebrush-covered hills fading into the distance. I was in LOVE with what I was doing.

Down on the flat, near my camp, were several decrepit buildings. The old log structures were all fallen in and dissolving back into the earth. I wondered about the people who'd lived there in the isolation of the area. I touched the axe marks on the logs, imagining the man in the long ago, chopping away.

Chapter 4
Northwestern Colorado
June 1 - June 9

June 1.

Reluctantly, I left the old homestead. The oasis was comforting, and met our needs well, but we were moving slowly enough as it was, having gone only thirty-one miles in nine days. Today, we walked along at a great clip for us. Libby was very fast on the flats, for a burro. She really seemed to enjoy striding off into the distance, but slowed down a lot on the uphill grades. She had a lot of speed, but not much power. Beanie was stronger, but slower. We had a very easy five mile walk around to the other side of Cross Mountain, reaching a place where we stopped to camp before noon. The reason we stopped so soon, when we really weren't tired, was that we had come to the Little Snake River, and the next water was a long way off. Slightly smaller than the Yampa River, the Little Snake River was still large for such a dry area. Its source was far away in the Rocky Mountains. The biggest requirement for a camp was an accessible water source. Water weighed too much to pack to a camp. The burros might each drink as much as five gallons a day, although they usually drank only two or three gallons daily.

Before choosing a spot for the night, I always took a walk around to check out all of the possibilities. I hated finding a better camp after I'd unloaded the gear. Moving the gear once I'd taken it off the burros was so much work that I'd only do it in an extreme situation. Finding the best, most practical camping spot available was crucial. If I was setting up the tent, and heard myself say that the location was good because of the view, a flashing red warning light went off in my head. The best tent-site wasn't determined by scenery, but by practicality.

Protection from the wind was the most important attribute, after water. Strong winds weren't much fun, and, at any time, could blow harder than my tent could withstand. Flash floods were also a potential hazard to be avoided. A flat spot that looked like a good place to set up a tent could become a pond after a heavy rain. Another big consideration was sunshine; did you want it, or were you trying to avoid it? During high mountain trips, where morning temperatures were cold, camping where the morning sun would hit was a huge plus. On lower, desert trips, one wanted the tent in shade. There was rarely a clear-cut best place to pitch the tent. Usually, I had to weigh all the different factors, and compromise on something.

Just before the bridge across the spring-swollen river, we found an adequate camp spot. Right along the river's edge was a grove of small cottonwood trees and an open grassy area for grazing. Everything else was covered with sagebrush. The grass was clipped a bit short, because of cattle grazing, but the spot had the all-important water.

A rancher in a pickup truck had passed us several times during the day's walk. That evening, he and his grandson pulled up to my campsite to see what was happening. He was seventy-four years old. His teenage grandson, who was helping out on the ranch for the summer, had broken his collar bone in football practice, but was still able to chase cows. When I mentioned that I'd camped at the old homestead, the grandson told me that his great-grandfather had homesteaded the property in 1917, and his grandfather had been born and raised at the long abandoned home-site.

He was a real local, still living within a few miles of his birthplace. A classic old-time cowboy, he was one of the few people living in that vast desolation. He'd really lived the life, and had a fine sparkle in his eye. When I told him how much I enjoyed hearing stories of life in the very isolated area from an old-timer, he was a bit offended. The tough old cowboy pouted, "I don't feel old." His life of constant activity had kept him very fit. He liked what I was doing: taking pack animals into the sunset. One of the joys of traveling with burros was meeting and conversing with someone like him. Driving through in a car, it wouldn't happen.

I sat on the bank of the hundred-yard-wide, slow moving river. A blue heron flew lazily by, landed just upriver, and stalked away for a meal in the shallows. A muskrat cruised downriver along the bank where I sat. It paused briefly in front of me, checking out what this tourist was doing, before diving and swimming away. A soft evening sunset; I was sure feeling good to be out on adventure.

June 2.

I set my little travel alarm clock for 3:45 a.m., wanting the earliest start possible. The next water source was a long, daunting fifteen miles away, across a desolate, dusty landscape, and it would be hot. Also, it would be our first two-consecutive-day walk, and our eleventh day on the journey. We'd reached my first big goal of the trip; we were still going on day eleven. I didn't believe going two days in a row would be much problem, since we'd moved only five miles the day before, finished early in the day, and had plenty of time to rest before the long walk.

We left at 6:45 a.m. I'd hoped to be packed and on the way earlier, but I still wasn't up to full speed. We crossed the bridge, and headed up through low gentle hills, eventually reaching a wide plateau, with a long straight stretch of road. A few miles to the south, a higher ridge of interesting rock formations and large ponderosa pines rose from the plain. Even this early in the day, it was already getting hot. It was obviously going to be a difficult day. I wore my large grass hat for protection from the hot sun. It was made in South America from palm leaves. I liked it because if it got crushed, it would pop right back into shape when wet. The extra-wide-brimmed hat was essential for keeping the blazing sun off head, neck and shoulders. I added a chin-strap to hold it in the wind.

We encountered several small bands of Pronghorn. Commonly called Antelope, Pronghorn are actually a species unto themselves. They are about the same size as deer, but have shorter legs and neck, and small, uniquely-shaped horns. Their coats were light brown and white. They were common in the wide-open, high deserts of the west. Whenever I'd seen them in the past, usually from a car, they were shy and kept their distance. I was quite surprised when, walking with the burros, these little groups of pronghorn were very curious about us. They not only didn't run away, they came closer to investigate this once-in-a-lifetime event. A lone Pronghorn followed us for a good quarter-mile, racing by to within twenty yards on numerous passes. It was magnificently fast and full of itself as it pranced proudly about, pausing some moments to give us a good look before bursting off again.

The sleek beast didn't care if Lucy-dog chased it, or that I was yelling at the barking dog to stop. It ignored her, knowing that the dog couldn't match its brilliant speed and, for some reason, wasn't at all afraid of me. I believed that what so interested the prancing Pronghorn was the strange sight and smell of the burros, which it probably had never encountered before. After several minutes, the lone speedster finally had enough of us, and disappeared into the sagebrush.

The direct sunshine was beating down on us, so after ten miles, we stopped to recuperate under a large roadside juniper tree. I took the equipment off the burros, so they could rest better. They just stood in the small spot of shade, instead of grazing. We hid from the burning sun for three hours, before I deemed it possible to continue. We had to get to water. I struggled to finish the last five miles through some low hills, finally reaching a dip in the terrain, which held a stream and a couple of small ponds. I was so glad to get to the precious water! The road was so isolated that we saw only two cars all day.

I had to find a place to set up our home-site for that night and the next day. I was hot and exhausted, and struggled to set up camp under a large juniper. One of the most difficult parts of the trip was that a day's work wasn't over just because the walking was done. I had to unload the animals, get them water and grazing, set up the tent, unpack the gear, and cook something, often when I was totally exhausted, and would've rather collapsed on my gear. Setting up camp at the end of the day took about an hour. Packing the gear in the morning usually took at least a couple of hours. Traveling days were very long; the difficulties of moving made vacation days just that much more delectable.

Cattle had grazed down the grass, particularly along the water, and the rest of the area was covered with sagebrush, making stake-and-rope grazing difficult. Near camp was an area where most of the brush was dead. I removed the deadwood with my lightweight pick-hoe, after a couple of whacks to the roots, levering it out of the ground with the handy digging tool. I was able clear out areas large enough for the burros to graze without tangling their ropes. I only staked one burro at a time, changing them every few hours, so they'd both get a chance to roam and find the best eats.

I took a very casual day off, resting by the tent in the shade of the tree. I was totally thwacked tired. Luckily, all I had to do was move the burros around once in a while, and get some drinking water. The headwaters of the stream were on private land; therefore, I had to filter water from one of the ponds. The water was clear enough to pump directly from the calm little pond. The water-filter was new, so it took a while to figure out how to get it working properly.

The burros were such good companions on a journey like this. They were like big dogs, loving attention, particularly being scratched. I used a big-toothed, metal comb, though a stout stick would also do the trick. The burros had very tough hides and loved to be scratched with a lot of force. Beanie's favorite scratch-spot was her butt. She couldn't get enough, and would back into me, trying to get me to scratch her. Each became upset and annoyed when I scratched the other, always wanting it to be their turn. The beloved scratching usually took place in the evening, after the girls were in their night-time spot.

Usually, I staked out each burro on a ten foot rope for the night. That way, they could graze and I could still find them right away if necessary. If I left one loose at night, it might wander too far away, and cause the staked burro to have a hissy fit and break loose. Beanie was strong enough to yank out the steel grazing stakes if she really wanted to. Theoretically, there was a long-shot chance of the burros being attacked by a mountain lion, so I liked to keep them close-by at night. Mountain lions were quite common in the wide opens of the rural west.

To be extra safe, I didn't usually tie the burros on twenty foot ropes at night. If something spooked them in the dark, they could get up enough speed to either pull the stake out of the ground, or hurt themselves when they hit the end of the rope. If I really wanted to keep an animal around, I'd put a half-hobble around one of its front ankles with a rope to a stake. This way, it couldn't yank hard enough to pull the stake, and it was a little less likely to get its legs tangled. I hadn't used that method in years, because the burros preferred to have the rope attached to their halter.

Burros have excellent hearing. Their oversized ears pick up sounds even better than dogs. That evening, they alerted me to approaching intruders with their distinctive distress call, a raspy guttural sound they made when something unknown or scary approached. This time, seven elk came down from the juniper-covered hills to drink from the stream in the last light of day. The burros didn't scare the nearly horse-sized animals, and I was hidden in the trees, so they came right in close to drink. To the north, low hills dotted with juniper trees glowed in the soft pink and gray twilight

June 4.

We started the day with a climb out of the drainage where we'd camped. Once on top, we were on a flatter mesa area with a few houses, so a few cars came by. It was another long, broiling stretch, with the sun on its Bright setting. We took a short break, a little more than halfway through the 12-mile day, under some juniper trees big enough to give us some much needed shade. On breaks during the middle of the day, I almost never took out the cooking gear, instead eating snack foods, usually just nuts or peanut butter. During the walk, particularly in the heat, I sucked hard candies to moisten my mouth and get a bit of an energy boost.

The side road rejoined Rt. 318, the road we'd followed through the town of Sunbeam several days before. Soon after that, the road crossed Vermilion Creek, the only water in the area, and, therefore, our camping spot. According to the BLM Land Use map, the entire area was public land, except for one tiny private block. We could camp anywhere we found a suitable spot. Grazing was extremely poor in all directions. I wanted to camp upstream, away from the highway, but after a thorough reconnaissance, I found the grazing too sparse. Below the steep road embankment, just downstream from the bridge, was an open flat spot with a couple of cottonwoods to cover our camp. The grazing was paltry, but it was the best available, so it had to do.

Lucy and I took advantage of the comparative coolness in the shade, next to the water, under the highway bridge. Occasional vehicles gave us a rumbling shock, speeding over the bridge above us. Lucy was obsessed with fetching, so I threw something for her at every opportunity.

Chasing a stick into water was extra-big-time fun for her, so I tossed a stick into the stream repeatedly as we waited out the heat of the day. Lucy had turned out to be the perfect traveling companion. My belief that she would stay right with me had turned out to be true. I imagined that, for her, the new life wandering the countryside with her person was a joyous adventure, after her previous years in the fenced backyard.

I went to the only nearby house, to see if I might be able to get some drinking water. The friendly rancher not only gave us water, but even brought over a bale of hay to give my burro-girls a treat. He refused money for the hay. Hooray for ranchers! He told me there were a lot of rattlesnakes in the area, and that his dog had recently been killed after a rattlesnake entered its pen, seeking the numerous mice living under the doghouse.

June 5.

I learned first-hand about the mouse infestation when I woke up at 4:30 a.m. It would be a very hot day, so I wanted to beat the heat. That plan went out the window when I found the panniers I'd left outside the tent infested with about fifteen mice. They'd already been building nests throughout my gear. It weirded me out, and ruined an early start, because I had to empty the panniers of all of my gear, to rid myself of invading mice.

I was frazzled and herky-jerky walking down the side of the highway. Being in a lousy mood was dangerous, so I put myself on alert, understanding that the commotion in my mind might detrimentally affect my performance. I also worried that Lucy would run out into the road and be hit by a car, chasing after the numerous rabbits in the area.

I kept her on a leash as we went on our way. This kept my hands full, holding the lead rope for the burros and her leash at the same time. A major concern when leading large animals was keeping my lead rope and the animals tangle-free. If an animal bolted and I was tangled the situation could easily be deadly. Although my burros were docile, if they started to drag me it would be bad, because they'd spook at the dragging, and keep running. Despite this danger, I often looped the lead rope under one armpit, around the back of my neck, and over the other shoulder. I did this so that I wouldn't have to carry the rope in my hand hours at a stretch, and if I did have to pull the burros, I'd have more leverage and grip on the rope. I tried to stay aware of the possibility of being tangled.

We dropped down into Brown's Park, a large valley through which flowed the mighty Green River. The lower valley was surrounded by relatively high mountains, and walking into it was quite dramatic. The Gates of Lordore, where the Green River flowed out of the valley, through a steep narrow ravine in the mountains, was particularly dramatic. A lot of early history had taken place in Brown's Park. The area's lower elevation made for a somewhat warmer winter climate. This part of the west had fairly harsh winters, so the pocket of milder conditions attracted early settlers to the valley. Before them, Native Americans wintered in the big valley. The area was also famous for the outlaws who hid out there, taking advantage of the warmer winters and the surrounding rugged mountains, where they could escape if the law was on their trail.

My map showed some side roads, but when I tried to find them, they no longer existed. I'd found maps to be wrong about smaller roads and trails many times in the past. It was important to keep that possibility in mind, to avoid getting brain-locked on information which might be wrong. In my circumstances, that could literally be deadly. This time it cost me only an extra mile. That extra was painful enough, added to the heat and weariness of a 12-mile day. I'd made it more difficult than necessary by leaving the spigot of my drinking water sack open, draining two gallons of the precious liquid onto the road. Luckily, I had two or three swallows of water in another sack, and only had to go another three miles to where I thought we could camp: being out of water made me feel thirstier than I really was.

There was a large wildlife refuge on the valley floor, along the Green River. The rest of the bottomland was mostly private, so the refuge was the logical place to camp. I was excited to have a chance to camp near the Green River, the major drainage for all of that part of the west. The campground in the Brown's Park Wildlife Refuge had the only cluster of trees available for camping, and I gladly set up under the spreading branches of the large cottonwoods. I made camp off to the side, so that the burros wouldn't foul up the campground proper.

Surprisingly, there wasn't any drinking water, but I was able to get enough for my immediate needs, as well as some fuel for my cook stove, from the few other campers. It was off-season, already getting too hot for most visitors. The rolling Green River was several hundred yards from our camp, so I had a workout going to the river for water. Three times I went with my dirty-water sacks, scooping water into them with the bottom of a plastic juice jug, and then lugging them back to camp. I got enough for the burros to drink all they wanted, and still have some camp water.

I decided to take a two day vacation, since we needed the rest, and we had a good camp. I still planned to move along relatively slowly, so that we'd keep getting stronger, and not risk injury. Temperatures were near ninety degrees, hot even in the shade. Thankfully, the wind cooled things a bit. I got more breeze than I needed one evening when a thunderstorm rolled through. Hammering winds broke one of my tent poles. I collapsed the tent, and hid inside, the nylon flapping wildly inches from my face, until the violent storm ended. Fortunately, I'd owned two similar tents, and had brought along some poles from them, to use as spares, and as supports for my ten by twelve foot tarp.

I had an older A-frame tent that I loved. It was rated as a four person tent, though it really only fit three. I used such a big tent so I could store my gear, have enough space for someone else, and, of course, have room for Lucy. It weighed only a few pounds more than a two man tent, so it wasn't an extra burden for the burros, compared to their entire loads. It was a huge pleasure to have the larger tent, especially over such a long time. If I was only going to be in a spot overnight, I'd usually leave my gear outside under a small tarp, to eliminate the effort of dragging the panniers in and out of the tent. I liked the A-frame design, because when it rained with the wind coming from the back, I could leave the front door open and see out. The stove had to be outside to be safe, and didn't work well when wet so, when it rained, I hung the tarp in front of the tent for protection. This allowed me to be out of the confines of the tent, and have a good place to cook.

Through the years, I developed an exact way to set up and organize my tent. It had a sloping rear vestibule, which I aimed toward the wind. Always, even if it wasn't windy, I pitched the tent in a place with trees, bushes, or some other protection from winds that might come up. I preferred a slight uphill slope toward the back of the tent, with my feet toward the door. That way I didn't mess up the head of my sleeping area going in and out of the tent. An inflatable foam mattress went in the center of the tent, with my gear in its proper locations to each side. A saddle pad was at the side of my sleeping bag, near my feet, for Lucy's bed. In town, I was an unorganized slob, but on pack trips I strove to keep my gear in its proper place, so I could find things when I needed them.

I met a lady near the campground, working on her Biology PhD, taking soil samples for the Park Service. She gave me a huge boost by bringing me some much-needed drinking water, dog food and other food supplies, when she finished her work. I gave her an art card as thanks for the help. I'd brought along some of my two-handed art work, mostly business-card size pieces that folded like a greeting card. The small artworks were really handy, because I could keep them in a notebook, inside clear business card holders, which protected the paintings and made them easy to view. There were also four eight-by-ten-inch paintings which fit into a five gallon bucket. I hoped to sell some artwork along the way for food money, or to use as gifts to people who helped me along the way.

Just seven feet in front of my tent, under a bush, was a huge nest of red-black ants. I didn't know their proper name, but the front half was red and the back half was black, so I called them Red-Blacks. Thousands of them roiled about on their large anthill of twigs. A parade of ants went off in one direction, marching to and fro on hive business. I hadn't noticed them when I first made camp. I could have moved my tent, but I wasn't too worried about them. I'd had a lot of experience with these ants, and found them to be uninterested in humans, unlike the common black ants that crawl all over you, if you are on the ground. Red-Black ants seldom climbed on me or any of my equipment. I'd gotten friendly with them on the rock formation where I'd lived in New Mexico. One of my favorite places to sit on the rock was right on one of their ant highways. Even though I'd sit right in the middle of them, they rarely crawled on me. They'd never bitten me, and I wondered if they could even bite. One day, I saw a cluster of them dragging a dead bug back to the hive. They were having a hard time pulling their prize past one twig, so I picked up another twig and moved the obstruction out of their way. The moment I moved the twig, an ant that was on me immediately bit me. I was amazed that the ant knew I was messing with its comrades. It seemed that they had some immediate communication, as if each ant was a cell in one creature, each knowing what was happening to the others.

It was particularly hot in the afternoons. Therefore, I wore my swim trunks, which doubled as shorts, and took quick dips in the cold water of the Green River. I sat on the riverbank, throwing sticks for Lucy, and enjoying the huge meandering river and the surrounding high mountains. I took two rejuvenating rest days, relaxing in the shade, reveling in my freedom.

June 8.

I was well-rested and anxious to be on the way again after our vacation, so we were up and on the road early. The Park road followed along the meandering Green River a few miles before rejoining Route. 318. We made good time, going ten miles by 11 a.m. I was excited to be nearing another big milestone, the Colorado-Utah border. A mile before the border was the Wildlife Refuge headquarters, where we stopped for a rest and water.

At the border, we would leave the area covered by my good map, and all I had for the upcoming section was a lousy copy of an insufficient map. I had been worrying that I wouldn't have an adequate map to guide us through the upcoming dry-lands. The best route, water, and good camping places would be difficult to predict using the map I had. I was hoping there might be better maps for sale in the Park headquarters. Officially, they had no maps of the upcoming section, but the lady working there had a spare of her own, and generously gave it to our cause. Wonderfully, it was the exact map I preferred, the BLM Surface Management Status type. While resting at the refuge headquarters, we met a kind gentleman on vacation from the Oregon coast. His ancestors had lived in the area, and he was trying to find some of his family's historical locations. We talked a good while, and out of the blue, he gave me twenty dollars to help us on our way. Yeah, the good people of the world kept on appearing.

The ten miles we'd already walked were enough for me, and I was hoping to camp by the stream near the Refuge headquarters, but the rules only allowed camping in designated campgrounds. There was a campground two miles away, totally out of our way, making a 4-mile detour. The campground had no shade trees, so it wasn't really an option. The lady at the Refuge headquarters told me where to find some good camping, six miles ahead, along the Green River.

With some excitement we left Colorado and crossed into Utah. The road changed from pavement to large gravel. Burros don't like walking on that kind of surface, so we mostly walked alongside the road on paths made by free-range cattle. It had always been my philosophy to go the way the burros wanted to go. I figured if the burros thought I was wise, they'd be more likely to want to follow me. If the burros really didn't want to cross a certain obstacle, I'd try to find a better alternative. The burros were in on the decision-making process, and I listened to them when I could.

Shortly after entering Utah, we came to a piece of fenced-off private land with a small stream and a good field of grass. I didn't really want to trespass, and since it had been cloudy and relatively cool all day, we continued on to the camping place I'd been told about without too much trouble. A cloudy day was a blessing. Under a blazing sun, the 16-mile day would have been on the harsh side.

I found the seldom-used side road leading to the river and the wonderful camping spot. There was a huge cottonwood tree above a picnic table, right on the magnificent Green River. Nearby were open grassy areas for grazing.

I was so glad for good directions, or I would likely have missed this perfect place to camp, being several hundred yards off the road. I was tempted to pitch my tent on the open ground beneath the spreading tree, but instead listened to my experience and tucked it amongst some nearby bushes.

I was very tired after the long day, and knowing we faced a thousand vertical foot climb out of Brown's Park, we laid over the next day. Up to that point, the burros had been walking unshod. I'd left their hooves as long as possible before starting the trip, to allow them to wear down on the long walk. Libby's hooves were softer than Beanie's, so it was time for her to start wearing her protective rubber boots. The boots needed adjustment, because burro's hooves are shaped differently than the horse hooves the boots had been designed to fit. Burros have a straight up and down hoof, horse's splay out at the bottom. It took several adjustments, using dense blue foam, to get them to stay on properly. I took out the sewing awl, and attached nylon straps that went around their ankles. They'd help keep the valuable boots on, and reduce the risk of losing them, if they did slip off.

I very much enjoyed our camp by the slow moving river. Lucy and I took some short sight-seeing strolls up and down the river. This would be our last opportunity to spend time along the Green River, in the wonderful valley, amongst the higher peaks. It was good that I'd hidden my tent in the bushes, instead of setting it up in the open spot near the picnic table. Late in the day, a storm moved in, and the wind came up. I would've had problems in the open. It rained steadily all night.

Chapter 5
Dam and Other Devils
June 10 - June 21

June 10.

We made the three and a half mile climb out of the valley very slowly, pausing about every thirty yards to rest. Burros like to go in short fast bursts up a steep hill, and rest often, rather than keep a slow plodding pace. Spurt-stop, spurt-stop was our rhythm climbing hills. The technique was developed over many years of burro packing in the high mountains of Colorado, with enormously long, hard climbs at high altitude. It was slow, but since the burros wanted to do it that way, it was the way we did it. I planned on a half mile per hour on the hardest, highest climbs. The best thing about the ultra-slow-climb was that we would reach the top of even the highest climb without being exhausted, a dangerous condition when packing animals alone, in the out-country. People told me early in my career that it required a lot of patience to take burros on trips.

Working with the burros was always better than trying to command them. I always tried to make going on walks a fun thing to do. Frequent stops gave me a better chance to look around at the sights, many of which I would have missed if I'd just been head-down walking. We'd stop for only part of a minute, and then Libby would start on her own, when she was ready. Being on the ground walking gave me a good sense of how the burros were doing. We got tired at about the same time. My burros were the perfect size for me, since we walked at the same speed. A large horse walks at a pace faster than a human, creating a problem, because they are always stepping on your heels, or trying to pass you.

The gravel road wound up a canyon along a tiny creek, with brush and small trees along its banks. We had the great fortune to have cloud cover for the whole climb. Otherwise, we would have roasted in the sunshine on the south-facing hill. I hooted and hollered in joy and exuberance when we reached the top of the long climb. I was filled with ecstasy at reaching another goal, and with the joy of wandering the world with burros. The higher ground had some scenic hills, and was even prettier than down below.

A man, his son, and two nephews from southern Utah pulled up beside us and stopped. They had paused briefly to chat earlier in the day, and now, on their way back up the road, they wanted to hear more about our enterprise. We talked for quite a while. They appreciated the freedom and adventure of my life. They took pictures and contributed twenty dollars and some sodas to our cause. After the man at the Brown's Park Refuge Headquarters had given me the twenty dollar bill, and these men had shown such interest in the trip, I thought I'd offer to put them on my Burro Christmas Card list if they contributed twenty dollars. I gave the Utah gentlemen this option, but selling my adventure didn't feel right, so I decided not to do that again.

I was surely having a great and joyous day, and bounced down the road in supreme happiness. The nearly empty morning road gave way to an unusual flow of traffic in the early afternoon. Several vans covered with fishing company logos came by, pulling empty boat trailers, all heading towards Brown's Park. The Green River held great fishing between the Flaming Gorge Dam and the Brown's Park Valley. The choice stretch of river ran through rugged mountains, in a deep canyon, and was only accessible by floating down it in small boats and rafts. The vans were going to pick up the boats and customers at the end of their float trip.

We came down into a valley filled with gas-field pumps and pipelines. The arid area was covered with sagebrush and felt odd for a camping spot with all of the industrialization. We crossed Red Creek at the bottom of the valley. Our need for water required us to camp somewhere near the river. The valley was called Clay Basin. The name proved accurate after I tied the burros to the bridge's guardrail, and began scouting along the river for a campsite. The rain the night before had turned the clay soil along the river into a total slimy mess. What looked, from a distance, like a good place for the night, was a totally unsuitable quagmire. The next water was a long way off, and we'd already gone about twelve miles, so I continued my search. In the sagebrush-flat, a quarter mile from the river, was a small, open green spot caused by a seep spring. I felt lucky to find the one little pocket, in the entire area, that was suitable for camp.

Red Creek ran muddier than chocolate milk, too filthy to filter, so I flagged down a car to get drinking water. The river water was so muddy that I chose water from puddles, for the burros and my gruel. Beanie drank it up, but Libby hardly touched it. This puzzled me until I ate gruel made with the water. The gruel tasted like I'd dumped a pound of salt into it. The valley soil was so heavily mineralized that even new puddles were heavily tainted. I wonder if the river was as salty? I tried to eat some of the gruel, wanting the food, but after just a little, I had to toss it; something hard for me to do, since I hate to waste food, particularly on a trip. My stomach cramped a bit. The minor discomfort didn't dull my good mood. I was very excited and upbeat. I'd reached a new, higher level of attitude.

June 11.

We started the day with a steady uphill westward trudge of four miles, climbing more than 800 vertical feet out of the valley. We eased down the other side of the ridge a few miles before turning south on a gravel side-road to a pond, where the burros gratefully drank up the fresher water. Thank God for the good map from the Brown's Park lady, without it, I wouldn't have known about the hidden pond or the side road.

The back road went over an intriguing, thin fin of rock which was the ridge-top above the next valley. At the top, we were rewarded with one of the most beautiful sights a walker in this withered landscape could see, a lush green oasis near the top of the drainage. As I saw the large bright green meadow, pond, and nearby aspen forest; I knew immediately that we had found our camping spot. The view from the ridge-top was majestic; the huge Flaming Gorge Reservoir, about fifteen miles away, and beyond that, the snowy High Uintas Mountains. I excitedly walked down into the oasis, knowing that we would have to take a day off to rest and enjoy the wonderful slice of heaven.

The several-hundred acre green zone was fenced off to keep free-range cattle from spoiling it. Three horses that were corralled inside the area ran about excitedly when they saw us. Horses that have never seen burros will usually become very excited and a bit scared. Most horses we passed usually gave us a good show of prancing, galloping, and snorting as they ran about, investigating us. The agitated beasts repeatedly came in close to investigate, and then bolted away in fear from the strange sight and smell of the unusual burros.

We took an excellent campsite on the meadow edge, in the shade of an aspen tree. A small clear stream babbled nearby, and the grass was great feed for the burro-girls. A while after our arrival, the cowboy who owned the horses came up the road in his pickup truck. Seeing us, he came over to hear our story. This was a real cowboy; living with his cows, out on the range, in his travel trailer, nine months of the year. We visited for a while, exchanging stories of being in the out-out. He used to ride rodeo bulls, but with the wisdom of age and his share of hurts, he only did team roping competition anymore.

I had a story about being bucked off, but I didn't tell it. He'd ridden huge angry bulls. I'd been tossed by Billy ... the little gray burro. I'd climbed onto Billy-burro, during the beginning of my first journey, to see what it was like to be atop an animal. He swung his head around, and gave me an intense glare, which I clearly understood as, "Get off!" I quickly dismounted. Early in the second half of that trip, when I had the horse Lady, I rode her a little; but, being out by myself and this being my first time riding, I felt more comfortable just walking her. I was still curious about getting on the burro. So once again, while Billy was loose grazing, I got up on him just behind the cross on his back. Billy gave me no warning this time. The wily burro made a little hop, tossing me to his butt, and then, like tossing a baseball in the air and hitting it with a bat, deservedly sent me flying. I landed hard on the small of my back and crawled back to camp.

The cowboy told me of a shortcut that would not only save miles, but bypass a stretch of paved highway. He told me to cut off the road less than two miles from camp, and follow an elk trail over a low spot in the ridge. We could follow the drainage down the other side, right into the small town of Dutch John. I wouldn't have trusted most people's ability to pick a route for us. Horses and burros can't move over rough terrain the way a human can. People are monkey-like, and can climb over obstructions that stymie equines. Knowing that the cowboy had ridden the route and was so knowledgeable made it a good choice. The shortcut would be a huge bonus for us if it worked. It was sure great talking with the genuine cowboy. I appreciated his love of being in the out-country with his animals, and living the true cowboy life.

Late in the day, Lucy and I walked back to the top of the ridge we'd crossed earlier, just to gaze at the sprawling view. A formation behind the ridge was like the steep, severely sculptured formations of the South Dakota Badlands. Everything glowed with color in the late-day light. I sat, taking in the wide-open views, until darkness drove me back to camp.

The next day at the oasis was wonderful. Lucy and I walked around the area, admiring the odd geologic features and expansive views. We followed the stream to its hillside source for drinking water. The cool, green aspen forest was ecstasy after all of the desert we'd been through. The burros grazed the day away. All was wonderful in my world.

June 13.

I found the elk trail, and followed it up the ridge. It was a bit rough with brush, and steep, but we managed to reach the top, and a grassy saddle in the otherwise rocky ridge. The other side sloped just gently enough for us to ease down. The bottom of the drainage was too rough for walking, so we stayed on the hillside, taking as steep an angle as we could. Occasionally, we had to take switchbacks to get past the steeper spots. There was no trail here, and no one would be likely to come through the area until hunting season, many months later. I put myself on high alert, aware that if I got hurt, no one would find me till I was a pile of bones, if ever. We were very much on our own.

I was accustomed to this situation, from all of the years I'd spent alone in the mountains. Traveling without a set plan made a serious injury "in the middle of nowhere" something that just couldn't happen. I constantly went hiking off-trail, where I might never have been found. Months might pass before anyone realized there might be a reason to look for me. I had to remain competent, and negotiate the terrain as safely as I could, one step at a time, staying in the moment.

A fire had burnt the area some four years before, opening the formerly forested slope enough to descend. Travel off-trail, through the rugged, lovely countryside, was a thrill. At the point where the burnt trees would have been too thick to move through, we found the abandoned gas-well road that led to the bottom, just as the cowboy had described. At one point, we almost walked right upon a coyote den, dug into the side of a dry riverbed. The coyote hopped up and sprinted away in a panic. We were all startled. Lucy gave a brief chase, until I called her back.

We came out of the skeleton forest, right at the small town of Dutch John. I was really jacked up and excited from taking the perfect shortcut through the out-country. Instead of a 14-mile plod, with much of it along a busy highway, we went seven fantastic miles, through some inspiring wild-country. HOORAY!!! ...for a great and wonderful day.

We went to the roadside everything-store: gas, groceries, rafting, fishing guides, motel and restaurant. I unloaded the burro-girls, and tied them and Lucy in the shade of some pines near the building. Seeing the burros, several people came over to talk, and like everyone else that I'd met along the way, they were very friendly. I bought supplies from the small store, and when the owner-operator heard what we were doing, she offered me a free lunch. She gave me two double-bacon cheeseburgers, an extra-huge pile of fries, and two sodas. Amazingly, I ate every last bit of the humongous meal. My body wanted every calorie it could get, and I hadn't eaten much pure protein lately, so I just gobbled it up. I was very trail-starved, after all of the walking, and eating only gruel, popcorn, and peanuts for weeks. I was very grateful for the much needed, huge meal. I would never have bought it, with my meager finances. She also gave me a sandwich to have later. I gave her an art card as thanks for her kindness and generosity, hoping that I might someday be able to give her some advertisement.

There was no decent camping close by, so we crossed an open field about a third of a mile, to camp in one of the few clumps of trees that hadn't burned in the forest fire. Most of the surrounding area had been consumed by the flames, except for the area close to town.

I assumed that the town had been saved by the hard, dangerous work of firefighters and some good luck. The campsite had no water, but I'd filled some of my water-sacks at the store, where I'd tanked up the burros. That night, even though I still wasn't hungry, I ate the meat sandwich, because I had no refrigeration. Lucy-dog was happy to help.

June 14.

I'd been anticipating difficulties with the next stage of our trip, since beginning to plan the journey. We had to take a relatively busy, two lane highway across the Flaming Gorge Dam. DAMN! It was the only place on the whole walk to Oregon where we had no choices, a bottleneck. The challenge was in crossing the Green River. The south was blocked by the High Uintas Mountains, impassable with snow, unless we went clear to Nevada. The next crossing north was way up at Rock Springs, Wyoming, where we'd have been forced into the desert along the Interstate 80 corridor. The way I wanted to go would bring us along the north slopes of the High Uintas, where we'd have plenty of water, grass, and trees. Also, the mountain route would be much more scenic.

I was tense and hyper-aware as we made our way down the busy, winding highway to the dam, keeping to the shoulder where possible, and avoiding the inside of curves. People cut closer to the inside of curves, and we'd be less visible. Thankfully, all of the vehicles that passed were careful to slow down, and give us as much room as possible. We made it safely to the dam only to find another dilemma; the dam was under repair. One of the two lanes was closed, jack-hammers banging. The construction actually worked in our favor, since the traffic could only come through slowly, one direction at a time. This left a few minutes when no vehicles were crossing the dam, while the direction of travel was changing.

When traffic approached again, we moved out of the way, ducking onto the lane under repair. The workers also helped, stopping their jack hammers to avoid spooking the burros. Slowly, we made our way across. Certainly, we made an odd sight: a traveler from another century on the mammoth, modern concrete-structure. A passing policeman even stopped in the middle of the road to take a quick picture from his car.

All of the distractions made us tense and jumpy, so a few miles later, we stopped for the day. We only went a little more than four miles that day, but I felt that we'd accomplished enough by crossing the dam to call it a day. There was a campground not much further on that didn't allow livestock; we camped close enough so I could use its water by making several trips with my water-sacks. We were now in National Forest Lands, which allowed us to camp wherever we wished, except in designated campgrounds, where they usually didn't allow livestock. This campground was operated by a private company, and had very good facilities, including hot showers. The showers were meant for paying customers only, but it had been weeks since I'd really bathed, other than jumping into the cold Green River, so I sneaked one anyway. Most people wouldn't like going without showers the way I did on pack trips, but I rarely missed them. It's a handy trait on a journey where getting filthy happens within hours, and warm water is a long way off in time and distance. I took a nap in the afternoon, and awoke disoriented and weirded.

June 15.

There were a few more miles of the winding uphill road ahead. We left early, trying to be past the dangerous section before the heavy traffic. There were sharp blind corners, with no shoulder, which would have been lousy in heavy traffic. Guardrails along these roads were among my greatest nightmares. There wasn't usually enough room for us to walk outside the guardrails, and on the inside we were trapped on the road with the traffic. We had one close-call on a sharp curve, but gladly made the top safely. Some campground workers stopped to take pictures and visit. They were excited to see such a sight, and to hear about our journey. They bought a couple of art cards, and gave me a cap with their company logo.

We'd entered a different climate zone during our climb, leaving the arid sagebrush and junipers for a forest of tall ponderosa pines and better grazing. I was relieved to be past the stress of a narrow, winding road. Here the road was straighter and the forest more appealing. We stopped to rest a while at the Flaming Gorge Lodge: rooms, RV spots, a little store and restaurant on a small chunk of private land within the National Forest. I unloaded the burros, set them out to graze across the road from the lodge, and went into the restaurant for some coffee and conversation.

We connected with Highway 44 shortly after the break. It was a busy road, fairly straight, with a shoulder, easy for us to travel. Vehicle speed determined my relationship with the passing people. On a dirt road, where people came by slowly, most stopped to inquire into what we were doing.

Fewer people stopped as their speed increased, although nearly everyone would happily wave to us. I developed the habit of waving to most of the passing people, unless it was a very busy road. That day, despite the high speeds, a young man stopped for a chat. A spice-company salesman, he loaded me up with a pile of his flavors to help my austere meals.

The map showed some small lakes, a mile or so off the main road, and even though it was out of our way, I decided to head there. We needed a day of rest, and wanted a good spot, so I felt that the extra distance would be worth it. A trailhead sign on the side of the road said that it went to the lakes, so even though it wasn't shown on the map, we took the trail for the last three miles of the 9-mile day.

Beanie-burro had been around the block as far as trail travel was concerned, after years of packing in the rugged Rocky Mountains. Libby, on the other hand, was a rookie. Burros don't like to cross water, mud, or do anything else they've never done before. Once they experience a lot of different obstacles, they learn to deal with them. On this trail, we came to a water-filled ditch with a small wooden bridge. Libby balked at the little bridge. I leaned forward into the rope. A steady, slow pull was more effective than jerking the rope, which greatly offends burros. She held fast in the classic stubborn-burro pose. After more pulling, she finally decided to cross. But instead of taking the bridge, she jumped the narrow ditch in a wild leap, losing one of her boots by breaking the strap. I removed the rest of her boots for the remainder of the day, so none of them would be sucked off going down the sometimes muddy trail.

Soon, we found a larger stream and another longer wooden bridge. I remembered a similar situation many years before in the early part of my burro packing career. Billy-burro was willing to cross a bridge, but the young rookie, Fanny, wouldn't budge. I put Billy in front, and started him across the bridge with Fanny tied on a long rope to his pack. When Billy was about halfway across the bridge, the rope went taut to Fanny, stubborn on the bank. A bend in the stream allowed Fanny to go along the water's edge without going in. The bridge had no handrails, so when Fanny was far enough to the side, resisting strongly, she pulled Billy sideways off the bridge and into the stream. Luckily, the fall wasn't far enough to hurt him and the water not deep, but he was on his side in the shallow water, thrashing about on his side, unable to get up because of his panniers. Thank God it was the mild mannered Billy! When I yelled, "WHOA!" he calmed down enough for me to remove the packs, and he regained his feet. Not only did I learn how not to do something, but also realized the need for a quick-release buckle system, so that in emergencies such as this, I could get the packs off the burros, fast and easy.

I'd since learned a better way to get a stubborn, balking burro past an obstacle. I tied the unwilling Libby to a nearby tree, and walked "Ol' Reliable" Beanie over the bridge and up the trail until she was hidden in the trees. Being separated from Beanie was more traumatic for Libby than crossing something she feared. When I untied Libby, she crossed the bridge hastily ... almost running me over. We finished the day without incident. Camping wasn't good close to the lakes, so we took a nearby spot in a Ponderosa forest. Several hundred yards away was the campground where I had access to water.

Nearby, at of one of the lakes, on a parcel of private land, was a resort lodge. The morning after our arrival, Lucy and I went over to the quaint little lodge. It was in a very scenic location, with a beautiful view of the nearby lake. I had coffee on the lodge deck, even though it was a little blustery and all of the other lodge guests were inside. It was like other times I'd visited lodges on pack trips. I wouldn't have been inside a building for weeks, finally get a chance for a meal inside, only to spend the whole time looking out the window. At moments like that, I understood how addicted I was to being outside. I met several friendly lodge employees. One of the cooks had seen us walking up the road several days before, as he was driving back from town. When he got off work, he generously loaded me up with all kinds of food: pasta, beans, cocoa, energy bars, and canned food; refusing any payment. Unfortunately, I didn't give him an art card or get his address, so that I could send a holiday thank-you card for all of his help.

We were all tired, after the first three-day walk of the trip, and still getting into shape. I didn't want to press any of us into an injury, so we took another rest day. I was enjoying the company of the lodge employees, and the scenery, so a longer stay was fine. The head-chef came out to visit and take pictures of my burros. He yearned for his own adventure.

June 18.

We left the fine social life of the lodge, and rejoined the highway for another seven miles, before turning off onto a gravel side road. This was a big move for us. We could have followed the paved road down into the flats of southern Wyoming. It would have been a shorter and much faster route. The open flats would be easier than the more convoluted route through the foothills, with its ups, downs, and many curves. But I wanted to stay in forests as long as possible. Soon enough, we'd be out in the dry flats for a long, long way.

We took the side road another mile or so before making camp beside a stream, in a pine forest. Being away from the busy highway and in the quiet protective forest along a clear running mountain stream was a relief. I ate as much of the heavy canned food as I could, to reduce the weight for the burros, and to consume as many calories as I could. All of the unaccustomed food gave me lousy farts.

June 19.

We traveled happily down into a pretty river drainage with tall trees and eye-catching rock ledges. The road crossed a fast-flowing, clear stream, and then climbed out of the valley onto a plateau, midway between the tallest peaks of the High Uintas and the low, flat, brown desert below. The plateau was beautiful, with forest, streams, and vistas of the craggy, snow covered peaks. We had easy going, over a flat, smooth-surfaced gravel road. Roads here were covered with small, slate-like rocks that were perfect for our feet. Some roads were hard-going, graveled with too-large rocks.

We came to a large section of forest that had burned the year before. Walking through the destruction reaching far up the nearby ridges, I wondered about the origin of the big fire. Lightning started many fires in western America, but we found evidence of a different source for this burn. A spot right on the roadside seemed to be the origin of the blaze by the way the blackened trees fanned out from there. Apparently, a crew thinning the small pines along the roadside started the blaze with a chainsaw, or some other activity. Right at that location, the tree thinning stopped. The crew had stopped thinning when the fire began, and never returned to finish the job. We kept good pace to another pretty stream for our night's stay. I was very tired at the end of the 10-mile day, though I felt much better in a few hours. Recovery time was shortening, as I was getting in better shape. A large meadow gave the burros great grazing.

June 20.

I purposely took a leisurely morning, sitting by the stream in the shade. I was hoping that the clouds might build up in the afternoon, as they had a couple of days before, for cooler walking. I also believed we'd have an easy 6-mile day to what looked, on the map, like a great place to camp, in a large meadow system. The burros' grazing needs made meadows our preferred camping locations, so I keyed in on them if there was also water. Usually, I found protection for my tent just inside the trees at the meadow edge. Meadows in this region appeared where the ground was too wet for trees. Overly wet meadows didn't work.

The burros didn't like marshy ground or the coarse grass which grew there. I could tell from a distance how swampy or dry a meadow was, by the color of the grass;

and could determine not only whether the burros would eat the grass, but if they could walk across it. They had very small hooves relative to their weight, and sank deeply into mud, which might cause a fall. They passionately avoided mud. I've had to deal with the "balky burro" routine with mud, more than any other obstacle.

We didn't leave the beautiful camping spot until about 1 p.m. My theory that some clouds would build up in the afternoon proved correct, making it perfectly cool for our walk. The meadow where I'd hoped to camp was infested with a large herd of cattle. I didn't like to camp among cows, because their grazing clipped the grasses short, and it wasn't as good for my burros. They also created a lot of flies, noise and poop. The burro-girls walked on the slow-side, and I was a bit tired and on the grumpy-side, hence the day wore me out more than usual. We went up the road a couple more miles, and turned off onto a barely-used dirt road running along another large meadow. Our easy 6-mile day had turned into a relatively grueling 8-mile struggle.

I found a great spot at the edge of a little clearing, in an aspen grove, just off the main meadow. It was just the perfect little spot, with a very homey feel to it. An old, well-used campfire ring betrayed the fact that others had camped there many times in the past. Whenever I was looking for an exact spot to set up camp, I looked for the old established campsites, figuring that the previous people had already found the best spot; though I always thoroughly checked other options, before deciding on the final location. I also looked at all of the trees around a prospective camp, to see if they'd ever been hit by lightning. Lightning left a top to bottom scar(e) in the bark where the charge traveled through the tree into the ground, unless the tree just exploded. I'd seen 10-foot-long splinters driven into the ground like mighty spears.

We'd been traveling for a month, slowly picking up the pace, growing stronger. I didn't plan to hit full speed until we left the High Uintas, so we stayed a day in our calm little spot in the aspens. Lucy and I followed the little stream running through the meadow a half-mile to its source. The spring flowed well enough for drinking water, even though it was a bit far carrying the heavy water-sacks back to camp. Wandering through the beautiful meadow was a joy, so we also took a scenic tour of the nearby forest, following some old abandoned roads up through the stately trees.

The burros took turns grazing free. Beanie wandered the furthest, sometimes a couple hundred yards away from her buddy. Libby would call her back, with a loud, mournful, lonely-burro bray, when she went too far. I only freed a burro while I was in camp, otherwise the curious critter would come into camp and rummage through my gear. While loose, they often took the opportunity to rub themselves on a tree. Still shedding their long winter coat, they loved being brushed, which extracted large clumps of fur.

I had a great view of the tall, rugged High Uintas, where I'd spent two and a half months two years earlier. The High Uintas were the toughest mountains I ever hiked, rougher than some of Colorado's ranges. Some stretches were tough because of a lack of trail maintenance. The most common problem was a large tree across the trail, requiring a detour. An obstacle on a steep, rocky, or forested slope could really be a problem. I carried a bow-saw and a hatchet so that I could try to cut out downed trees. I also had a small, light pick-hoe to dig out trails on steep side-hills. I always knew that we might come to a place that could stymie us on mountain trails.

What made the High Uintas so difficult were loose rocks and boulders. The peaks were covered with crumbling rock, and, particularly in the passes, we had to negotiate long stretches of extremely rocky trail. We were on the High Line Trail, which stayed above 10,000 feet throughout the wilderness area. Thousands of lakes and ponds dotted the rocky vastness. We crossed six major passes that summer; all were jumbled rocks and boulders. There were places on the high, rocky extremes where the trail was only a narrow ledge, on a cliffside, above a sheer 1000-foot drop. Getting an animal through the rough terrain was a challenge. Fortunately, I had the highly talented and experienced Fanny-burro in the lead, her good buddy, the strong and steady Beanie, following wherever she went. Fanny was very spunky, sometimes obstinate for the sake of being a burro. She was a true character, who understood travel, and seemed to love the high mountains where we wandered so often. Fanny loved expansive views. In the highest places, she always stopped to take in the panorama. Burros were sure-footed, but if they didn't believe they could do it, would refuse to try. The intelligent animals were hard to hurt. When we found a tough spot, Fanny would look at it, study the options, and choose the best path. She really seemed to love figuring out a way through challenging terrain for her own satisfaction. Beanie, her beloved burro-buddy of fourteen years, would dutifully follow along, if Fanny led.

That whole summer in the High Uintas, was a challenge. At each turn, without a balk, Fanny chose a way through the rocky terrain. The last pass was one of the easier ones we'd encountered that year. We carne to a spot where the way was squeezed by a constriction of boulders. Since the burros were short, the panniers hit on both sides, stopping them from passing. I could have done the safe thing by unloading them, guiding them through the tight spot, and reloading them. It would have taken about fifteen minutes. Fanny moved to go around the downhill side, off the trail, onto the steep slope. It looked acceptable. I didn't think it through, or look closely at the possible dangers. We moved around the boulders onto the steep slope. It was loose gravel on a hard surface. One of Fanny's boots twisted off, and she fell ... breaking the link to Beanie. Fanny struggled to get up, losing her balance; and to my complete horror started rolling down the mountainside, packs and all. I knew she was dead. It was the worst day of my life.

Now, reliving my huge failure put me into a foul mood about myself. I thought of my many failures in the "real world." I'd done things of which I was ashamed; though at least I'd come to understand why I'd behaved so poorly. I'd put myself and my life above others, considering myself more important. I'd learned the hard way that selfishness made people do lousy things. The corruption that comes from believing that "I am what am most important" also infects groups, nations, religions, and the species. Humans that believe they are the most important thing on earth, do rotten things to the rest of the planet. I saw my wants as supreme, tweaking my priorities out of whack. Misplaced priorities, believing that your "----" is above all else, causes most problems.

That shortcoming weighed heavily on my mind. I felt terrible about myself, and vowed to do better in the future. I noticed that, the worse I felt about myself, the harsher I was with myself and others. Actions follow beliefs, creating self-fulfilling prophecies; if you believe you're no good, you'll do bad things. My negative self-image caused a continued negative relationship with the world. The cure for behaving poorly is a good self-image. Believing that you're a pile of crap will not produce sweet-smelling results.

The one solace I gave myself was a plan to reward everyone who had helped me. Many people had assisted me with jobs, in difficult situations, and through other acts of kindness over the years. I hoped and yearned for my investors to be glad that they'd helped me in some way, since, in my envisioned future prosperity, I'd be able to give them a big payback.

Chapter 6
High Uintas
June 22 - July 7

June 22.

The next morning, I was still depressed as we rejoined the gravel road, descending 800 vertical feet, to find that the road I'd planned to take was closed. It looked as if it hadn't been used in a long time. I was in a turmoil as to what to do. The map showed the only alternate route going far out of our way into the dry plains to the north. I tied the burros to some trees and walked along the road a little way, hoping to find a nearby newer edition of the road, going where we wanted to go, but found nothing: devastating. At that moment, the first vehicle we'd seen all day came along. I flagged it down to see if they might have an answer to my dilemma. The driver and his young son knew the area well. They were just the perfect people to come by, at the exact moment I needed them. I learned that there was a new road that would take us where we wanted to go. It was back up the hill a couple miles.

I sank with disappointment. I hated to backtrack, particularly since it meant we'd have to go back up the large hill we'd just come down. The locals proposed another option. They thought we should go with my original plan, and take the abandoned road. The map showed what looked like a good meadow, where I really wanted to camp, ahead on the old road. The newer road would miss what looked like a prime location for us. The old road had been closed for fifteen years, so we might well encounter downed trees, but the terrain was mild, so they thought we could probably work our way through it. This crucial information and encouragement, right when it could most help me, was a reminder of the rightness of the journey.

I took the chance and headed up the defunct road. Piles of dirt had been bulldozed onto the road to keep vehicles from using it. We easily passed those obstructions, several times coming to downed aspens across the road. We were able to work our way past with some effort. Several times, I had to separate the burros and take them through the tight forest individually. The route was a convoluted maze with tight, sharp turns. If I'd kept them tied together, I would've risked the back burro, Beanie, hooking a tree. It was worth the extra work to avoid possible problems. We got over the forested hill to a more open, easier part of the road, an absolutely beautiful route through meadows and scattered evergreens. The road lead down into the meadow where I'd hoped to camp; we'd gone nearly ten miles by then. The excitement of taking the road not traveled turned my dismal attitude into exuberance. Accomplishing the fairly difficult task made me feel better about myself. The intensity of the experience also helped me focus on the mountains where we were, instead of the past tragedy. It was just what the doctor ordered.

We camped among a small patch of evergreen trees at the edge of the wonderful 300 acre meadow, with a small stream nearby. Lush green bottomland bordered by low forested hills on three sides, faced a steep wooded ridge capped with forty-foot cliffs of light rock guarding the top. There were some very old fire-rings around the edges of the meadow, but it didn't look like anyone had camped there in the fifteen years since the road had been closed. We'd probably have this sizeable slice of heaven to ourselves. Our ability to use the road westward out of the valley was a concern. So, after setting up camp, Lucy and I took an exploratory walk in that direction to scout out the possibilities. I found that, with some creativeness and a bit of trail work, we'd be able to get through to the main road a mile or so away.

The wonderful meadow was such paradise, in its beauty and solitude; that I decided right away to take a 3-day vacation. I was glad to take some time off from the rigors of moving along. Simply not having to break down and set up camp for a few days would be a big bonus for me. These mountains would be some of the most scenic of the trip, so I wanted to move slowly. Bypassing the new road had turned out to be a huge positive. The new road passed a reservoir instead of our meadow. Had we gone the "right way" through the woods, I would have missed this perfect vacation place.

Taking the "wrong way" had turned out to be the right way for me on past burro trips. During the second half of my first trip, with Lady the horse and Billy-burro, we were just into the Colorado Mountains above Telluride. I planned to take a trail over the jagged mountains to Ophir Pass. Partway up, I took the wrong trail, ending up at the ski area.

I was very mad at myself for taking the wrong route, leading us back to a main highway, before eventually reaching a side road up to Ophir Pass. The wrong route was not only less spectacular than the trail I'd originally chosen, but much longer. The mountains outside Telluride were the first real rugged up-and-down country in my animal packing experience. I learned an important lesson soon after reaching difficult terrain. The horse had most of the gear in its panniers; and, because of her body shape, this worked well. Burros, on the other hand, are shaped differently. A burro's chest narrows toward the front, unlike a horse, whose chest widens toward the front. This combined with a horse's withers (the hump at the top of the shoulders), kept packs in place going down a steep hill; but when Billy-burro went down hills, his panniers slid over his head. It was good that I discovered the problem before getting deep into the mountains, though I still didn't have the equipment or knowledge to fix the problem.

The climb to Ophir Pass took us through the tiny mountain-village of Ophir, where some professional animal-packers lived. I went to them, hoping for help with the problem. The very friendly people immediately took out tools and old parts to rebuild my equipment. They not only created a britchen system which went around the burro's butt to keep the packs from sliding forward, but were full of good advice for a struggling greenhorn. If I hadn't taken the "wrong route", and had my gear made right, my first trip through the mountains would have been a disaster.

Now, early on the second day of our vacation, a lone horseman came through our wonderful High Uintas meadow. He was camped at the reservoir, about a mile away, and was exploring the wonderful country on horseback with his son, who had stayed at their camp. Later in the day, Lucy and I took a walk up through the forested hillside to the reservoir.

It was a good sized body of water set against the backdrop of the higher mountains. It was a pretty spot, but I was glad we'd camped in our hidden Shangri-La. The horseman I'd met earlier was camped on the pretty side of the reservoir, near a little clear inlet-creek. We went to their camp hoping to acquire some food to augment my dwindling supplies. They would be leaving the forest soon, so I was able to get their excess energy bars and canned food.

During the next two days, I heated water in my black water-sacks by placing them out in the hot sunshine. By afternoon, there was enough hot water for laundry and even some rare personal bathing. Some of the gear needed repairs. The burros placidly grazed in the meadow. Lucy was constantly finding me sticks to throw. When I'd first gotten her, I tried to break her of the habit, but she loved it so much that I gave up. While I lazed around camp, we played stick until, in her maniac zeal, chasing the stick as fast as possible, she tore a large gash in her leg. I cleaned it out and kept an eye on it. Of course, she still wanted me to throw the stick, not caring that she was injured, but I made her do without her addiction for a while.

I enjoyed having campfires during those nights. Surprisingly, they were the first fires of the trip. Most of the places we'd stayed during the trip weren’t suitable for campfires, often being on roadsides. The hard work of the traveling made me tired enough that I hadn't particularly wanted the work of getting firewood. The biggest reason I hadn’t had fires was that I liked having them when it was dark, and it'd been staying light until 9 p.m., rising early in the morning made me ready for sleep in the early evening. This vacation finally gave me an opportunity to enjoy caveman TV. I stared into the flames, late into the starry nights.

The logo on the hat given to me by the Flaming Gorge Dam camp workers had, among other words, AMERICAN. For years I'd abhorred wearing commercial names on my clothes. Either I didn't wear clothes with logos, or I removed the name before wearing them. Sometimes, I just pulled out part of the advertisement to form another message.

When I first arrived in Steamboat, Colorado I got a town hat, pulled out the S and the b, and went with "team oat", a big favorite with the equine set. Now, having some free time, I took my knife and a needle and pulled out all of the words but AMERICAN. Being so hardcore about not wearing labels, I was even a bit unsure about wearing AMERICAN. I was in disagreement with many things happening in America. What I found most upsetting was that the country had been so overrun by greed. Big money ruled and corruptly controlled everything, including the government. I believed that democracy was supposed to take power out of the hands of the few and spread it among the many, because of the "power corrupts" principle. America had rightfully eliminated royalty but had replaced it with "power through wealth" which was similarly corrupt. I had no problem with American ideals. Freedom was my greatest need. I'd tried to expand my actual freedom as much as I could. One of the biggest draws of the mountains was "actualized freedom", doing exactly what I wanted to be doing at each moment. Wandering the high mountain wilderness satisfied that need. Living in a country that, at least in theory, allowed freedom was essential. That the U.S. had 5% of the world's population and 25% of the world's jail population indicated that something was askew.

In the late 1980s, on a trip in the Colorado Mountains, I met a man from China. He was fascinated with what I was doing. I asked him if anyone in China did what I was doing. He scoffed, "no way" would or could anyone do what I was doing in the China of the times. He thought I must be a rich man to be able to take off into the mountains for months at a time. I assured him that I was actually quite poor. I didn't try to explain that I was just too irresponsible and selfish to lead a "real life." I could afford to go off into the mountains for extended periods of time, because I had nothing to lose. Not going to the mountains for the summer would be the bigger loss. Just staying physically fit, hiking up and down 10,000+ foot high peaks all summer, was enough reason to go; not to mention going (more) nuts, if I didn't go to the mountains. I was so much happier, wandering with a couple of burros and a dog, than trying to survive in town. In the mountains, I was a celebrity; in the world of possessions, I was the lowest-of-the-low.

What really made my wandering life possible was not only freedom, but all of the wide-open public lands of the rural west. The huge tracts of public land that we could roam freely were better than owning it, since I didn't have to worry about being an owner. I could just enjoy the tremendous, spectacular countryside. What a very lucky person I was, to be when and where I was. At my better moments, I appreciated it.

The third day of our stay in the magic valley, Lucy and I hiked up the cliff-topped ridge that had been beckoning from across the meadow. It was a steep climb without a trail, so I slowly cut back and forth across the slope, working my way through the brush, trees, and sometimes uncertain footing of loose rock. Lucy took her own trail, but stayed close, as we climbed toward the rocky ridge top.

There were gaps in the cliffs, so we were able to reach the summit. I sat for quite a while atop the craggy outpost, taking in the outstanding view of my meadow below, and the mountains beyond. I was also able to see off to the other side of the ridge, into the lower flat lands to the north; the area through which we would've walked had I decided to leave the mountains. Some of the flats were greened by irrigation water from these mountains. That way probably would have been o.k., but I was glad for time in the mountains, with great campsites, trees, and water. After a thorough tour of the ridge top, we returned to our wonderful camp. I finally found a good drinking-water spring hiking back to camp. I'd walked close to the spring several times, but hadn't seen it. I went back later to fill a water-sack for the next day.

June 26.

We left our wonderful little meadow via the unused road to the west. I'd cleared most obstructions during my vacation, so we had an easy passage to the rough-rock road which was the main route through this section of country. At one point, there was a rare steel bridge over a large, fast-moving stream. Libby didn't like the steel surface, so I used the Beanie-first method to coax Libby across. We passed charming Hoop Lake. I'd hoped to find a place to camp there, but seeing nothing suitable in the windy, exposed area, we continued on down the now much improved gravel road.

The road dropped lower and lower till, after eight miles of walking, we came to the unique "Hole in the Rock" formation. A narrow, vertical, two-hundred foot high, fin of rock pushed through the surface. Near the top, a forty foot wide circular hole opened completely through it. Nearby, the road passed through a narrow gap in the long, high wall where a stream had breached it. Beyond, the road entered the flats and private land. We found a place to camp where the land was still National Forest just before passing through the gap. Right above us was the Hole in the Rock. Interestingly, there was also a 4-foot-wide cave at the very bottom of the rock with a stream-sized spring flowing out. I filled a water-sack, and sat down to enjoy the unusual place with its cold, clear stream springing from the rock. I felt blessed to be camping in such a "holey" spot.

Our campsite was tucked in a lush aspen forest filled with light-blue and white Columbine flowers. Leprechaunville, for sure; slow moving, 5-inch-long gray-brown salamander made its way through the grass near the tent, and crept under a log. Light rain fell early in the evening, and I napped while hiding in the tent, waking right at sunset.

Having slept awhile, I stayed up later than usual, listening to my little radio. During the day, radio reception was questionable, depending on our location. I might pick up a few stations, if there were no mountains in the way. I marked our progress by the different stations that came in and out of hearing. At night, the AM dial came alive. I tuned-in stations from all over the West, some even from Mexico and Canada. Politics was my main interest, but if I woke in the middle of the night, I often listened to trucking-stations with live, all-night broadcasts and good national weather reports. Weather reports were very important to my plans, helping me make intelligent decisions about whether to go or stay. Before sunrise, when the AM stations disappeared, I usually got "local" weather forecasts with the morning news. Many times I had to modify the forecast for our locale. If they were calling for cloudy skies in the valley, it might mean rain in the mountains.

Knowing when stormy weather was coming saved me many times in the mountains. On my second trip along the Continental Divide through the Wimenuche Wilderness, I was stalled at one of the longer above timberline sections when the weather was worse than the normal awful afternoon thunderstorms. I waited days for the weather to change. Just when I was going to give up the planned route and loop down through lower terrain, I heard on the radio that the weather was going to clear. We waited another day, and crossed the high section on one of the prettiest blue-sky-days of the summer.

One time, I walked a long, high, exposed section after I heard that it was going to rain all day. There'd been hardly any lightning the previous day, so, when the radio said it would be ten degrees cooler, with steady rain, we traveled in the rain. Normally, I'd never cross a section like that in a rainstorm, but I figured that, with the lower temperatures, there'd be no lightning. I decided that it would be better to cross the high ridge in a steady rain without lightning, than in a pounding thunderstorm. My prediction was correct, and we traversed the difficult high section without a problem, other than wet clothes that I peeled when we made camp.

June 27.

We walked out into the flats after leaving Hole in the Rock, getting a slight taste of the treeless low-country. It was a relief to quickly turn off onto another Forest Service road winding back up into the foothills. Our route followed the outer edge of the foothills, giving us expansive views of the drier flat-country to the north. We were beyond the area covered by the good map, and just as I was beginning to wonder if we would find water, we came upon a small, clear stream running through an aspen grove and a little meadow. The water looked so inviting that, instead of taking drinking water only from a flowing spring, filtering, or boiling, I decided to trust it, and drank straight from the bubbling stream next to camp. We were in a very unused part of the forest, and had only seen one car all day, and that was only after we were already camped.

All of the winding around, combined with the ups and downs of the mountains, while wonderful, was slowing our progress to Oregon. Originally, I'd planned to pass through the mountains and hills along the western Wyoming border, before cutting through the Sawtooth Mountains of Idaho, hitting Oregon near Boise. I had an atlas showing most of the smallest roads in Idaho. I studied the maps, looking for our most likely way across, but found only very convoluted routes through the challenging mountains of central Idaho. All of the visible routes would've had more winding ups and downs than we were taking in the High Uintas. I began to wonder if that route would slow us too much to make it to Oregon by fall. The other alternative was crossing southern Idaho; more direct and flatter, but with less water or public land, fewer trees, and much hotter temperatures. Elevations were much lower, and we'd be crossing in mid-summer. Shade would be rare.

Most of my past trips had been in the high mountains which I loved, and where I felt very at ease. Mountains were more technically difficult, demanding care, often literally with each step, on the sometimes brutal terrain. Figuring out how to pass numerous obstacles and deal with the usual harsh weather could be challenging. I was starting to lean toward taking the southern desert route. Crossing an open desert in the heat of summer worried me. It was more unknown to me. I wouldn't be able to make a mistake with the route, or a plan that left us at the end of a day without water. I couldn't blow the strategy or tactics. I wondered if we could we make it. I would leave the final decision till later, when the crossroads were at hand. It was my habit to wait until I was literally standing at the "fork in the way"; to finally decide which way to go. At that point, I had the most information that I could gather about the different options.

My cooking fuel was down to a half-quart so, to conserve the little gas left, I cooked my nightly gruel over a campfire. This was quite a chore. It took a lot of attention to keep the fire at the right, consistent height, to avoid burning the gruel. It took nearly an hour to cook, and burned very easily at the end of the process, when it was thick. Burnt gruel tasted terrible, so I had to keep stirring to avoid having to eat an unpalatable pot-of-plop. Also, I'd failed to bring a grill to hold the pot, so I had to balance it on rocks without spilling. It was still fun to play with the fire, though I was glad it wasn't my regular cooking method. I had run out of one of my other staples: popcorn. I'd eaten popcorn almost daily for many decades, and felt very deprived by the lack.

June 28.

We had a relatively short 5-mile day, partly on the back dirt road and the rest of the way on a much improved gravel road. There were a few gas wells in the area. We'd gotten to an area where I wasn't sure which way to go. My insufficient map showed that we might have to go far out of our way to the north, to get around a blocking mountain ridge. I just knew there must be a shorter way over the obstructing ridge. When a forest ranger drove by, near the end of the day, I flagged him down. He was very friendly and helpful, and said that there was an ATV trail over the ridge that would take us right where we wanted to go. Unfortunately, he'd switched trucks, and didn't have his usual pile of maps, to more accurately show me the way. Later in the day, he found our camp near the large, rapidly flowing, valley stream. We had a good long visit. He said he'd be back in the morning, to give me a map of the area.

June 29.

Our ranger friend came back to visit in the morning, with the map to show us our way over the mountain. He also brought some popcorn. Yay, I was no longer deprived! Thank you, good friend. The shortcut was excellent, climbing a thousand vertical feet in a series of switchbacks, taking us up to about ten thousand feet in elevation. Switchbacks really make climbs a lot easier. If we climbed slowly enough, it was hardly an effort. Steep trails were more tiring. We took a beautiful meadow-trail from the top of the mountain, down into the valley on the other side, right into the wonderful China Meadows area. We'd gone about seven miles.

I barely had my tent pitched, before it started raining. A successful shortcut, along with having camp set up, just before it rained, was the definition of a good day. HOORAY for good timing! It rained quite hard, which was good because it had hardly rained at all recently, and the forest was getting very dry. I'd spent years in the Colorado Mountains during droughts, with fires burning all around, so I was happy for the rain. Some of my gear got wet when I set my panniers and pack saddles on a flat spot that became a puddle during the heavy downpour. I chastised myself for the foolish mistake, though no real harm was done.

The rain stopped that evening. This part of the High Uintas was more accessible to people from the Salt Lake City area, hence there were many more people in the forest. Lucy and I walked around to see if I could find some much-needed gas for my stove. It was the beginning of the 4th of July weekend, and the pretty meadow area with road access was filling up with campers. I walked over to a group of people who had a couple of large RVs and a slew of ATVs. They had once raised and packed mules. We had a good talk about packing. After many years, they'd finally traded in their mules for ATVs, because fueling an ATV was so much easier than all of the year round care and expense mules required. I've heard similar stories from people many times before. Animal packing was getting rarer all the time. They had plenty of gas along for the ATVs, and were happy to help out my gas supplies. My cooking stove burned either white gas or regular gasoline, which surely came in handy in situations like this. White gas was fairly rare and expensive. With so many ATVs in the forest, finding regular gasoline was easy. The only problem with using regular gasoline was that after a while the burners began to clog.

A lady who camped in the RV closest to us came out to inquire what I was up to with the burros. She was a school teacher waiting for family and friends to join her for the holiday weekend. She was impressed with what I was doing, and gave me an armload of food, without any hints from me. People were so friendly, trusting and giving to someone traveling this way. This was one of the best parts of burro packing.

We'd just traveled four days in a row, so the next day we just relaxed around the camp. It was Saturday of the holiday weekend. With all of the happy campers around, the area had a festive feel. Two families arrived early in the day to join my neighbor, the school teacher. They had a pretty good clump of young kids. Their exuberant voices and yells filled the woods as they played. We had camped away from the road, somewhat hidden in the trees, so we were unseen for a while, but they eventually found us and came over to visit. They ran about grabbing clumps of grass to feed the burros and give them a scratch.

At first, I feared that their parents would worry that I might harm the youngsters. But the children kept coming back after being called to their camp, so I figured no one was too worried about it. I talked with them about the dangers of visiting with strangers, but they kept assuring me that I was their good friend, and would do them no harm. I relaxed, and we had a great time. They checked out my camp, had some food with me, and were as cute as could be. I gave them all an art-card. The big entertainment was throwing sticks into a nearby pond for the fetch-loving Lucy. I was invited over to their camp that night for dinner and visiting around the campfire with the adults. It was a big party for me.

July 1.

My young buddies came over to my camp first thing in the morning, and we had breakfast together. They gave me some flowers and one of their little plastic bracelets as a token of their friendship. The burros, Lucy, and I stopped by their camp on our way out, to say our goodbyes and let them take some pictures of the burros and me, all packed-up and "heading down the road".

The walk down the gravel road was wonderful. It was a blue-sky day, with a few white puffy clouds for accent, a forest of tall trees, and great views of the higher peaks. I was in a celebrating mood, and bounced down the road smiling at what we were doing ... HOOTING and HOLLERING ... with the JOY of the day. I thought to myself that, with each passing day, my confidence was increasing, and concerns and anger were slipping away. Quite a few people drove by, all with smiles and waves. When cars stopped, windows down to ask about our journey, sociable, curious Libby-burro would stick her head into the car, to check them out. Her big head and ears made a large impression on folks.

The High Uintas were a relatively unknown mountain range, visited primarily by the people of Utah, unlike the Colorado Mountains which got visitors from all over the country. At one point, a couple of scruffy young guys drove up in an old pickup. When I first saw the truck, I heard in my mind, "Maybe these people will help." They stopped and were very intrigued with my adventure. We talked for a good long while, before going our separate ways. They were going fishing. My expedition continued up the scenic way for another mile or so, when the young men pulled up beside us again. They said they wanted to talk more about burro travels, and handed me a fifty dollar bill. I was astounded. The most unlikely people, in terms of wealth, had given me the biggest contribution of the trip so far. I thanked them profusely, assuring them that they had helped us greatly on our journey. They were welders. Fifty yards further up the road, we crossed Steel Creek, confirming the miracle. My attitude soared to a most wonderful high. I decided that further worry about needs or outcome on the adventure would be foolishness. We found good camping nearby in a forest, next to a large meadow and stream. We walked about seven miles that day.

Having a large flat meadow of lush green grazing for the burros was tremendously beneficial. Mountain grasses were the best grazing the burro-girls could have, and I didn't need to move them often, or worry about them getting snagged on brush. This spot was far enough from the road that I was again able to let one of them run free, which they really loved. They were very curious about their new surroundings, and toured the area, searching out their favorite fare. They preferred just the tops of their selected foods, and in these ungrazed areas, they had the best of the best. Sometimes Beanie, who'd been around the block, would run away from me when I tried to catch her for her turn on the rope. I'd have to give my burro-call to make her stop and be caught. When I made the call, I gave them a treat of grain or peanuts; that way, they'd stop and come over to me for a treat. I carried a small supply of grain for bribes when needed.

When I awoke the next morning, I just felt like staying in the excellent spot. A good spring was in the nearby meadow for drinking water. The welders, who were camped nearby, found us again, and as they were leaving, gave me their excess food.

July 3.

We had a great day, finally making the turn north out of the mountains, and getting just a tiny way into Wyoming. Evanston, the big town along our way, looked to be about five days away. I planned to do a major re-supply there, since the small campground stores didn't have much of what I needed. I was also excited about getting close to Evanston, because once we were past there, it seemed that we would really be getting somewhere. It was a milestone on the journey.

We had gone ten miles, with Libby and Beanie thrashing about, because nasty horseflies were bugging them greatly. I'd run out of bug repellent, and really wanted more to help out my girlies. A family stopped to visit just as we were pulling off the road toward a prospective camping spot. They were leaving the woods, so they piled a load of food on me, steaks and everything. As they were about to pull away, they asked as an after-thought, "Do you need any bug spray?" After they left, I realized that I hadn't given them an art-card or gotten their mailing address, after all they'd given me. I'd collected addresses so I could send holiday cards to people who'd helped me, but it still wasn't a habit. I missed many that I should have collected. I vowed to do better. There was a good campsite, near a large reservoir. A little forest-protected alcove had a large meadow, stream, and spring nearby. I was awake enough that night to have a good long campfire to enjoy after I cooked the steaks.

July 4.

The next day turned miserable after we hiked a couple of miles to find that the road I'd planned to take to Evanston was a closed private road, even though my map said it was public. I cursed the gate and the incorrect map soundly. While it wasn't a fatal mistake, it was going to take much longer to reach Evanston and much needed supplies. Nearby campers, who knew the area well, said that the way north was convoluted and dry, with questionable water availability. They recommended going back into the mountains, and continuing west for a while, before taking another road to the north.

Disgruntled, I backtracked up the road down which we had so joyfully come. My attitude was saved when the school teacher I'd met several days earlier, and her husband, came looking for us. He was a commercial truck driver, who had joined her after I'd left China Meadows. She'd wanted him to meet me, so our detour had some benefit at that. They cheered me up greatly, giving me a chance to unload my gripes. The burros, Lucy, and I returned to the fork in the road where we'd turned north, went a little south, and found a place to camp near a river. The error on the map had cost us a 12-mile detour, back into Utah, a full day out of our way.

July 5.

We had a bit of a job leaving the camp area, because, still being frustrated the day before, I'd just plowed us through a swampy area and down a steep hill with no trail. We had to take a longer route bypassing the obstacles to reach the Forest Road. It was a long 7-mile climb to the top of Elizabeth Ridge, the "high point" of the journey at 10,243 feet. The summit was significant for more than its elevation.

It divided the Green River drainage, which joined the Colorado River and eventually flowed into the Pacific Ocean, from the Great Basin Drainage, where water never goes anywhere, but simply evaporates. We were entering a different world.

We'd climbed the long hill very strongly; all of us were really getting into shape, right on schedule for our push across the flats. I had a good, long view to the northwest, lower hills and flats stretching into the distance, where we'd be heading after we left the comforting mountains. I felt a thrill of anticipation, "Here we go, out into the vastness, the meat of the trip." All of the journey, so far, had been a prelude, a warm-up for what lay ahead. Five-and-a-half miles downhill, we camped at Mill Creek. It was busier here, near the edge of the Forest Lands and close to a main highway.

The following day we laid over, having trudged thirty-two miles up and down over the previous three days. I slept a lot during the day, enjoying our last forest camp before moving on to the next part of the journey. We were at a much anticipated change in the trip. I imagined that it would be much more difficult and probably less enjoyable. We were leaving the beautiful mountains, with all of their wonderful trees and abundant water, for the arid, open flatlands with only occasional stunted deciduous trees for shade. In the Forest Lands, we camped anywhere we wished. Amongst the private lands, we'd have to camp where we could. Water would be much scarcer, with fewer good springs for drinking water. The mountains were my Home. The land ahead was more alien and unknown. We'd been used to walking along nearly empty gravel roads, with an occasional slow moving vehicle full of happy campers on vacation. Now, we'd be creeping down the side of paved highways, with fast moving cars carrying people of all walks of life. I took a deep mental breath, "Here we go!"

Chapter 7
Out into the Wides
July 8 - July 17

July 8.

That evening, a family set up camp near us. The next morning, they made me a hearty breakfast to properly send me on my way out of the forest and into the Wides. We walked the final six miles of gravel Forest Road easily. A short traipse along Highway 150 brought us to a lodge with a camp store. I hadn't been around cars moving at any real speed since the Flaming Gorge Dam, so suddenly being out there with cars zooming by was unsettling. Life on the pavement was pretty tense after the quiet woods. It was like casting out in a little sailboat from the safety of shore … onto a VAST ocean.

One of the lodge managers bought me lunch at the store-café, and later a visitor bought me an ice cream cone for dessert. I bought a few supplies, getting only the necessities, since the bigger stores of Evanston were only a few days away. The store manager gave me a discount on the supplies, since it was a pricey tourist attraction, and I was part of the entertainment. A biker and his son gave me a twenty dollar bill to help us on our way; being treated so well as soon as we hit the highway really boosted my confidence. Since we were still in some hilly terrain, the road was narrow and winding, with a very inadequate shoulder. This made it difficult for drivers to see us, and made me very tense. Fortunately, conditions improved when we reached the flats, where the road straightened, and people could see us from a distance. Of course, we wore orange to be more visible.

We passed two large bands of sheep, of about a thousand head each, heading up the road to the mountains. I'd met the shepherds of these large flocks many times in the high mountains. They took the sheep into the highest, most remote meadows during the summer, usually keeping them above timberline until it snowed. The shepherds were always from foreign countries, usually Mexico or South America, and once, I met a pair from Mongolia. The Mongolians and I became particularly friendly, spending many hours at camp trying to converse across the very difficult language gap. Shepherds were my peer-group in the high mountains, since we all lived for months in the same harsh and challenging climate. They had a much more difficult time than I did. During the frequent violent thunderstorms, with driving rain, hail, and terrifyingly close lightning strikes, I could hide in my tent, while they had to stay out in the cold-wetness tending their flocks.

Passing the two flocks on the road, I looked closely at the shepherds to see if I knew any of them, but saw no familiar faces. The huge, slow moving herds clogged the highway, forcing cars to creep slowly forward through the masses of sheep, waiting for them to part, so they could drive ahead. We had it easier; the sheep were frightened of the burros and Lucy, and moved out of our way. I kept Lucy leashed so she wouldn't chase them, not only because of the chaos which would have resulted, but because the shepherds had large guard-dogs that might attack Lucy just for being near their sheep.

We were passing a shepherd riding a horse, when Libby for some reason let out a LOUD BRAY! The horse must have never been around burros, because it completely FREAKED OUT!!! … Bucking and trying to run away. Only the shepherd's great skill as a horseman kept him on the berserk animal. He eventually controlled the skittish animal, looked at me … and we both laughed. If his fellow shepherds had seen a meek-little burro nearly cause him to be bucked off his horse, they would have teased him about it all summer.

The burros kept up a good pace, moving us a few miles back into Wyoming before the end of the 15-mile day. Reaching the Wyoming border was a bonus, because from there on, the road had a full, wide shoulder we could travel without much worry about passing traffic. Also, there was a hundred-foot-wide zone running along the roadside between the pavement and the fenced-off private land. We came to a thick row of trees, with a strip of good grazing between the trees and the private land. The roadside spot was as good as we could hope to find, since the row of trees hid us from the road. A ditch flowed with water. The grazing was actually quite good, since it was beyond the reach of any other livestock. Often, the area right along the road is the best grazing around, which is the reason many deer eat along the highways at night.

The curious cattle on the other side of the fence came over to investigate. Lucy went berserk, lunging and barking at what she considered an intrusion into our home. The fence was sheep-wire she couldn't get through, so she had to be content with being belligerent from our side of the fence.

I wouldn't have let her chase the cows anyway, since it would cause problems with the rancher, but I was glad she discouraged the cows. My camp stove was barely working, so I took it apart to see if I could fix it. The fuel line to the burner was clogged by all of the regular gasoline that I'd been using. I was unable to fix it. A new stove, or at least that part, was needed. Luckily, we'd soon reach the relatively large town of Evanston, where I should be able to find one or the other.

July 9.

I kept looking back at the mountains with a twinge of nostalgia for the great peaks we were departing. We clipped along at an exceedingly fast, "burro sonic" speed of 3-m.p.h. The open straight road through ranch country, with its good wide shoulder, gave us no problems, until a fast moving pickup pulling a trailer with a loose tarp blew by. The loud flapping tarp spooked Libby. I was just barely able to hold her from bolting off in a panic, which could have been a total disaster. This was where holding an animal smaller than a horse made a huge difference. If she'd been any stronger, I would have lost them both. The truck pulled off onto the side of the road ahead of us. When we came up to him, he apologized for scaring the burros. I helped him fix the tarp, and he took some pictures of us on my camera.

The pace was tiring, in the hot sun. We stopped after eleven miles, where we had water, grazing, and trees for shade. I was able to coax one last hot meal out of the stove, before it completely died. Cooking pasta over the very low, sputtering flame took a long time. I was so overheated from the fast, hot walk I could barely eat any of it. Even Lucy only wanted a little of it, so even though I was very low on food, I uncharacteristically tossed the rest away in some tall grass.

We took a long break, hoping the temperature would cool before heading down the road another five miles or so. It was a rough day, and I kept looking for a place to camp. I got so tired I finally just had to stop somewhere. The sun was about to set, and we were passing more buildings as we got closer to Evanston. We came to a stream in a steep little ravine, with a clump of trees and a ditch running along the top of one bank. I agonized for quite awhile over where to camp. Nothing seemed that good, but after seeing no other workable option, we went through a gate onto private land without an invite. We crossed the ditch at the top of the bank and hid in the trees. We were on commercial land. The building was a hundred yards away, and it was Saturday night. I figured we wouldn't be bothered by anyone, but I still didn't like the situation.

Not seeing much chance of rain, I didn't set up the tent. We'd be less visible, and we could leave quicker in the morning. With the stove not working, all I had to eat for dinner was peanut butter. I sat on a log, eating spoons of the goop … looking at my meager pile of gear. I felt desperate; maybe because of the difficulty in finding a place to camp, or because we were going to walk into a large town tomorrow. Big towns were dangerous and disorienting, with all the distractions and traffic. I looked at my situation rationally; walking alone down the highway, with a couple of burros, a dog, and a hundred dollars to my name; trying to move somewhere I'd never been, and where I knew no one. Doubt and fear settled over me. I was on very thin ice; a homeless person with some animals.

One of the worst things that could happen to me was happening in the middle of a burro pack trip. I'd regained my city logic. The magical faith that it would all work out because the Maker wanted me walking burros across the countryside had turned into a rational scientific outlook. All of the dangers and possible bad luck that I could imagine came crashing down on me. There were a hundred ways in which I could be hurt or stranded, while trying to walk cross-country to Oregon. At that point ... the whole idea seemed such a foolish ... improbable undertaking. My loss of faith was like being on a high-wire without a net ... and suddenly becoming afraid of heights. I'd lost my balance and was about to fall. I was homesick for somewhere safe and comfortable. I couldn't go back to Steamboat. As weirded out as I'd been the winter before, I was convinced that I couldn't survive there any longer. I had my good buddy in Cortez, who would let me live there, but I couldn't imagine living there again. Tres Piedras, where I'd lived for ten years, and had been so happy had the strongest pull. But when I'd left there, I felt like I had to move on. I had to find something more. All of those options were so far away, and I didn't have enough money for trailering, even if I thought I could go back to any of them.

I remembered what had pulled me up out of desolate dark-holes in the past: the vision I'd had at my highest moment decades before, that reality was being PURPOSELY crystallized at each moment. Physical reality was like the flames of a campfire, seemingly solid, but actually being created anew from an inner source at each moment. The Maker was creating every bit of reality: NOW!!! Visualizing that as the way reality was formed ... washed away my doubts and fears. Thank God, I was crazy once more.

July 9.

Having no tent or cooking gear to pack, we made a quick start in the morning. I just had some peanut butter for breakfast. We rejoined the road without anyone apparently aware of our stay. It got more and more built up with houses with every mile toward town. We came right into the heart of the Evanston business district. Even though it was 10:00 a.m. Sunday, it was still quite busy with the hustle and bustle of traffic Beanie was her usual mellow self, but Libby was spooky going under the interstate highway bridge. The echo of all the traffic was very disconcerting to her. I held tight to the lead-rope next to the halter, and stayed beside her head. The burro's necks were so strong, that if you were behind their front legs, with a long lead-rope, you wouldn't have enough leverage to turn their heads, so they could pull free and run off. It took some effort to hold her till we passed the new obstacle.

I'd learned early in my packing career about burros panicking in town. Moving through the small town of Fountain Green, Utah, late in a long day, we'd just turned off the main street onto a side road, when we came upon a lawn sprinkler. The little sprinkler made a hissing sound, which the burros mistook as a snake! Both immediately turned and bolted! I tried to hold them, but I was quickly behind them. At the end of the rope, instead of them stopping, I was pulled off my feet and onto my face. I held on stubbornly, not wanting them to run loose. After being dragged for about forty feet, I finally saw the wisdom in "letting go". They ran up the road a hundred yards before they stopped and some helpful folks grabbed them. Fortunately, my ignorance only cost me a hole in my pants and some minor scrapes.

Among all of the big chain-stores, near the highway exit in Evanston, was a little strip of unused land. I unpacked the burros, staked them out to graze, and tied Lucy to my gear-pile with her long leash. If Lucy couldn't be with me, she liked to be with my gear, our Home. I would just have to have faith that no one would mess with my world as I hurried through the stores to find supplies.

I wanted to get enough food for a while, but not so much it weighed down the burros. We'd be going through small towns, where I could get some items as we went along. I got a new stove, not being able to find the part to fix the old one. The stove was such a crucial piece of gear that I was glad to have a new one for the rest of the trip. All of the expenditures took me down to twenty-five dollars, but as we were heading through the parking lot, away from the stores, someone with whom I'd talked about our journey came running over and gave me another twenty-five dollars. That act of kindness immediately doubled both my bankroll and my confidence.

Much to my tension, we took it right down Evanston's main street, with people stopping to stare. I got confused on the way through town, but eventually found the highway out of town to the northwest with the help of friendly locals. We'd walked along busy Highway 89 just a quarter mile and were near some of the last buildings in town, when a booming thunderstorm hit us face-first. The wind was blowing so hard sideways that we avoided most of the wind and driving rain, by simply standing behind a large building. The business was closed for Sunday, so we stayed behind it for two hours; hoping that we'd be able continue on our way, once the rain stopped. The rainstorm ended late in the day, and not knowing anyplace further on to camp, I decided to bivouac where we were. I tied the burros, and Lucy and I took a run around the immediate area. There was a rare parcel of unused land amongst the commercial sprawl, behind a nearby convenience store. I decided to stay there for the night, rather than head out into the darkening night.

Libby was so fried by coming through town and the storm, that when I tried to move her a couple hundred yards to the camping spot, she wouldn't even step over a simple curb. She was out in traffic with me doing the classic pull-the-stubborn-burro routine, to no avail. This was where being alone was difficult. There was nothing to which I could tie her, and I couldn't let her loose. After a struggle, I finally got Beanie untied from Libby, without letting go of Libby. The second I got Beanie over the curb, Libby also came along. That struggle and near-panic was the final note of a difficult day. We'd only gone about six miles, but all of the tension had made it exhausting.

I was relieved to get us behind the store and into our odd little camping spot. It was a very lush spot made almost swampy by the downpour. A little hill and clump of trees hid our presence from anyone passing by, and the grazing was good. There was even a ditch full of water. I set up the tent, in case it rained again. We were all very wet. In fact, I was so soaked that even my hands were clean.

July 10.

We were up early, so we could leave before we found out if we were welcome or not. Right from the beginning, I was very tired. Two long days, topped by the town stress had really worn me out. I needed a day to recuperate. We needed an early camp.

Highway 89 was a relatively busy road made barely tolerable because of a narrow shoulder to walk along. There was usually a little strip of gravel right along the edge of the pavement which made a good walking surface. We headed northwest through mostly flat country with a few dry hills to our north, passing occasional businesses on the otherwise rural road. I wondered if there might be a route we could take to avoid the main highway, and stopped at one of the buildings for advice. The people didn't know about the road I hoped to find, but they had an extra U.S. road atlas to help us. I tore out the pages of the states we'd be going through, and threw the rest in a dumpster.

When I saw two men sitting in a barn, fairly close to the road, I stopped to ask them about the best route we might take. They said the side route I was considering wouldn't work, unless we were willing to wade a large river. They also said that the last water for a long time was only a mile ahead. The owner offered us the use of one of his corrals for the burros, hay, water, and a place to camp for a couple of days, if I wished. It was just what we needed: someplace we could take some time off, other than just the roadside. The owner raised and trained racehorses. They had prime quarters in the barn, where I could muck out the stalls, if I wanted some work. The other man lived just up the road, and said that he also had a day or two of work, if I wanted to earn more. I gladly accepted both offers, needing money for future supplies.

We settled into the barn area for a couple of days of fine hospitality, and much needed rest from walking. I mucked the stalls in a couple hours that afternoon. When the owner handed me a twenty dollar bill, I declined it, saying that a place to stay was enough compensation. He dropped the money at my feet and walked away. He gave me a big pile of leftover pizza in the afternoon, and his wife brought me out a good plate of homemade food that night.

The other work was sanding paint off a deck so that it could be refinished later. A short time into the job a rainstorm rolled through, soaking the deck, ending the chance to complete the sanding that day. I decided to stay another day to finish the job. He offered to trailer the burros and me up the road a way, to ease our burden, but I passed, wanting to walk. He had to leave town the next day, and left his house open to me so that I could finish the work. He left me money at the house. His trust was admirable. He joked that the reason he trusted me was that, with two burros, I couldn't get away very fast or far if I did something devious.

Sanding the deck in the sun was mighty hot, and I hadn't quite finished when his son-in-law stopped by to give me a ride back to camp. I accepted, thinking I might finish the last little bit of work and clean up the mess the next day, on the way out of town. I left twenty dollars of the money the owner had paid me, just in case I didn't get back to do it. The racehorse owner's wife brought me a large tasty meal each night, trying to fatten me up. She was concerned about my skinniness. I sure had a good time hanging out with them, enjoying good conversation, friendliness and food

Walking with the burros in the rural west was like having an ultra-diamond-encrusted credit card. The burros opened all doors. People were friendly, helpful, and trusting. If I'd been walking alone with just a backpack, people would have been much more leery of me. Trust in a generally untrusting society was very noticeable and consistent throughout all of my burro trips. It made my prospects exciting. I might meet any kind of person, get any kind of offer. Burros made people trust me, even though I was very scruffy. My beard had grown substantial, and my clothes were getting more and more trashed and dingy. It's a dirty world out there. Spending time and effort keeping my clothes clean would've diminished my ability to complete more important tasks. To accomplish my main goal, superficial cleanliness was just too trivial.

July 13.

The next morning, as we were leaving, he insisted on giving me another twenty dollars to help us on our way. They were truly good people, and, even though I'd only been there a couple of days, it felt a bit like leaving home. My bankroll was up to an astounding two hundred and twenty dollars!! I felt like some rich guy! When we reached the turnoff to the deck sanding jobsite, I hesitated. It would be a half mile or so out of our way, and an hour or more to finish the job. It seemed too much extra time and effort. We had a long 15-mile day ahead of us, and it was already getting hot. I decided it would be better, particularly for the burro-girls, to get on with the walk, so we stayed on the road. I'd send a letter from the next town to apologize for not finishing the job.

I'd planned to get more water at the jobsite, so I had to stop at one of the last houses before heading out into the desolate wide-open stretch awaiting us. I tied the burros and dog to the fence in front of the house, and gingerly went to the door. I was leery of going to someone's door like this, unannounced and unknown, not wanting to scare the occupant. A woman who was home alone answered the door, but instead of being afraid, she was glad to meet me. She'd seen us walking down the road, days before, and was happy to hear my story. Being so noticeable, it was quite common to meet someone who had seen us along the way. Sometimes, people would see us over the course of several days and finally have to stop to inquire about our mission.

We crossed back into Utah, and immediately lost our good wide walking-shoulder. This put us back out into fast-moving traffic, if we stayed on the pavement. There were several small hills and dips along the way, making us invisible to drivers at times. To be safer, I took us off the road and into the ditch in the worst spots. This was difficult owing to the tall, uneven clumps of grass that made lousy footing. Also, lots of trash was scattered along the roadside, forcing us to pick our way through broken glass and garbage. Most of the time, we walked on the pavement, and hoped we wouldn't get squished. It was a very wide-open dry stretch, with no shade for a break. A small area of trees at the town of Woodruff, visible eight miles away across the desolate valley, was our "destination of the day." Like a mirage in the desert, it seemed to get no closer as we trudged along. I kept thinking we were closer than we were … and longed to be there. It was broiling, and I was fighting fatigue. I was surprised at how hard the day was, even after a couple of days rest. The tension of the narrow road was adding to my weariness. The burro-girls had a hard time with a cloud of flies near the end of the day, close to a marshy section. I doused them with bug spray to help them with their chore.

I was so very glad to walk into the town of Woodruff ... after our many steps finally got us there. The only commercial enterprise in the tiny town was an auto repair garage. We stopped there for water, and I asked if they knew somewhere in or near town where we might camp for the night. The garage owner said we could use his vacant lot behind the shop. It was a flat field with no trees. That late in the day, not having shade wasn't a problem. There was no chance of rain, and wanting the earliest possible start, to avoid as much of the next day's heat as we could, I slept under the stars. A Salt Lake City radio station was forecasting near 100 degree temperatures for the next seven days. The afternoon cloud build-up that we'd enjoyed for a few days was over; therefore, leaving early was imperative. Our camp was right in the middle of town, so to get some privacy, I plunked my gear down among some large sagebrush. A neighboring dog took particular exception to our intrusion into his territory, and came over to bark at us. He would periodically stop barking, leave for a short time, only to come back and start again.

July 14.

We were up at 5 a.m., and gone by 7:30. During the 10-mile walk to the next town, Randolph, I had the urge to splurge on lunch at a diner which several people had told me had good food. Shortly before town, some men stopped to take pictures and gave me seven dollars, so I felt that I really could afford the rare restaurant meal. We got to the cute little town of Randolph by 11:30. Big shade trees along a side street, right across from the park, made a good place for the burros. I left Lucy with the gear, and went into the diner to pig out. Lucy and I spent most of the rest of the day hanging-out in the park, and wandering around the little town.

I checked out their local historical site, one of the first settler cabins in the area, where I picked up a more detailed map of our upcoming route. The very rural town hadn't grown much since those earliest days. One of the locals told me that it was because of the mosquitoes. These little towns were hardcore Mormon-country, and like all of the other Mormons I'd met along the way, they were very friendly and helpful. I asked if there might be another route through the hills running along the west side of valley, so we could avoid the highway. They said that no practical way existed for us to go through the hills, because of the lack of water.

I packed up the burros at about 6 p.m., to try to get a bit more distance on the day, and find a good place to camp. After another six miles down the highway, we found no decent camping spot, and it was getting too dark for us to continue. We pulled into an abandoned ranch for the night. We just had to stop somewhere. It was private land, but it didn't seem that we'd be doing any harm by camping there. I moved past the old house, intending to set up behind the old barn, out of sight and away from the road; but when we crossed through some tall grass in a marshy area, a huge cloud of mosquitoes rose up and attacked. The burros were covered with thousands of the swarming, obnoxious horde. I moved us back near the road, and set up camp. Even away from the marsh it was still about the worst spot for mosquitoes I'd ever seen. I emptied about half a bottle of repellent on the burros, and even put some on myself for the first time in years. Fortunately, I'd gotten more repellent in Randolph. I usually just wore long sleeves and pants to keep the mosquitoes off. I also put on gloves and a piece of mosquito netting under my cap and over the back of my neck to help protect me. The simplest way to protect my neck was to unfurl my long thick hair. I still got bit a lot, but after all of the time being chewed in the woods, I'd developed an immunity to mosquitoes. I didn't get lumps, and hardly noticed that they bit me. These mosquitoes were over the top even for me. I hurriedly set up my tent, and dove inside to escape the persistent pests. I just ate peanut butter so I wouldn't have to go outside to use my stove. I understood what the man in Randolph was talking about when he said mosquitoes kept the area from growing. I'd thought he was kidding.

July 15.

I set my alarm for 3:33 a.m. to try to beat the mosquitoes as well as the heat, but I failed to set my alarm properly, and awoke a little after 5 a.m. I thrashed myself for the mistake, and hurried to get my gear together, before the impending sunrise mosquito onslaught. Peanut butter for breakfast saved cooking and repacking time. We were gone by 7 a.m., record-speed for "get up and go." I was filled with true dread as the large red-orb appeared on the horizon … understanding that being under its influence was going to be a torturous event.

We went three more miles up the road to the junction of Highway 30, and headed west. This was the "fork in the road" for our two main-route options. Going north up Hwy. 30 would have taken us along the Wyoming border, to central Idaho. I'd already decided fairly strongly to go across southern Idaho, so didn't give the northern route much thought. Soon after we turned west, some people stopped to talk. The Texas family had seen us several times the previous day, and were overcome with curiosity as to what we were doing. They took pictures and gave me a twenty dollar donation.

After the junction we had a grueling, 7-mile climb. My road map from the atlas didn't show terrain, so I didn't know how long the hill was. I kept thinking we were getting near the top, only to come around yet another turn with another long uphill section in front of us. This was so disheartening! It was an east-and-south-facing hill, so we were pounded by the early sun. The rolling hills were bare of shade-trees.

We finally achieved the top of the FOREVER-hill, but I was so overheated I didn't have much joy at the accomplishment. The water in my black water-sack was hot as tea from the blazing sunshine. I was desperate for something cold to drink, to bring my body temperature down. Some people stopped to take pictures, and gave me five dollars. I asked if they had anything cold to drink. They did, and I guzzled it down. It was veritable ecstasy, though I was still staggered.

Shortly after the summit, we came to an old abandoned homestead off the highway. The original road had gone through the property. I thought that the fenced-off section was probably public land. No signs on the gate said otherwise. I moved us in without much hesitation. It was an excellent place to camp: aspen trees for shade, a spring for water, and excellent grazing. The fence had kept range cattle out of the property.

I collapsed in the shade after our blazing 11-mile day, and dozed for an hour. I felt bad for not watering the burros immediately. After getting water for the thirsty burros, I pitched camp. The spring was good enough for my drinking needs. After another hour of rest, I was feeling pretty much recovered. All of the miles we'd traveled had gotten me in good shape, so my recovery time had shortened a lot. I remembered that after the first, relatively easy day of the adventure, it had taken me a full day to recover.

There were large burrows around the area. The size of the holes made me think that they might be badger dens, but I hadn't been around badgers enough to know. I hoped that, whatever they were, they didn't mind guests. It was such a fantastic location. It seemed logical to stay a day there, but I had a feeling that we should continue on the next day.

July 16.

I tried to talk myself into staying in the wonderful spot another day, but kept getting the very strong feeling to move on. We headed down the narrow snaking road through the rugged rocky ravine toward Bear Lake. This early in the day there wasn't much traffic to worry about. Even with all of the curves, I was able to hear cars far enough in advance to keep us safe.

We walked out of a gap in the rough barren hills, and into the large valley holding Bear Lake. About 7 miles across and 16 miles long, Bear Lake is surrounded on three sides by high steep mountains, with an open plain to the north. It was an extremely impressive place, though it was obscured and marred to some extent by a thick haze of smoke hanging in the air. Several fires were burning across the western U.S., some of them hundreds of miles away, and the whole region was covered by the bluish haze. I could hardly see the mountains on the far side of the lake.

Soon after we hit the flats of the valley, we came to an older couple gardening in their front yard. Most of their yard was covered with a beautiful flower garden. They seemed to want to talk, so we stopped. A few days earlier, they'd been out for a drive and had seen us on the road, therefore they were happy to find out our story. We talked for quite awhile. I was interested in hearing their stories, since they'd lived in the area their entire lives. I wanted to hear about the changes that had occurred during their lifetime there. They bemoaned all of the recent growth in their paradise of water and mountain scenery. By their account, Garden City, a town we'd have to walk through, was particularly built-up with large houses and condos for people from the cities.

The happy old couple had chickens, and since I couldn't carry eggs, because of their fragility and the heat, the woman went inside and made me a delicious egg sandwich for breakfast, while I filled up my drinking-water sack. The burros didn't want water. They never liked to just sip a little water, but only drank when they were thirsty enough for a couple of gallons. They did get several apples, which of course they were more than happy to inhale. It was a very pleasant stop for breakfast and conversation.

We took the pavement to the south of the great lake, finally getting right close to the water on the west side of the lake. It was Sunday, in a resort area, at the peak of the season, so there was a fair amount of traffic. People were crowded into a lakeside RV park, and the beaches were covered with people. The temperature was a bit cooler along the large lake, but it was still hot enough to convince me to take short breaks, under the occasional shade-tree, as we made our way along the shore.

I was concerned about where we'd find a place to camp amongst all of the houses we were approaching. Not only would we need our usual grazing and water, but we'd also require shade for the burro girls, if we were going to rest a day in the blazing heat. We definitely needed a rest, and supplies. Doing laundry would be great if I got the chance. The biggest challenge ahead of us was a large, tall mountain-ridge. The last hill had really toasted me, and this climb was going to be even tougher. I'd been looking at this spot on the map as one of our major problem areas, since I began considering this direction. We could climb a major highway over the mountain pass to the west, and turn off onto Forest Roads. I'd been asking advice along the way from people who knew the area. It was my habit to learn about different possibilities from as many people as I could. Anyone might have a little bit of information that could greatly help, like a good camping spot, water, etc. They might know a better choice or a reason why we wouldn't want to take a particular route. One way might be perfect on a warm sunny day, but a nightmare in bad weather. It was best to have as much information as I could gather. I'd learned the hard way to never entirely trust any information, because sometimes people can be wrong about what they believe. Many times, I'd gotten incorrect information about distances; people driving in cars can easily misjudge distances by several miles shorter than reality. In a car it doesn't make much difference, but on foot, several miles longer, when tired, is miserable.

Everyone said we shouldn't go up the highway. It was the major route between the Salt Lake City area and Bear Lake, so traffic would be heavy. Most people advised me to take another route to the north, but it would be far out of our way, and wasn't appealing. One suggestion was a route on side roads that avoided some of the busy highway. It seemed like our best option, but it didn't entirely eliminate being on the busy, winding highway with the burros. With the length of the climb, and the heat, it looked like we were in for a difficult time, whichever way we went. First was the challenge of making camp in the built-up area. I didn't think that the city people with vacation homes would be as inclined as rural people to let the burros, Lucy, and I plunk down in their yards for a day or two.

The highway was just turning away from the lake and into the town, when a pickup hauling a horse trailer pulled over. A young man got out and came back to talk. He was a rodeo clown on his way back from a gig in Evanston. His wife and young son, who were part of the rodeo intermission show, were with him in the truck. He was very excited to meet someone traveling with burros, since he had burros himself. He also had a few mules that he rode in the mountains. We talked for a short while, when he made me the amazing offer to load the burros into his nearly empty horse trailer, drive us to the top of the hill, and drop us off at the Forest Road. He only had his show gear in the trailer, so there was plenty of room for my burros. The rest of my gear would fit in the bed of the pickup. We'd not only avoid having to find a place to camp in the resort town, but we'd skip climbing the long grueling hill in the blazing heat. The trailer ride would save us about fifteen miles of hard walking. For the burros' sake it seemed like the thing to do, but I really wanted to walk all the way to Oregon. Would taking this ride be cheating? Would it corrupt my walk? A dilemma; I hesitated.

I followed my usual method of choosing a route when I wasn't sure which way to go. In my mind I imagined taking the ride up the mountain in the pickup, and being dropped off on top. Then I visualized walking the burros up the mountain. I examined the feelings I had as I imagined each option. I did this several times, and definitely had a better feeling when I imagined taking the ride up the mountain. I believe that the brain is a sense organ … a radio … that picks up "The Mind". Using this method, I tried to tap into the universal knowledge, rather than just the physical information at hand.

I gladly accepted his wonderful offer. Quickly, I popped the gear off the burros, loaded them into the trailer, piled my gear in the truck bed and, in a flash, we were being whisked away up the mountain. Since our time to the next town would be shortened, and we had enough supplies, the only thing I would really miss was a chance to do laundry. I could live with that; being dirty was a beloved part of the business. What a true blessing it was to avoid the long climb up the mountain in the oven-like weather. We caught a great view of the lake below, as we drove up the long hill. I thought to myself, "So this is the reason I had such a strong feeling to leave the good camping place last night." If we'd stayed there an extra day, we would have missed our ride up the mountain. I believed that the very welcome ride had been arranged.

The good soul of the rodeo clown totally showed through when we passed a vehicle broken down on the side of the road. He immediately pulled over onto a wide spot, and walked back to see if they needed help. Sure enough, their tire had blown apart, and they had no jack, tools, or knowledge of how to fix the problem. The rodeo clown got out his tools, but didn't have the proper lug-wrench to remove the rim and tire. I flagged down a passing vehicle, finally getting the fifth one to stop. They had the proper sized wrench and were happy to help. The clown took charge and soon had the blown tire off, and the spare on, so that the city-dwellers were able to drive away. I was so impressed with this clown's character! The rodeo family dropped us off at the dirt road leading into Franklin Basin. They gave me Gatorade, grapes, cherries, and a couple of bananas. I thanked them heartily. They left me with a joyous glow at my good fortune, and at having met such good kind people.

We were high enough now to be in an evergreen and aspen forest. I lounged a while in the shade, hungrily gobbling the much needed fresh fruit, and contemplating such a wonderful day. We'd been transported into another world. I relished being in the green of the high country. My mood was just spectacular.

We were fairly close to the highway, so, after resting, I repacked the girls, and we headed up the dirt road into National Forest Land. I happily strode into the trees and mountains, with a bounce to my step … and a smile on my face for sure. Thankfully, it was quite a bit cooler at the higher elevation with the shading trees. We went several slow miles up the drainage, sometimes near the rushing stream, sometimes not. We made camp near the happy, clear-running mountain stream, in the high valley. I guessed that we'd walked about 10 miles that day, not counting our miracle-ride.

Vacationing by the stream the next day was good medicine. I'd put the tent close to the wonderful, rushing stream. Trees grew right along its banks, so I was able to stay in the shade, next to the sparkling waters. It was a lazy day, listening to the radio and soaking my feet (for brief spells) in the icy water. Dunking my feet in the cold water was very refreshing, after all of the heat we'd been suffering. It wasn't totally idyllic though, since there was a cloud of extremely annoying tiny black-flies harassing me all day. They didn't bite, but there were about a hundred of them buzzing around me at all times. Also, the grazing was sparse and pretty chewed down, because of the range cattle everywhere in the forest. I blamed the flies and poor grazing on the cows. Frequently, I switched which burro was untied, giving each of them a chance to roam and find the best eats. Mostly, I just sat there, entertaining Lucy by throwing sticks into the fast-flowing creek

Chapter 8
Entering Idaho
July 18 - July 25

July 18.

Skimpy grazing forced us to move on the next day. We moved north up the primitive road, finally getting to a long anticipated landmark: the Idaho state border. YAY, we were really starting to get somewhere! Things actually changed a lot after we crossed the border, marked by a fence and a small sign. Instead of cattle, once we crossed the border, there were only sheep. Sheep grazing was better for us, because sheep stay in a herd, so you are either in the middle of a huge group of them, or there are none at all. Cattle spread out all over the forest. Also, sheep didn't graze on some of the plants that my burros liked to eat, leaving more eatables for them.

We went seven miles up through the beautiful country, getting into large meadows, with higher, forested hills to each side. The basin we were traveling up was basically a plateau atop the high mountain ridge. A side trail took us west up another drainage. We followed it a mile to the highest water source, a little seep pond, and made camp in a nearby group of large fir trees. The huge trees gave good shelter from any possible weather. Initially, we'd passed the spot, hoping to find more water higher up, but backtracked when there was none to be found.

It was a good camping spot, with an ample meadow and the large trees to protect the burros from the sun and any rain. Beanie particularly liked big trees. When she was loose, and wasn't eating, she'd stay under them. At night, if there were trees available, I'd stake the burros so that they could stand close to trees for shelter and scratching posts. They took advantage of the trunks and various branches to rub different parts of their bodies. One would think that they'd want to spend the night in a lush green meadow, but they preferred to stay where the soil was dry and dusty, so they could roll on the ground; one of their favorite activities. Several times a day, they liked to roll in the dust, particularly if they were sweaty from packing gear. They were quite comical doing this, raising a big cloud of dust, and having a noticeably good time as they rolled from side to side, happily grunting … legs to the sky.

We were now on the maps of the Idaho Road Atlas that I'd bought before starting the trip. It showed all the little roads and some of the trails. The maps weren't as detailed as the BLM maps, which I preferred, but they would do for this part of the trip, since we would mostly take back-roads across Idaho. The atlas, covering the entire state, was a great thing to have along, because I could change my route as I pleased. I'd taken this side trail because the more detailed map, which I'd picked up in Randolph, showed that it would connect to roads on the other side of the ridge. The trail would save about ten miles, and probably be more interesting. I asked people about this shortcut, but didn't meet anyone who'd actually used it. It wasn't a major trail, and maintenance was a question.

I tried to answer that question the next day. Lucy and I left the burros, and took a stroll up the trail to see what we could see. The trail was used occasionally by ATVs up to the top of the ridge. We had an amazing bird's eye view of the valley where we were headed on the other side of the ridge. It was a large, long valley running north-to-south, with a lower brown ridge about fifteen miles away to the west. The center of the valley was pocked with green irrigated fields. Whatever wasn't watered artificially was desolate brown. I could see the streaks of the roads we'd soon be traveling crossing the valley. Clumps of trees betrayed small towns in the valley bottom. The next ridge paralleled the higher mountains where we stood. I noticed a notch in the ridge where we'd probably cross over to the valley beyond. Running across the bottom of Idaho were four north-south ridges, which we'd have to cross on our walk to Oregon.

I sat awestruck, gazing at the tremendous view into which we were going to be walking. It was going to be a huge transition, from forests and streams to the parched barrens of southern Idaho. We'd had a taste of the lower country after leaving the High Uintas, but this was much, much bigger, drier, and more desolate. With forecasts of hot-and-hotter weather, the walk across southern Idaho seemed ominous. Would we be able to do it? It was my "Cowardly Lion Moment". As in the "Wizard of Oz", when the Lion SHRUNK BACK at the view of "The Wicked Witches Castle"; I was knowingly APPALLED at I was looking at; the view we were about to walk into was 300 miles farther than what I could see, and soundly implied: several months of REAL hardship by heat and desolation.

The big question at the moment was still whether we could get through to the valley floor, on the trail before us. While several ATVs had come to the top on our side, few had gone over to the other side. I wondered if we should gamble on the seldom used trail. It would be brutal if we got stuck halfway down the mountainside, and had to backtrack up the mountain. Also, judging by the lack of travel on the trail, we'd be on our own and couldn't screw up. No one would be coming through, or know we were there.

Lucy and I walked back to camp through the beautiful forest and meadows. I tried to soak up the green-lushness of the high mountains as much as I could while we were still there. One thing I wouldn't miss was the constant cloud of black flies that harassed me around the camp. I'd get fed-up with the menacing horde, and dive into my tent for protection. Each time Lucy and I plunged into the tent, about fifty flies got inside before I could zip the tent door shut. I'd have to open the door again, take my large atlas of maps, and try to shoo the intruders to the outside. They don't call it "being bugged" for nothing.

Late in the day, I sat against a particularly wide, soaring fir tree, considering our trailer-ride. I thought back and forth about whether it had been the right thing to do. Did the ride somehow foul the adventure, or not? While churning this in my mind, it came to me. The trip was as much about the wonderful people I was meeting, and who were helping us, as about us. The Helpers were as important to the story as we were. The trailer-ride and all of the other great favors people had given was an opportunity to show their great-goodness. The adventure was way bigger than just us.

July 20.

It rained steadily all night, drenching the forest with welcome water, and stopped a bit after first-light. We weren't in a huge hurry to get going, since the only goal for the day was to get down the mountain, where the roads started again. I'd decided to try the shortcut. The forest twinkled, happy with last evening's moisture. The trail was slippery from the drenching, forcing us at one point to leave the trail where it was too steep and slick for the burros to negotiate. I cut them back and forth across the open face of the slope, instead of chancing the slippery trail.

We paused at the top of the ridge. I tighten the burros' britchens, so the packs wouldn't slide over their heads; took a DEEP breath and headed us down the hill. I knew I was gambling, and questioned my decision. The beginning of the trail crossed the steep forested face of the mountain ridge. It was a slow, easy descent. Once past the trees, and onto an open section of the mountain slope, we had great views spreading before us. There was a recent ATV track, so I felt that the trail might go through. As we dropped lower and lower, I kept looking back up at the top of the ridge, very much hoping that we wouldn't have to go back up the ever lengthening climb.

About halfway down the nearly three thousand vertical foot decent, we got into a thick tangle of undergrowth where the ATV had turned back. Soon after that, I lost the trail. Range cattle had made well defined trails of their own. We got onto a false trail. DISTRESS began to well up inside of me. My worries that the trail wasn't maintained were true. I tied the burros to some trees. I had to "SLOW DOWN and figure it out" before I did something stupid in a spot where I was very much on my own. I followed the trail without the burros, and confirmed that it wasn't the trail we wanted. Then, I backtracked until I found the old road. Dense, tall ferns had obscured the trail. I was relieved to find the trail again, but still uncertain if we'd be able to get through. We were still several miles from the bottom of the hill.

I retrieved the burros, and we got back on track. At one point, a log barred the way. I surprised myself when I easily tossed it out of the way. Adrenalin had made me stronger than usual during the trying challenge. The old road had been washed-out into a 3-foot deep gully. Dense underbrush on each side forced us to stay in the bottom of the narrow trough. Not only was it narrow, it was muddy from the rain the night before. The burros skated down the slippery trail. Fortunately, with four-leg-drive, they kept their balance. We were all drenched from pushing through brush that was still soaked by the rain. A tense while later, we crossed the stream running down to the forested valley. The trail improved somewhat, and I saw the most wonderful and joyous sight: Fresh Horse Poop! ... YES! I felt fairly sure that the horse-people had come up from the bottom. It was far less likely that someone had gone on a day-ride the way I had come. My spirits lightened up greatly. Over the years of trail travel, horse poop was a welcome sight. If horses could get through, so could we.

We weren't "out of the woods" yet. We had to cross the stream repeatedly. Several of the crossings were really lousy, since the trail still wasn't maintained. I put Beanie in front to get us past the most difficult spots. I was very glad to have the old girl along. At one point Libby hooked a pannier on a large dead branch. She kept pushing, and tore the pannier from the pack frame. Quickly, I popped off the other pannier, to level her load. When you make them, you can fix them. I took out my spare parts and replaced the torn straps. This time, the repair was relatively simple. The strap holding the buckle to the pack frame tore off, instead of ripping from the pannier, which would have been a brutal repair. I'd made a good design feature without planning. Twenty minutes of trailside repair later, we were again on our way.

With much "tussle and toil", we got down to a fork in the trail that wasn't on my map. It showed our trail going up and over a ridge into another drainage, and then rejoining this drainage further down. The trail not shown on my map followed our drainage, with another difficult stream crossing, just past the junction, so I decided to try the trail on my map. Up, up, up we went on the side ridge. After about a mile, it was still climbing, which didn't make sense? According to my map, we should have topped the ridge and been into the other drainage. Also, the trail was petering out. I tied the burros, and went ahead with Lucy to scout it out. Not too far ahead, the trail disappeared in a tangle of fallen trees. I should have recognized that we were on the wrong trail earlier. I was getting frustrated by all of the difficulties of the day. Usually, I preferred trail travel, but after all we'd encountered on the way down the hill, I was going to greatly appreciate getting back on the easier roads.

I retrieved the burros, backtracked down to the junction, and followed the rough trail down the valley. The trail in many places just followed right down the middle of the stream for hundreds of feet at a time. We stumbled and slipped over the slick river-rocks. Happily, the weather was hot, so wading the cold mountain stream was refreshment rather than torture. I soaked my boots again and again. I couldn't tippy-toe around everything while leading the burros through difficult places. Wet feet were part of the business. We finally reached the end of the trail, at a traveled road. A sign facing back up the trail said, "CAUTION trail washed out ahead." I exclaimed, "NO SHIT!!"

The trailhead had grazing and some shrubby little maples for shade. Further down, the land was private, and camping uncertain. It was hot enough even in the shade, that I soaked my shirt in water and put it back on wet, cooling myself. Being pretty thwacked, I collapsed under the trees and took a nap. Even though the walk had been downhill, and we'd only advanced maybe six miles, (plus a couple of miles on the wrong trail), it had taken us seven hours to negotiate the unkempt trail.

Late in the day, a young fellow on an ATV came up to our camp. We talked for a while. He was staying and working at a house not far down the road. He took me down to the house, and then back up to my camp, on the back of the ATV, to get some drinking water. Later, he brought me a good dinner to help me on my journey, which he admired.

July 21.

Two months on the trail. The beginning of the day's walk was pure delight. The lightly traveled, winding country road leisurely descended the scenic valley through shrub maple trees. The shady way abruptly ended when we came out of the drainage, and onto the valley bottom, where we walked by an older gentleman in his yard. He waved us over, and told me to take a break. He had horses and mules corralled across the road, and had ridden and driven wagons with animals all his life. He was very knowledgeable about what I was doing, and we talked for an hour about the small details of equipment and procedure. The old gentleman loved what I was doing, and said that if he wasn't married, he'd pack up his mules and head off with me. "Ah, what a time it would be …" he lifted, old eyes sparkling. We parted good friends.

Soon after this very enjoyable stop, the burros, Lucy and I made it into the little town of Franklin, the first town to be settled in Idaho. The business district was a convenience store, restaurant, and a bar, all on the corners of the main intersection. The bar and convenience store were owned by the same people. They gave me permission to put the burros in the yard by the bar, with shade trees and plenty of grazing for our afternoon break. As always on the long breaks, I pulled the gear from the burros.

The temperature was 100 degrees. I waited for the temperature to drop by going into each business for a part of the afternoon. I took lunch in the restaurant, newly owned by a Mexican lady.I could tell by the care that she put into each plate, before sending it out to the customers, that she was the owner. She'd seen us walk by her window, and gave me my good meal for half price, even though she said the new business had been extremely challenging. Because of her generosity and friendliness, I hoped she'd do well. The convenience store had a large walk-in beer cooler; the coolest place in town during the stifling hot day, where I loitered as long as I could. I told the workers in the store that I should bring my burros into the cooler with me. I went into the bar last, though it seemed hotter inside than out.

I packed up the burros and finally left at 6:30. Technically, it was cooler. Walking west, directly into the setting sun, it was still plenty hot. We headed out through the flat farmlands of the valley bottom on a back road. The roads here were one mile grid squares, north-south and east-west. The sun sat, and we still hadn't found a place for the night. We'd already walked fourteen miles, and needed to camp soon. It looked like we might just have to take a place at the edge of the road, when the mother of a young couple I'd met a few miles earlier, pulled over to see how we were doing. Her daughter had told her about meeting the strange sight along the road. I told her I was looking for a place to camp. Her yard was right across the road, but it was too small for us. She knew the owners of the land next to us, and called to ask them if we could stay in their pasture that night. Her friends went along with the idea, so we set up in the field behind the house, by a water trough.

The elderly man was a jolly jokester, despite his ailing legs and eyes, and loved my adventure. He had a good chuckle thinking about how long we'd been walking, and how far we still had to go. It was dark by the time we pulled in, so the jokester's wife made me a quick sandwich for dinner. We planned to have a good chat over breakfast the next morning. I was warmed and overjoyed by these good hearted people and our continued good fortune.

July 22.

I was very tired and slept until dawn, much later than usual. The tiny town of Weston, our next "clump of trees", was only three miles away, so we could afford a late start. It would be treeless for a while after that, so Weston was where we'd take our mid-day break. I'd gotten a good idea of what was ahead from the ridge top several days before. I'd rather have gone farther in the morning, but the need for shade in the afternoon ruled our agenda. One hundred degrees in the shade was cool compared to walking down black pavement in the blasting sunshine.

The old couple brought breakfast to my campsite in the morning. We had an enjoyable talk out in the field. He told me about all of the interesting jobs he'd done throughout his life and, with a sparkle in his eye … how he'd met his younger wife. Before we left, a neighbor came over with gifts of peanut butter and more.

We made the short hop to Weston easily. Our patron had told me the park supervisor's name, thinking that he'd let us stop in the park for our afternoon break. A large, brick Mormon Church with a fine trimmed lawn adjoined the town park. I didn't want to literally mess with the park, and forgot it after the perfect spot appeared at the edge of town. A row of large deciduous trees on the right side of Main Street, close to the center of town, had good grazing beneath them. I unpacked the burros in the shade. The only business in town was a small grocery store. I went inside for a few items.

Next to the burros was a good tree to sit under at the edge of a field, overlooking the pastoral valley. I fell asleep in the heat for awhile. An older gentleman who owned a couple of properties in town, stopped by to visit; he drove back and forth between his properties on his riding lawn mower. I walked over with him to one of his properties for water. We visited while he moved his lawn sprinklers around the fresh-cut grass. He threw the stick for Lucy a bunch of times. We talked for a long time, while he advised me about upcoming sections we might walk through.

Late in the day, I collected myself and we took to the road, to make a few more miles. We ambled up a pretty side valley, climbing slowly out of the larger main valley we'd crossed. We were heading toward the gap in the ridge I'd seen from high up on the mountain. As we neared the mouth of the narrow canyon into the hills, we passed a ranch with many horses, mules, and a burro even larger than mine. The owner was waiting for us, on an ATV, when we came walking by the end of his driveway. He was alerted to our approach when all of his animals perked up, looking in our direction. We were too far out for him to see exactly what we were, but he figured by the way his horses were acting that it must be someone with animals.

He was very friendly, and immediately offered us a place to stay on his pastoral property before I could ask about a place to camp. It was a good location for us, with interesting people to boot. They had all kinds of animals, with a large contingent of dogs, cats, horses, mules, peacocks and the burro. We walked only about seven miles that day, having traveled such a short distance in the morning. I set my tent on their green lawn, and put the burros in a nearby corral. Their burro was a male. His purpose was to make mules. Burros have a very loud bray that can be heard from at least a mile away. The male and my girls serenaded each other from their separate corrals, with loud and mournful brays, emotional delivery on maximum.

I had a wonderful dinner with the ranchers in their comfortable farm house. They knew I was o.k. when their old dog, which sometimes bit visitors, was very friendly toward me. The ranch couple and I got along very well. I saw something I had not observed in a long time: TV. The hearty, delicious home-cooked meal was a huge treat, not only for flavor, but for all of the calories my body needed.

We rested from walking the next day. They let me do laundry. It was the first time during the trip that I'd done laundry in a real washer and dryer. Up until then, I'd used five-gallon-buckets with the water heated on my stove or in the sun; an arduous process that only gets things somewhat clean. I also took a shower, my first real clean-up in about a month. Ah, dirt! Thank God I loved the earth!

The rancher took me on a drive around the area, to show me a couple of different routes west that we might take over the upcoming hills. It was a very helpful tour. He knew the terrain well, having hunted all over the hills. He knew all of the different routes, and where there was water. I learned that there was much more water in the hills than I'd guessed, which freed up my route and camping alternatives a lot.

One possibility (other than the main road) was to go up a minor drainage. That trail would take us to the top of the ridge, after which it stayed on the high ground for a fairly long distance, before dropping down the drainage to our next destination, Malad City. From the top of the high ridge there were great views, east and west, into the large valleys and beyond. The drawback was that the only water was on the uphill side about four miles into the day; too short to really call it a day. After that, there was no water until miles later on the downhill slope. That would make a 15 mile day with nearly two thousand vertical feet to climb, which seemed a bit much for one day. It would be more scenic than walking the main highway. The highway covered almost six of the thirteen miles it would take to reach the same place. Besides, there was a really good camping place at eleven miles. We could also water at a reservoir on the way. I just mulled the options, planning to choose the route when we got to "ye olde fork in the road."

July 24.

I awoke at my usual 4:30 a.m. to rain. Luckily, it was just a mist, because I didn't have the rain-fly over the tent. Another fine home-cooked meal for breakfast, before saying goodbye and thanks to these good new friends; we were on the road a little after 7 a.m., heading for the hills on a farm road. At the fork in the road, I paused, visualizing going both ways, but didn't get a real clear feeling of which way to go. I started toward the ridge top option. Libby uncharacteristically balked at starting. I gave her a stronger pull. She kept balking. I turned toward the main drainage … and she started right away. I figured she'd answered the question of which way to go. A mile later we rejoined the main road up into the hills.

Thankfully, it continued to be cloudy as we made the steady climb through the rounded hills of the area. We climbed the hill fairly quickly, since we were well rested by the day off, and helped by the coolness of the cloudy day. The road was nearly empty of cars, since it was the Mormon Holiday, Pioneer Day. Southern Idaho was primarily inhabited by people of the Mormon faith. The holiday celebrated their ancestors who'd originally settled the region. I could appreciate the hardships that the early pioneers went through, a century and a half ago, using wagons and livestock to make the long journey west.

Partway up the hill we came upon a large rattlesnake warming itself on the dark pavement, in the cool of the morning. Lucy made a move toward it. The snake coiled and rattled. Even though Lucy had probably never even seen a rattlesnake before, she instinctively moved away from it, much to my relief.

Years before, on a burro pack trip in a desert section of southern Colorado, I had a stout little Blue Heeler named Gypsy; we were crossing the only water in the area, a small stream with thick brush and tall grass along its banks. I could just feel the rattlers all around the area, so as we made our way through the stream bottom, I purposely stomped my feet to let the snakes know that there was a large creature around. I hoped that the snakes would want to avoid me, and move away, or at least rattle to show their presence. I should have had Gypsy dog on a leash through the stream area, to keep her out of trouble. Sure enough when we got to the other side, she had two small blood spots on her nose. I went into denial at first, calling the blood spots pricks from a cactus. But her rapidly swelling nose betrayed the truth. Fortunately, my beloved little buddy weighed only thirty pounds, and was small enough to strap to the top of my backpack. We hastened to a potato farm, several miles away. The owner of the farm scoffed at my worry. He said his dogs got bit all of the time and never died. Gypsy didn't die, but her head swelled hugely. We were near the end of the trip, so a friend came and took her home to save us from having to stop for a long time waiting for her to heal.

Gypsy was quite a character. She would aggressively challenge any dog, no matter how big, that got close to me, even one of my other dogs. I was her guy for sure. She was very overweight in her older years, so when we were on the forty day pack trip in the Colorado Mountains, I decided it was a good opportunity to put her on a severe diet. The whole trip I just fed her small amounts. I'd miscalculated my own food needs, and was nearly out of food ten days before a homebound trailer was going to pick us up. Since I was skinny to begin with, not eating wasn't such a problem. We were deep in the wilderness, during black-powder hunting season, when four hunters came into the backcountry, riding horses and leading pack stock. They'd been coming to the same location for seventeen years, only to find us camped in their favorite spot. Because of the trees and rugged terrain, there was no other decent place to camp in the area, if you had horses. We made a deal; I'd let them move in right next to my camp, if they'd feed me for a day or two.

That night they broke out a 5-pound smoked ham for sandwiches. I was quite hungry, and definitely appreciated it. The next morning they were going to make breakfast, but couldn't find the ham anywhere, until they looked at squat little Gypsy. Her belly was literally dragging the ground. She'd eaten the whole four pounds of leftover ham! It was not only a big part of their food, but she'd blown her month-long diet in one meal. Luckily, one of the hunters shot an elk that first morning, so they had plenty to eat.

Back in Utah, we stopped at the reservoir so the burros and Lucy could drink. Several small groups of fishermen were enjoying the holiday weekend along the shore of the pleasant mile-long body of water. I tied the burros to the fence between the road and the nearby water, and took one of my 5-gallon buckets to fetch water. Lucy, who was also tied to the fence, so she wouldn't mess with the fishing, was the only one who drank it.

A couple of miles past the reservoir, we left the highway for a gravel Forest Road. A mile past the turnoff we reached the aspen meadow which would have been a great place to stay, but the next day's goal made me consider another plan. We'd be going into Malad City after we left the mountain ridge, about seven miles away. A short day would be best just before going into Malad City. Since we were walking so well, we bypassed the pretty green spot, and continued up and over the ridge. This was where having discussed routes with a knowledgeable guide came in handy. I knew there was water on the other side, so we could continue on. The road went downhill close to the bottom of the ravine, just above a little steam with a forest of maple trees and dense brush along its banks.

Our mountain ridge was National Forest Land, so we could camp where we wanted. The land was divided by fences into different grazing allotments. They could be used at different times of the year, or not at all, hence each allotment could have much different grazing conditions. We had been traveling in an ungrazed allotment, when we came to a fence with a heavily grazed section on the other side. We were about a third of the way down the hill, and didn't know if the conditions farther on would be better, so we stopped to have the best grazing. I pitched the tent under a maple tree, even though it was right next to the road. The spot worked, since the one lane mountain road was infrequently traveled by just a few slow moving vehicles. I rested in the shade by the trickling stream. I figured that we were approximately four hundred miles into the journey.

July 25.

We had an easy walk down the narrow drainage into the wide, flat valley with a freeway running through it. We walked the frontage road for a mile, before going under a bridge and coming into the middle of Malad City; actually just a town by most standards. I always felt a bit odd and out of place whenever we came into a fair sized town. Nearly everyone stopped to look at us. There was an abandoned house, with a yard full of tall grass and shade trees, right across from the grocery store. I asked someone in a nearby yard about the abandoned property. They said that in the five years they'd lived there, they'd never seen anyone there. I figured it would be o.k. to hang out there for a few hours. The lawn needed trimming anyway, and it was a perfect location for us.

I did my town-thing of grocery shopping and a quick tour of the rest of downtown, a couple of blocks away. Several people stopped to hear about our story. It was about 100 degrees when I told one woman that we were walking from Colorado to Oregon. She looked perplexed: "On purpose?" I admitted to being a sort of refugee, having very little money. This was just a way of moving somewhere new, having no other means to do so.

I'd heard that an old-west movie was being filmed in the area. Someone working as an extra, said that with my look, I could also probably get a part. I saw the sign directing people to the site, thirty-eight miles north. I looked at the map. There was no good route west from the movie location. It would have been fun to walk into a western movie set, doing what I was doing, but I didn't get much of a feeling to head that way. My mission, walking to Oregon, was way more important than a bit-part in a movie. Also, it wasn't a sure thing that I'd get a part, so I gave up on that idea. Acting as if I was in the old-west didn't seem like that much fun when I was doing the REAL THING anyway.

Late in the afternoon, I repacked the burros. While I was doing that, someone in the neighborhood brought me a couple slices of pizza. We took the main highway west for five miles, into the small cluster of houses and trees named Pleasantview. The road went up into the dry hills beyond the little town; consequently, we had to find somewhere to camp near the houses, where we'd have water and grazing. A man who was cutting his lawn stopped, and asked about our mission. His wife had seen us earlier, while driving home, and they'd wondered when we'd come by. He was sort of waiting for us, and asked if we wanted to stay in his yard, after I told him that we were looking for a place in the trees to camp. He stopped cutting the lawn, so the burros would have more to graze. He and his family had already eaten dinner, but promised me a hearty breakfast the following morning. They invited me in that night for a shower. I took them up on bathing, even though I'd just showered five days before. Such rare luxury! I appreciated the courage and real "action on faith" that these people showed by inviting someone as scruffy as me into their family home. Burro Magic: I couldn't imagine anything else I could do that would get me such good treatment and trust.

Chapter 9
High Heat

July 26 - August 4

July 26.

I packed my gear in the dark so we'd be ready to leave right after breakfast. The morning family-feast was made by one of the young daughters. She cooked her special-occasions meal, a sort of pancake in a deep baking pan. I'd never eaten anything like it, and gladly partook of the wonderful meal. I very much appreciated the privilege of sitting with the good family and sharing their meal. The young cook blessed the meal, and included in her prayer a request for our safe journey to Oregon. As she mentioned us in the blessings, I included (under my breath) a wish for some cloud cover. The upcoming section was going to be truly trying. Ahead was an 18-mile day, through country barren of trees and maybe water. About halfway, there was a possibility of water at a spring-fed cattle trough, but no one knew for sure if it was flowing now. I scrambled to leave as quickly as possible after the wonderful breakfast. We surely wanted to be gone before it got too hot.

My prayer was answered. A cloud formed above us. I was in high spirits as we pulled away. The man of the house was in the front yard, to bid us goodbye. I thanked the kind, trusting gentleman, and pointed to the sheltering cloud as proof that his daughter's prayer for us had worked. As I looked back, a short distance up the road, the homegrown man went across the road to the small-town cemetery … for a talk.

The first five miles were uphill through barren, rounded hills. Because the hill faced east, the climb would have been brutal if the sun wasn't hidden. The difference between walking up the road in sunshine or shade was HUGE, particularly on a long day. The owner of the land with the water troughs stopped to talk. He said there was water in the troughs, and that we were more than welcome to use it.

I was glad to top the divide. From there, it was all downhill into the distant town of Holbrook. We paused for a few minutes at the top, before heading down the other side toward the next valley. Our protecting cloud continued to block the killer sunshine all the way to the water troughs, a couple of miles after the ridge top. I took the buckets over the fence to retrieve water for the burros. We took another 15-minute break, while I spooned-up some peanut butter for energy.

As we departed the water troughs, the cloud passed us by(e). It really had been a miracle having the sheltering cloud. The sky had been clear everywhere ... except over us. It was near the middle of the day, with the sun high overhead ... immediately harsh. Just a couple of hundred yards past the water trough, I realized that I should have soaked my large grass hat and t-shirt, evaporation would help cool my body for awhile. I paused to look back at the water. At that moment, I wasn't overheated, so I decided not to retrace the distance, a decision I soon regretted. The heat built up fast under the pure sunshine. I started to bake and flounder.

The highway followed the bottom of the dry drainage west, with rounded, treeless hills on both sides, brown in the summer heat. There hadn't been any dwellings, except for a few abandoned homesteads, since Pleasantview. The decrepit structures were crumbling back into the earth. I considered trying to find some shade beside the old buildings, but the sun was too high for protection, so we passed them. A better idea was to get to camp. It would still be hot later in the day, walking into the sun. We just had to keep plugging forward, down the long, broiling highway.

Many miles later ... could it be? YES, the sound of a water pump in the distance. JOY! The noisy well pumped the precious liquid into a large trough. I hurriedly hopped over the barbed wire fence, not caring if I was invited or not, threw my hat into the water to soak, stripped off my t-shirt, submerged it in the trough, and put it back on, dripping wet. It was shivery cold, but I took the chill with an "Ah" of relief. The wet wide-brimmed hat gave me a welcome shower. I got the bucket for the burros, but they didn't drink.

The water-treatment helped for awhile, but I dried off quickly in the heat. (Later I analyzed: my best action would have been for me to submerge my body completely in the water trough until my core temperature had dropped.) Periodically, I used a little bit of my drinking water to wet my hat again. It helped, but I was still overheating in the stifling temperatures. The burros didn't show any noticeable signs of overheating, but we all HAD to be wishing for some shade. After a long struggle, we left the hills for the broad bottom of the main north-south valley. FINALLY … I saw our next oasis: a clump of trees in the open valley … the town of Holbrook … four miles away. I was surely glad to see salvation, but at two and a half miles per hour, we still had to endure over an hour and a half in the CAULDRON. Staggering with extreme fatigue and heat exhaustion … I was having a hard time focusing my eyes … struggling to see straight … telling myself that I not only had to keep going, but that I had to do it without screwing up.

A mile later, we came to a group of Mexicans, working on a farm near the roadside. They were interested in what I was doing, and helped me greatly with a couple of cold drinks. They told me how great it was to come to America to work, after the true poverty in their native land; though they remarked that if they could make a decent living there, they would rather have been home in Mexico.

I stammered down the last long straight stretch of highway. Keeping a wanting eye on the saving trees … we inched our way … step by step … nearer to our SALVATION. FINALLY … we reached the turnoff to the little town, a mere half mile away.

Just past the turn, was an abandoned house with some trees and grazing. It would work for a camp, if I could get water. I tied the burros to a fence, and walked across the street to an occupied house, hoping that it would be o.k. for us to camp at the old place, and get some water. I went to the front door, though it was obvious that no one used that door. Family and friends went to the side door, but being unannounced and as scruffy as I was, I thought it was best not to go to the family door. I hesitated, not wanting to scare anyone, and finally knocked. I heard a woman's voice, "Now, WHO could that be?" An older gentleman answered the door. Quickly, I told him I was walking burros through the area, and wondered about camping across the road from their home. He smiled broadly, and said he'd seen us coming down the highway, earlier in the day, and was glad I'd come to his home so that we could talk. He would've stopped earlier, but was bringing his wife back from the hospital and couldn't. He liked my story, and told me that a better place to camp would be at the town park in Holbrook. There was water, grazing, and shade, and he was sure that no one would care if we camped there. He said, that if anyone gave me a hard time about it, to tell them that he said it was alright. The small-town elder had some say. Later in the day, he'd come to visit and hear more of my adventure.

I stumbled the last little bit to the center of town, totally spent from the work and horrific heat of the 18-mile day. The park was right next to the Mormon Church. I didn't want to spoil the park, and the grass was too short for good grazing, so we went to the far end of the block, where there was an uncut field and a row of shade trees. I was unloading the burros when a man riding a bicycle-built-for-two stopped to talk. I told him what we were doing as I unpacked the gear. Immediately, he invited me to dinner. He had friends visiting from Salt Lake City, and he was sure they'd love to hear my story. He told me where they lived, just a few blocks away, and that dinner would be in an hour and a half. I watered the burros from a faucet in the park, staked them out to graze, and then just collapsed, limp against my gear, too tired to do anything but lie there in a heap.

When dinner time arrived, I barely had the gumption to get up and go, in my extreme fatigue, but the thought of a good meal with friendly people was just too inviting to pass up. I got there just as dinner was being served. The delicious and hugely satisfying meal with great company fulfilled me. I'd already determined that we'd take the next day to rest, and they generously invited me to come over for any meal I wanted.

They had a couple of special kids. I understood the situation well, since at one point I was a teacher's aide in a special-education program. My experiences with special kids taught me something about my own peculiarities; I was a "smart" one of them. The teacher confirmed this, "Sometimes I wonder, are you one of them, or one of us?"

I went back to the park fulfilled and refreshed by the feast, and finally had the strength to set up camp. The gentleman I'd met on our way into town came by with his son and four grandsons. The young boys kept Lucy running, throwing the stick for her, rapid-fire. We talked about my trip, and the best route ahead. His grandparents had settled in the area during the 1800s, so he knew much of the area and local history. He described the half-deserted town when it had been much larger. Years earlier, a man could only farm a small plot of land; now with all of the new equipment, it took far fewer people to work the land. People had left the hard life of farming for opportunities elsewhere, so the rural town had lost its stores and post office. He bemoaned the loss of people and businesses.

He told me how, as a young man fresh out of high school, he'd planned a horse pack trip of his own. He'd wanted to ride his horse to the large wilderness area of central Idaho with his younger cousin, but didn't take the trip, because it would have prevented his cousin from graduating high school. He added, sadly, that his cousin didn't graduate anyway, so he'd missed out on his adventure for nothing. We had a great bond, because of his dream of doing what I was doing. Mormons in these little towns had close ties with the history and ways of their communities, since they were direct ancestors of those who had originally settled the area. They were the most genuine, kindly people, as I imagined their forebears had been and needed to be; struggling to make it by helping each other. The kindness and appreciation of the people in this region, made it a perfect place to travel through with pack animals. I was sure that their ancestors would be proud of these truly wonderful people.

The following day, I went over to my other friend's house for lunch, dinner, and good company. I brought some of my two-handed art, to give their kids some cards, and to show them how I did it. The rest of the day, I lounged in the park, trying to keep cool by lying directly on the cement floor of the shaded pavilion. The cool concrete felt great against my back. Several other kind folks stopped to visit, treating me to candy and sodas. One man went home to get all of his maps of the upcoming area we'd be traveling. He studied the maps, trying to help me choose the best route through the desolate, mostly dry hills. We had three different maps to consult; each showed different roads.

I'd asked many people how to get through this questionable section, and had gotten about as many different answers. Holbrook was the junction for many different routes. Most people recommended that I go west on a major gravel road, but that way had no water to anyone's knowledge. It seemed that there would probably be water in the valley on the other side of the ridge, but it wasn't certain. Also, if we went that way, we'd end up walking the frontage road beside I-84 for quite a while. Questionable water and having to walk near the interstate eliminated that route. I opted for a route that some recommended against, because it was so isolated. If we got into trouble, no one would be coming by to help. The man with the maps knew a lot about the area. With his maps and knowledge, along with the other information I'd gotten, I was pretty sure of the route we should take. A big question mark was a gap in the road where private land interrupted the route. The map man knew the owners, and was sure that they wouldn't mind us cutting through.

Holbrook had been the most wonderful town for us! Everyone had been beyond friendly and helpful. The couple who'd treated me to all of the great meals rode over on their bicycle-built-for-two, in the last light of the day, with a gift of some home dried fruit and forty dollars in the bag.

July 28.

We went straight north up seldom-used Highway 37. The map showed it closed in winter, not because it went over a high mountain pass, but apparently it was just so little traveled that they didn't bother to plow it. Much of the area was in the Curlew National Grassland. From what I understood, it had been farmland, which the government had repurchased for a wildlife area. The sun was shining, so it was hot again. We'd surely need shade in the afternoon. The valley was wide, with low sagebrush covered hills on both sides, much closer on the west. There was one farm up the valley from Holbrook. No water flowed in the streambed beyond the green fields, since it all went for irrigation. After we passed the green patch, brown hills pinched in from both sides, and stream and road wound through a narrow, rocky canyon. The winding road would've been a problem if there'd been any traffic. What few vehicles did pass was easy to hear far away in the extreme quiet.

Eight miles up the road, we reached the old farmer's grandparents' homestead. We needed cover. The temperature in the shade was going to be in the mid-nineties, and much hotter out on the road. There was a stream, spring, and a clump of large poplar trees which the homesteaders had planted more than a century earlier. We took happy refuge under the grand old trees. The soft green spot was a relief in the otherwise harsh brown environment. It would have been a perfect place to camp with its water, big trees and ample grazing meadow, but the following day we were going to have an extra-long day crossing the ridge to the west. Therefore, I wanted to get as far as possible today. A few miles more would bring us to the certain water of Twin Springs, and a place to camp. I'd heard there weren't any shade trees there, so we needed to wait out the afternoon heat under the old homestead's trees.

Logistics of crossing the landscape dictated the agenda, not ascetics. It was best to shorten a long, hard upcoming day as much as possible, even if it meant passing up a great campsite. I'd learned about shortening a hard day while climbing high-mountain passes in the Rockies. They were such difficult and dangerous places to be, particularly during the predictable afternoon pounding by lightning-and-hail-heavy thunderstorms. The best choice was to find the highest practical spot in the trees to camp and rest a day. This "Make the Hard Dangerous Day as Easy as It Can Be" philosophy maximized the probability of success.

Sticking to this principle, we rested for a couple of hours at the shaded green oasis, before heading up the road a few more miles to Twin Springs, a relatively famous spot on the old Oregon Trail. The Hudspeth Cutoff Trail to California left the Oregon Trail near here, when gold was discovered in California in 1849. Twin Springs was well known to the gold-seekers, because for twenty-two miles to the east, the trail was devoid of any water. A historical marker said that the long trudge to Twin Springs was one of the toughest days the pioneers faced along the entire length of the Hudspeth Cutoff. They, like me had to reach water each night, so they were more than happy to get here. Water was even more imperative for them than us. My burros were desert animals, needing less water than the cattle and horses the settlers had. Apparently, the old-timers could cover about the same distance in a day as we could. Twenty miles was about our practical limit, particularly in the heat. The last day of my first trip, when one of the animals was a horse, we went thirty miles, but that day was extremely harsh. Fifteen miles was about the right amount of walking for a comfortably long day. If it was hot, it was harder, much harder.

Twin Springs was a marshy pond in a narrow valley. Rocky, sagebrush covered hills rose up near the green oasis. There was a campground with no visitors, which looked seldom used. A sign just inside the entrance to the campground stated in large letters: "NO HORSES ALLOWED."I thought about opening the fence, bringing the burros inside, and photographing them next to the sign, as if it were an exclusive burro-resort with "No Horses Allowed", but left the joke undone. I put my camp close to the campground, so that I could easily take water from the old fashioned hand-pump. I pumped good clean water into a five gallon bucket, carrying it back to the campsite covered, so that the water wouldn't slosh out onto my leg. To protect the tent from possible wind, I set it up next to some 6-foot high sagebrush.

The burro-girls had great grazing along the road between the campground and main road. Livestock hadn't been in the area, so the grass was at full height. The burros happily grazed about, just nipping off the tops of their favorite grasses. They were far enough from the seldom traveled highway, that the free burro didn't go out onto it, though as always, I kept an eye open. They took turns being "Free Bird."

The next morning, I woke up extremely tired, and decided to take the day off. The radio weather report said it was supposed to be cloudy all day. This meant that the burros wouldn't need any shade, making it alright to stay at the treeless spot. I was glad to have the opportunity to stay at the historic camp. I felt a great affinity to those who'd come through 150 years before, since I was traveling in much the same manner. I understood, first hand, what they'd gone through. We had the same problems with water, grazing and all of the other challenges of traveling long distances with large animals, though the old-timers had it much harder. I had many more water sources available. Modern ranchers and farmers had drilled wells, and dug irrigation canals across the landscape, where there had been none. Modern road surfaces were also a huge advantage for us. They gave much better footing, either graveled or paved, than the rough, sandy, or muddy wagon trails the settlers followed. The old-timers would also have had a much harder time finding grazing for their many animals, particularly after many wagon trains had come through. They traveled with hundreds of hungry animals. The best grasses would've all been eaten, so they would've had to go far off to the side of the trail to find decent grazing. I'd found it mentally brutal to go extra miles on a long journey.

The grazing issue grew larger and larger on a long journey, where any long-term deficiency of food for the animals would eventually take its toll. Having burros on a long trip sure helped. They had slower metabolisms, needed less food, and also ate a wider variety of food: brush, weeds, etc. They were overweight when we started the journey, and at this point, they didn't look like they'd lost any weight at all.

The other huge hardship the old-timers had, that I didn't, was that they had to make it all the way to their destination in one summer, or be trapped by winter, out of supplies in the middle of nowhere. I could stop for the winter, and figure out how to make a living, or even get a trailer ride somewhere else. On many trips, I'd needed trailer rides, and found them easily. It was actually probably easier to get a ride with the burros than hitchhiking without them. Many people in the rural western states had trucks and trailers. This combined with their love of someone traveling with animals made finding a ride easy. They were happy to be able to assist, to join in "The Adventure."

It stayed cloudy all day, which kept the temperature reasonable. Lucy and I spent much of the day relaxing at a picnic table. Having the table was a luxury. I usually had to sit on the ground. I continued to be very lethargic all day, despite having walked only one day since our last day off. I guessed that the extreme heat was sapping my strength more than usual. During the day, I retired to the tent for a couple of naps.

The old Hudspeth's Cutoff trail climbed the sagebrush covered hill, right beside our camp. Markers placed every so often, traced the old route through the brush. The original wagon road was a very visible trough in the ground. I was very excited to see the old road still so intact, and by the latter part of the day had the energy to explore it. It was a rather steep hill, right out of Twin Springs, and I imagined that it must have been a hard start to the day for the animals pulling the heavy wagons. A newer one-lane, four-wheel-drive road paralleled the original wagon road. Lucy and I walked up the hill, as I imagined the original pioneers coming through. The rough tracks in the sagebrush crawled up the hill, higher and higher for a mile and a half, until the trail disappeared into a wheat field on private land. The more modern jeep road followed the fence line. I presumed it joined the road I was trying to reach. My map showed that following that route would add two miles to what was already going to be a long day. The wheat field fence had an unlocked gate, if we wanted to take the shortcut. I left the decision for the next day.

July 30.

I was happy we'd taken the day of rest. I felt much better and full of energy as we climbed up the hill out of Twin Springs. Walking the old trail, thinking of the original pioneers, was joyously inspiring. Without much hesitation, we took the shortcut through the private land. As we passed through the wheat field, the burros wanted to stop often to pick the tops from the grain. I relented a few times, but didn't want to dally on private land or disturb the wheat field too much. We passed a vacant farmhouse. The landowners must have lived somewhere else in the area. It was common to find abandoned home sites, since a lot of the smaller original farms had been absorbed into larger operations. We were out of the driveway and onto the public road without seeing anyone, but I wondered what might be thought of the unusual tracks through the field.

Roads on my map were marked with county road numbers, but on the ground they were strangely numbered like city streets. We were on something like the corner of 20,000 Street West and the Middle of Nowhere. The difference in road markings made me question whether I was taking the right road, but since it led to a low point in the hills and not up the mountainside, I was convinced that we were on the desired route. The road through the hills of the Sublette Range was very unused, continuing to follow the markers of the old wagon-route westward. Shrubby trees, even some pockets of aspens and conifers were in the folds of the hills. We came across several springs with livestock troughs. I offered the burros water, but they weren't interested.

We were having just the most wonderful day meandering through the very pleasant hills. The primitive road went up and down through four different drainages, before coming out at water on the other side. I was impressed that the original trail-blazer had found such an intelligent passage through the complex topography. As hard as their chore was, I knew that the pioneers would've made sure they had the shortest, most practical route through the huge landscape. There was much more water in the hills than I'd anticipated. We could've stopped along the way, but continued on, since grazing was skimpy from range cattle, and we were having such a great day walking. Far into the day, I almost stopped at a spring on top of the ridge. A fence kept cattle out of the next allotment, but as I was considering camping, a large horsefly started harassing Libby. She weirded out so much that I could hardly hold her. I considered it a bad omen, so we continued on.

The old passage made its way down a narrow, scenic valley amongst the steep-sided hills. It was just a joy following the road down the other side. We passed many side canyons, some with primitive roads up them, but no surface water came from any of the higher drainages. The Sublette range, while not really high, was a very pleasant, complex place. We finally moved far enough down the canyon to find a place where several springs collected into a strong flowing stream. Shortly below the spring we came upon a great place to camp; a flat, lush, green grazing area, in the bottom of the pretty valley, close to a steep, wooded hillside. Most of the hills in the lower reaches were barren of trees, but this one was so steep and north-facing, that it stayed wet enough to keep the trees growing. We were in National Forest Lands, so I didn't have to worry about trespassing. The stream bubbled right through the spot, making water easily available. Also, singing water was good entertainment, a sweet bonus flowing by. Perfect. Perfect. Perfect.

It had been the best walking day of the trip so far; seventeen miles up and down over the hills, finished by finding a fabulous campsite. I'd felt great and exuberant all of the way, all day. HOORAY! I was so glad I'd taken the rest day at Twin Springs. If I hadn't, the whole day would've been a struggle, which would've increased the chance of a lousy or tragic incident. Our unscheduled vacation had made this wonderful day possible.

It was such a fantastic camping place, and right along the old pioneer trail, that I figured it must have been a popular spot for the early settlers. The area was so wonderful that I just couldn't pass through it too quickly, which made another vacation necessary. I heard no complaints from the burros, who had plenty of green grass and cooling shade. The clear stream curled on by(e). Lucy cajoled me into throwing the stick as I lazed around camp. Not having a rigid plan was such huge advantage! If I'd followed a set plan, I would've forced myself over the hills, tired and disgruntled. We would've had much less fun, and the walk would have been far more dangerous, being physically and mentally tired. I always tried to keep my mind open to "the way we really wanted to go", rather than being brain-locked on "the way we were supposed to go." I never knew exactly what I'd encounter, until I was actually there. I found it much wiser to have a list of probable-possible plans, and keep the options open to what might unexpectedly happen, or what I might learn along the way. The complex journey required decisions "on the fly" when the unexpected happened. If I needed all the answers before leaving, I'd be so bogged down with all of the details I'd either never go, or follow a less than optimal plan. Following a rigid plan, I could easily miss out on the best way to take the journey. A plan made with little knowledge of the way was less likely to succeed than one made at the actual "fork in the road", where there was more information about the options. Of course, I could usually backtrack, if I found the route somehow deficient. Along with other unknowns, weather could destroy a set plan. Some days were great for moving, others were not.

August 1.

We walked west down the valley, as more streams joined the main creek further down, bringing together enough water to create the Sublette Reservoir. We ambled along the north shore of the half-filled, mile-long lake. A handful of anglers dotted the shore, and a few were out in small boats. The reservoir was a jewel in the scarce-water area. Beyond the reservoir, the road passed out of the dry hills and into fields greened by the reservoir's irrigation water. I talked to several locals along the roadway. They were happy to have a traveler such as me come through their area.

The town of Sublette was just a small collection of farms and a few houses, with no business district. The farmers used up the stream before it made it very far into the grand expanse of the Raft River Valley. The impressively huge valley was fifteen miles wide, and stretched north beyond the horizon; bracketed by the low hills we'd crossed to the east, and higher peaks to the west and south. Black Pine Mountain rose impressively, starkly, over 4,000 feet out of the valley floor. Along the base of the western peaks were the Raft River and the town of Malta. We'd be there the following day, I hoped.

A spot on the map with a name didn't necessarily mean there was actually a town there. Sometimes, there was just a road junction which at one time was settled, but had long since been abandoned into nothingness. I'd heard that

Malta was a real town, and even had a small grocery store, crucial to my food plans. The middle of the valley was flat and desolate. Human habitation occurred mostly along the edges, where the mountain streams flowed in and could support farming. I'd hoped to find somewhere to camp in Sublette, but found nothing, and continued on into the main part of the valley floor. The road went dead west. We walked it until I-84 crossed our path, with a truck-stop just off the exit. We'd already walked thirteen miles, and had little prospect of a place to camp further on; after the truck-stop, the next sure water source was a full day across the vast valley.

Next to the large parking lot of big-rig trucks was an abandoned trailer house with a few trees in a field of dry grass. I inquired at the truck-stop convenience store, if we might camp there and got an o.k. I was glad to have been able to come so far out into the wide valley floor and camp, since it shortened the next day's long dry section. It felt odd next to the interstate highway, with all of America rolling by. Mostly, I'd just encountered local people. I was sure that, to the people stopping for gas and food, two burros and a tent, just off the edge of the parking lot, was quite an odd sight. I splurged on a meal in the truck-stop café. I was sufficiently tired to sleep soundly all night, even with big-rigs coming and going, and others idling all night.

August 2.

After the truck-stop, we went straight west for five miles, across the heart of the sprawling valley. A few cars came by. I could literally see them coming from miles away. Impressive mountains rose up ahead, 5,000 feet higher than us. Our route would take us through the beautiful peaks. The straightaway finally ended at a few bends in the road, near the west side of the valley, and metropolitan Malta. A sign at the edge of town stated “City of Malta, population 171.” I chuckled at the “City” part, and photographed the sign. With the mountains to the west, and the huge valley to the east, it was a postcard town.

Lucy came within inches of being hit by a fast moving car just outside town. The close call made me realize how much I'd become attached to my new companion. I heartily thanked God that she was still with me. It had been 9 miles to Malta, as a result, I was plenty ready for a break in the shade. We found a spot behind one of the few stores in the commercial district, and I got permission to use the space from the store clerk, a relative of the owner. Part of her duties was babysitting a handful of younger relatives. One, (the owner’s grandson) standing in front of the store, had a particularly astonished look on his face when I paraded by with the burros. I had a sling-shot in my gear that I'd brought along for no good reason, and had been looking for someone to take the excess baggage. I didn’t want the burros to carry anything unneeded. The boy seemed the perfect recipient.

He was astonished and thankful to get the prize for free. I told him that I gave it to him, because of the favor of letting me park my burros and gear on the land. A gas station-convenience store and a small grocery store-restaurant made up most of the rest of the commercial district. The town was far enough from any major shopping to support the local grocery, where I picked up a few supplies, and had a sandwich in the restaurant section. The business was owned and run by a young local couple, with four very young kids. The children alternately cried and laughed their way around the place. One of the young boys raced his tricycle around the store aisles, in gleeful abandon. Generally, I was very much into giving owner-run small businesses my money, rather than chain stores. In that regard, this business was the ultimate place to patronize. I ate my sandwich, enjoying the small town family scene.

On the wall, in large letters was: “PIZZA CHALLENGE”. Beneath it was the “Pizza Hall of Fame” and pictures of three young guys. I asked what it was about. If you ate a large, two-topping pizza and a liter of soda in less than an hour, you got the huge meal free; if not, the meal would cost fourteen dollars. It was too late to try the challenge, since I'd just eaten a sandwich, but I was tempted to try it later in the day. The key to attempting the great challenge would be getting permission to spend the night where I'd left the burros. I'd be in no shape to walk up the road after such a huge meal.

I was napping on my gear, in the heat of the afternoon, when the store owner came out to talk with me. His young grandson was with him, proudly toting his new sling-shot. The owner liked what I was doing, thanked me for giving his grandson the gift, and gave me permission to spend the night behind his store. YAHOO … I could do the Pizza Challenge!

I spent the rest of the afternoon psyching myself up for the mighty event. I knew from eating huge meals on past burro packing trips that I had a good chance of success. Not really being able to afford a fourteen dollar meal gave me extra incentive to complete the challenge, once started.

At 5 p.m. sharp, I went back into the restaurant to face my ordeal. I warned the young owner that I was really hungry, from eating so little, so long, but he didn't seem to think that a relative oldster could do it. I ate the cheese, pepperoni and onions first, and then took to the crust, chewing it as thoroughly as possible before swallowing. I didn't touch the soda until I had the whole pizza down, not wanting the sugary soda to ruin my appetite. Not being much of a soda drinker, the large volume of beverage, after all of that pizza, was the hard part of the challenge. I swallowed the last of the soda with ten minutes to spare, and asked what was for desert.

There was a table of young local men nearby. The owner teased them because I'd beaten the Pizza Challenge. I stated, "It pays to be starving." They chuckled. The owner took my picture, promising to put it on the "Pizza Hall of Fame" wall with the other three winners. I felt bad about taking advantage of the friendly business owner, with his gaggle of young kids and told him I'd try to give him some advertising. I went back to my camp, to lie down for a couple of hours and recover from having the massive pile of food in my stomach. I wondered how many calories I'd eaten. This ultimate pig-out must have added a couple of pounds to my skinniness. I'd barely been maintaining my weight until then.

August 3.

We headed west, up a side valley that narrowed as we went higher and higher into the next north-south mountain range. The forested mountains were over 10,000 feet high, and with the valley floor being at 4500 feet, their rise above us made it an extremely impressive place. We rose steadily up the beautiful farming valley, for twelve miles and a thousand vertical feet, to the wonderful little town of Elba. The charming green spot was surrounded by low hills, between the two highest peaks in the range. One of the majestic mountains had a ski area. A couple of snow patches still clung to the highest reaches of the sharp rocky peaks. Elba was an extremely impressive location for a town. The little hamlet didn't have a commercial district.

It was early afternoon when we came to Elba's pretty little town park. We needed a break at the least, and the large trees, green grass, water and picnic tables made it a natural spot to stop. Livestock wasn't allowed on the green park lawn, so I dropped the gear against the outside of the fence. The burro-girls had plenty of lush grazing and large shade trees outside the fence, along the side of the quiet road. The park turned out to be a hugely advantageous place to have stopped when a powerful thunderstorm built up over the high peaks. I took cover from the pounding rain and wind in the covered picnic pavilion, and the burros had some shelter under the large trees. If we'd been walking in the open, we'd have been soaked. The storm convinced me to stay the night at the park, not knowing where we might camp further up the road. National Forest Land was about six miles away. We'd likely find a place to camp there, but it was too far to go that late in the day.

I threw the gear I needed for my campsite over the low barbed wire fence, and set up my tent along the inside edge. A huge cottonwood tree and some bushes for wind protection made it an ideal spot for my tent. I had a deep respect and love for the big trees. The burros stayed outside the park, grazing the tall grass along the fence. I sat contemplating the sparkling stream twinkling through the edge of the park.

It was a pleasant enough place for the night, but I had it in mind to go up into the National Forest the next day. I was feeling a general fatigue, and needed a few days of vacation to recoup my energies.

Chapter 10
South Central Idaho
August 5 - August 14

August 5.

It was good that I was ready to leave the Elba town park. There was going to be a large family reunion on the grounds that day and the next. They'd rented it for the event, and I wasn't sure it would be good for me to be there. Also, I really wanted to find a place to take a much needed vacation. All-of-me yearned for a rest. I met an early arrival at the party, who really liked what I was doing. He was an outdoorsman, and loved the idea of traveling out across the countryside like we were doing. I encouraged him to take up the sport if the opportunity arose.

The road west of Elba continued uphill through the smiling countryside; greenness, and more and more trees. Right from the beginning of the day I was looking for a good place for a vacation. Early on, there were several good spots to camp, but they were on private land. I didn't particularly feeling like trespassing, so we continued on to the public Forest Lands. At one point, I thought I'd found a good enough place to camp. I tied the burros to a tree so that I could check out the area, only to find that it was a bee-tree. We moved, quickly! Thankfully, I noticed the bees before they got riled up and attacked the burros. It would have been a real mess to have them go crazy carrying all of their gear.

As we got to a fence with a sign denoting it as the Forest Land boundary, an ATV pulled up with three young people on it. They were the children of the man I'd met in the park. They'd arrived after we'd left. Their father wanted them to meet us, and bring me some lunch. We chatted for a while before they moved on to further explore the beautiful forested landscape. I hungrily ate the fried chicken they'd given me. The food boosted my energy, and we continued to hike up the road through the evergreens and meadows.

It was marvelous country for us with all of the trees, meadows and water. The only thing wrong with it was all of the cows. The grass was grazed down, and places I wanted to pitch the tent were infested with cows. Unfortunately, they liked to hang out in the same places I wanted to camp, protected from the wind. We kept coming to decent camping places, but none quite hit my fancy. Several of the spots would have been fine for us to camp, but I was being extra picky. I kept thinking that there might be another allotment ahead that would be less grazed. Consequently, we kept climbing. Our short easy day was growing longer and longer. I watered the burros at what looked like the last spring on the east side of the mountains. Cows were still everywhere. Passing motorists said we might find a good place to camp, in a small valley on the other side of the ridge. They didn't believe there were cows there. I decided to try the other side of the mountain.

After climbing several thousand feet, we reached the top. I really struggled all day. Our efforts were rewarded with grand views to the east, into the valley from which we'd come, and to the west, where we were going. There were trees and greenery to the east, and an empty brown valley to the west. The way ahead looked very austere from our green, treed perch. On the other side of the valley ahead, were low crinkly hills with a few trees. I'd studied my maps, looking for possible routes through the complex terrain, but only saw very convoluted ways through the hills. I was planning to take another route directly northwest, through the valley at the bottom of our ridge. This would be the shortest route, and we could take advantage of the few streams flowing out of the hills.

This would be a big turning point on the journey to Oregon. Not only was it time to start heading more to the north, but this would be our last mountain ridge to cross all the way to Oregon. After this high point, the way would basically be flat as it followed the Snake River. The concept buoyed my spirit. The expanses were certainly spectacular, but they also looked hot. I hoped for cooler weather than we'd been enduring.

The west face of the mountain was barren, except for scattered clumps of trees in the ravines. The road first cut across the steep mountainside to the north, and then switched back to the south, toward the valley far below. I saw cattle below us. My heart sank. Grazing would be rotten on this side too. At the small side drainage with our prospective camp, we took a rough little road up to a water trough. There was a clearing among the low bushy trees, but it was small. Since the spot was right at the water, it was grazed bare, and the slope was too steep for the burros on grazing ropes. I stomped around in frustration, trying to figure out how to make the spot work for us. I felt too tired to go on. I hadn't seen anything on the mountainside ahead that looked much better, particularly since I was really looking for a place to rest a couple of days. For that, the burros would need more grazing than what was available.

I pulled off Beanie's panniers, figuring that the sketchy spot would just have to do. I paused and looked around again. I really did need a few days off, and this would barely do for the night. I put Beanie's panniers back on, dismal and emotional with my plight; being so tired and not having a place to camp. I thought back to all of the suitable spots on the other side of the mountain. We should have stopped somewhere along the way. I cursed myself for being so picky and not stopping. I was paying a hefty price for not wanting to shack up with the cows. Wearily … we headed down the road toward the valley floor.

We descended into a side valley off the main valley floor, separated by a low brown ridge. The smaller side valley was greened by streams trickling down the tall, steep mountainside. The small town of Basin was a sparse collection of houses and farms in the valley bottom. I saw it from above, and figured we could find water, and, hopefully, a place to camp. Our short day's walk had turned into a 15-mile ordeal. I was having a hard time focusing my eyes. Deep fatigue had set in. A vehicle stopped about a mile before we got into town. They said they'd just killed a huge rattlesnake lying in the road.

We entered Basin with rain in the air. I desperately scanned the area for a place to camp. Finally, we found a small lot fenced off from the surrounding fields, with no fence between it and the road, grazing, a ditch of flowing water, and some trees along the road for privacy. Apparently, the lot once had a trailer on it, because there was a faucet for drinking water. I moved in without much thought about my blatant trespass. I just HAD to stop. As I unpacked the burros, I looked back up toward the mountain, to see a full double-rainbow glowing in the rain shower that had just passed. The beautiful sight warmed me. I thought we must be in the right place. I flopped on my gear, exhausted. A short time later, a car drove by, quickly stopped, and backed up. It was the property owner. I told him about our long walk from Colorado. He replied that it was perfectly fine for us to stay there for as long as we needed. His ancestors had been in the area since Brigham Young had sent them there 150 years before.

The next day, even though we were right in the middle of town, we took the day off. I did some laundry and repair chores, but pretty much just laid around in the shade. I was very tired. It was a pleasant day in the scenic green valley with high mountains above.

August 7.

For several days, clouds had built up in the early afternoon. Counting on that pattern to continue, we took our leisure in the morning, waiting until 2 p.m. to leave town. Another reason I left late was that I planned to go only the seven miles to Oakley, the next town on our way. My prediction was correct, and we headed down the valley under wonderful cooling cloud cover. The ridge separating the two valleys was a rib of volcanic rock. The road passed through the obstruction, following a stream that had breached the wall.

As we entered the outskirts of Oakley, I had an unexpected challenge; we had to pass a small male burro corralled by the roadside. My burro-girls very much wanted to stop and visit. Both sides of the equation made quite a fuss, braying and stomping their hooves very intensely. It was a good fence, or the male burro might have gone through it, to reach his desire. My very strong girls were extremely persistent in wanting to go over to him, making it difficult for me to pull them past.

On Sunday afternoon, all the businesses were closed, so we passed through without stopping. Another few miles brought us to the last irrigation ditch. After that, the land went from irrigated green farm fields into a dry, desolate, natural landscape. We paused at the transition to ponder options; as we did, a car with a couple of tourists stopped to talk. They were driving an RV around the west for the summer, pulling their smaller car behind it. They were on one of many day-trips, touring the local area in their little car. They loved their road journeys, and were very impressed with my adventure.

Refreshed by their encouragement, I decided to continue on into the desolate landscape another eight miles, to where a stream came out of the hills. Even though it was fairly late in the day, I figured we should be able to get to the stream by sunset.

Finally, after following the southern border of Idaho west so long, we were making the turn to the northwest. Ours was the only road in the valley not in the compass-grid system. I really liked having a road going the exact direction I wanted to go. It was always frustrating having to take the grid roads, when I was trying to angle across the land. Years before, while traveling with burros across a wide sagebrush plain with a similar road design, I wanted to go to the southeast. Instead of staying on the roads, and going straight south and then east, we took a shortcut across the landscape, directly to the southeast. A little ways into our diagonal across the sagebrush desolation, a coiled rattlesnake buzzed its warning right next to me. I involuntarily jumped about four feet sideways away from the snake in a moment of pure instinct. When we came out of the brush onto the next road, I took the rattlesnake's suggestion, and went straight south and then straight east on the road.

The turn to the northwest had buoyed my excitement. We moved quickly, late into the day, across the arid plain. The 6-mile straight stretch, through the vast, wide open beauty, was exhilarating, particularly since we were making such progress. The lonely road was fairly close to the stark rocky volcanic hills rising several hundred feet above the valley to the west. We reached a major drainage, Big Cottonwood Creek, flowing out of the hills. It was our most likely place for the night, so even though it'd be a couple of miles out of our way, we took the side road up the drainage to find a decent camp. The one ranch in the area was at the edge of the valley where the stream left the hills. We passed by it, and the BLM buildings for the public lands we were about to enter. A large flock of wild turkeys fed in the field and among the cottonwood trees, by the small stream. I was glad to see that there was actually some water in the tiny creek.

I was going to camp along the stream, but at the gate into the prospective camp, there was a skunk in the tall grass. We were lucky not to be sprayed, being only about five feet away. I got the message and moved quickly further up the road. Horseflies were bugging Libby, and just then some loose horses came running up behind us. Libby weirded out, and I was barely able to hold onto her during the commotion. At the end of the road, a trail continued up into the hills. We were farther off the main route than I'd wanted, but we needed a good camping spot. Up in the mouth of the volcanic valley, I found a great place! There was a little flat spot for my tent, right along the clear stream, under some large cottonwood trees, next to a big field of tall grass. The sun was just setting over the western hills. I was so relieved to have finally found a righteous place to camp. I made camp and settled in for a much needed two-day break. I really appreciated having the skunk, flies and horses move us to this perfect location.

Since I was on vacation, I awoke very late, 8 a.m. It was wonderful having the scenic isolated spot, where I could just relax and recoup from the constant needs of traveling overland with the burros. I took my sleeping pad, radio, water, snacks, and maps to a sandbar along the far side of the stream. The soft sandbar in the woods, by the pretty streamside, was just the perfect little spot for relaxing with my entertainments. I put some larger flat stepping-stones in the shallow stream so that I could go back and forth from my sitting spot to the tent, without wetting my feet.

The weather was still hot, but it was relatively cool along the babbling stream in the shade of the wonderful cottonwood canopy. Lucy insisted that I throw the stick into the stream on a regular basis. I dozed off from time to time, listened to the radio, filtered some stream water for drinking, and studied our upcoming route on the map. I luxuriated in the quiet tranquil nook, knowing that we'd soon be in much different surroundings. The substantial town of Twin Falls was near the route I wanted to take. The area would be built up with houses and farms. I could tell by the way roads were laid out on the map which areas were populated or more rural. Where the roads were in square grids, the area was farms and towns. If roads followed the terrain, it was more isolated.

I staked out one burro at a time. The field was big enough that I was able to clip all of my grazing ropes together to make a 60-foot length. The tied burro had a huge circle to graze, and could still reach the shade of the cottonwoods growing along the edge of the field.

By the end of the second day of our vacation, I'd fully recouped my energy, so Lucy and I took a walk further up the canyon-bottom trail. The geology of the area was all volcanic. The canyon walls were forty foot high, brownish-black cliffs, above steep rubble slopes. Scattered dry-country brush dotted the hillsides. The valley bottom, along the small stream, was green with brush and deciduous trees. It was good to be on a trail, in the wild countryside, after all the roads on which we'd been walking. Rattlesnakes seemed likely, so I kept my eyes open for them as we walked up the narrow trail. I worried some that Lucy would stick her nose into one.

August 10.

We left our isolated oasis in the mouth of the rugged canyon, having seen no-one for two days. It had been a very happy rest along the shaded, clear-running stream, and I was invigorated. We left early, but instead of following the road we'd used coming in, we followed primitive, barely used roads through the brush. It was a small shortcut, and a little more adventurous. We reached the main gravel road, and followed it through the parched landscape for another six miles, before we abruptly came out into farmland. Quite suddenly, we were in the heavily farmed and populated greater Twin Falls area.

The difference between the dusty, austere natural countryside, and the ordered rows of the croplands couldn't have been more profound. The whole huge area was lush from large irrigation canals coming from the far away American Falls Reservoir. Smaller and smaller ditches branched off the canals, so that literally every square mile was watered. Irrigation had turned rocks and sand into a plush green carpet.

We were close to the original Oregon Trail. I remembered reading about this section of the old trail as being a boring, brutally toilsome desert. When the original pioneers came through the area, they wrote of a hot flat land of sand, sand, sand. Their accounts told of difficult tiresome footing, and fine sand getting into everything. I hadn't originally wanted to walk across southern Idaho because of those early accounts. So much had changed over 150 years! It was now a garden. We passed through many different crops: wheat, corn, alfalfa, potatoes, beans and sugar beets in separate squares. The corn fields were 8-foot-high walls along the roads. It was field corn used to feed animals, and wasn't sweet enough for humans.

We were able to use relatively vacant side roads part of the way, but sometimes had to go along a busier paved road. Farm trucks and other cultivation equipment made up most of the traffic on the long, flat, straight roads. All of them gave us plenty of room, since they were slow moving, and could see us far away. The vast majority of workers were from south of the border and very curious about us. Several stopped to ask what our business was, some hardly knowing any English. They were amused to see the burros, which reminded them of their native countries.

We paused several times for short breaks, wherever there was shade and grazing together, but mostly just kept walking a long 17-mile day, to Lake Murtaugh. The lake was several miles long, made by Snake River irrigation water and a long dam. Being close to Twin Falls and easy to reach, it was a popular place on a hot summer afternoon. Two camping and picnic areas were on the lakeshore. The larger was far more popular and developed. Both had signs at the entrances forbidding horses. Theoretically, I could have ignored the signs, since I didn't have horses, but took the hint and camped in a spot between the two. It was a good grassy area, just off the road, surrounded by marshes. A Russian Olive tree gave my tent some protection from the late day sun and wind, and privacy from the road.

I made several trips to the small campground for water. After I finished my chores, Lucy and I went back to the smaller campground to enjoy the lakeside view. Lucy particularly liked fetching sticks in the water, so we played her favorite game. She repeatedly dove from the pier, with her usual zeal, at full intensity with every throw. Eventually, some boaters pulled up, to use the picnic tables by the water. They were local farmers, using the lake for boating and picnics during the summer heat. Lucy cajoled them into throwing the stick for her. I told them our story and pointed out my camp and burros. They gave me some fried chicken for dinner. Later in the evening, I went over to the larger campground for entertainment. Laughter from parties and barbeques filled the air. Powerboats raced by, pulling water skiers and tubers. I left the festival after sunset.

August 11.

The road ran straight west from the reservoir. Occasional rolling hills kept the visibility to no more than a mile. We soon ran into a problem, a section of freshly oiled and graveled road. The burros wore their protective rubber boots, so the loose gravel didn't hurt their hooves, but cars and farm trucks could spray gravel at us. I stayed in the ditch where I could, to avoid flying rocks and an uncomfortable walking surface. Drivers seemed to understand the problem, and most slowed way down when they passed us. I studied the map, hoping for an alternative route, but there were lots of gaps in the grid, so getting around it would be far out of our way. We traveled the 5-mile section of freshly graveled road without being pelted. It was still really hard walking, after a late start on a hot day. I sought shade and rest after seven miles.

We found shade trees and a swath of grass at a fairly major intersection, which worked for our afternoon rest. I'd heard that there was a convenience store about a mile to the side. I needed a few things, so it was the best place to stop. I unpacked the burros, and left them near the road, while Lucy and I walked to the store. I didn't like leaving the burros and my gear at the busy roadside spot, but I also didn't want to make the burros walk an extra couple of miles, so I just trusted that everything would be o.k. The road had no shoulder, and the ditch wasn't passable, so Lucy and I had to walk right on the edge of the road. Cars zipped by us. It startled me that drivers weren't giving me the space or the slower speeds that they gave us with the burros. I got spooked a couple of times, by cars coming fast and close, on the relatively short walk. It made me appreciate, even more, how privileged I was to have the burros. I got back to the girls, sat in the shade and ate lunch. I was still in the foul mood I'd gotten into when we hit the fresh gravel, and stayed grumpy throughout the day.

Late in the day, we started again. Several people had told me about an old stagecoach stop which was now a state park and museum. They thought we could camp there, but we were turned down. I got even grumpier. The hot sunshine in my face wasn't helping. As the sun was about to set, we found ourselves next to a golf course and a bunch of new houses. We were in a scary place: suburbia. I'd grown up in suburbia, and knew that its paranoid inhabitants wouldn't want us camped on their fine trimmed lawns. My lousy mood was making my negativity even worse. I wasn't getting the usual smiles and friendly waves from people.

I just stood there at the "street corner in the wilderness", the burros grazing the roadside. I tried to collect myself. The golf course clubhouse was right across the road, a neon beer sign in the window. I felt like getting drunk. I imagined going into the lounge to drink, filthy, hairy and sweat-soaked, amongst the tidy golfers. An amusing mental scene, certainly, but not a solution that would help, and could really hurt.

There was a gap in the road grid, so for the first time in the 10-mile day, we turned and headed north. A tiny distance later, we found a large irrigation ditch beside a service road. I contemplated following the service road to find a place to camp. A woman came out of a nearby house, to find out why her dogs were barking. She exclaimed about how lucky I was to be traveling with the burros. I told her that, actually, I was having a lousy day, and bemoaned my situation. She was only care-taking the house and pets, and the yard was just a tiny square, so she couldn't help me with a camping spot. I told her that I was going to follow the ditch, looking for a place to camp. She said she wouldn't complain. Her friendliness gave me a lift.

We all walked up the service road. Someplace next to it was just going to have to do, in our situation. We were near one of the last fields in the new suburban sprawl, when we came to a wide spot in the road, and an unused field that the burros could graze. I tied the burros to the fence and was just starting to unload them, when a man on an ATV rode up. He was the owner, and was just coming out to adjust the irrigation. He was surprised to find such an odd sight on his land. I was very relieved when he said it was fine for us to stay there. I told him the day's difficulties, and how tired I was, and thanked him hugely for saving my ass(es) from having to walk further. He was happy to meet me, being a throwback himself, refusing to sell his farm to the waiting developers. He said we could stay the next day if we wanted. With no shade, and more heat in the forecast, I declined his kind offer. Our day had gotten better right when we needed it.

August 12.

We'd gone just a couple of miles in the morning, when another farmer, driving an ATV, stopped to talk to us as we passed by. We had a long conversation about what I was doing. He told me about farming, saying that, at the moment, beef was the best investment, all other crops being so speculative. He bemoaned all of the new houses in the area.

His farm being so close to Twin Falls, with a stream flowing through it, made it very desirable for development. He didn't want to sell-out, even though farming didn't pay. He was hoping that his daughter would take up the profession.

His wife came by, also on a handy ATV. We chatted before she went to their garden to get me some fresh cucumbers, peppers, squash, and broccoli. Some of their neighbors also paused to talk for a minute as they drove by, and gave me some fresh ripe tomatoes. The man in the truck said he wanted to come along with me. I said he could if he was an ass-dragger. He replied that he'd done some of that, and I said that he was qualified. We all laughed. His wife told me to stop at her sister's house, just up the road, for some more vegetables and to meet her. She called her sister to tell her that I was coming.

Burros, dog, and I went up the road a piece and found the sister. She piled us with fresh sweet-corn and some new spuds, all just picked from her garden, and we talked for quite awhile. It was obviously a good time to be walking through farm country. I was very glad to be having such a sociable day with all of these good people. HOORAY! It was just what I needed after the previous day, when I only saw sour faces. The correlation between my mood and my experience was evident. When I was having troubles and my mood was lousy, I consciously tried to change my attitude, hoping that my experience would also change, and it did, with a great flow of happy helpful people. The friendly farm lady gave me a handful of dog treats for Lucy as we left.

It was already noon, and we'd only gone three miles, because of stopping for such long talks. Socialization was what was happening, so I went along with the larger plan, instead of forcing a walking day. Another mile west, the road dropped into a rough little canyon, with a flat spot and trees along a good flowing stream. It was another scorcher, so we'd hide from the sun in the afternoon, and maybe even camp here. There was a steep hill to negotiate, to get into the bottom of the rugged ravine. I was barely able to get the burros down the steep incline, because of a thick growth of high weeds that kept the burros from seeing where they were walking.

I pulled the gear from the burros, and set them to graze in the lush canyon bottom. The steep hill between us and the road above made us virtually invisible to people driving by. Even though we were in the middle of a built up and farmed area, we had this hidden little oasis, secluded and beautiful. There was even a waterfall over the far cliff, where an irrigation ditch emptied into the ravine. There was only one visible house overlooking the canyon. I appreciated the fine spot so much, particularly after having such a hard time finding a place to camp the evening before.

I perched on a boulder, in the shade of a tree by the rushing stream, and gobbled down some of the fresh vegetables. The fresh ripe tomatoes were the best I'd eaten in years. Oh, it all tasted so good! My body really wanted some fresh, live food. I put my sleeping pad under a tree, and took a righteous nap, until late afternoon. When I woke, I decided to spend the night there. I'd figured earlier that I'd probably stay because the spot was so perfect. I didn't dare leave a good place that late in the day, when I might not find anything else in the built up area.

I cooked a huge pile of the corn, squash, broccoli, and hot peppers for dinner, a wonderfully satisfying meal. I was exuberant after such a fine day. We'd only walked four miles, but with my change in attitude, it was perfect. Being in a better mood was worth 20 miles; actually ... a lot more than that.

August 13.

We popped out of our secret oasis, onto the road, and continued our westward journey. Twin Falls was only five miles to the north, so most of the farms had been replaced by houses. I found a relatively unused road, so traffic wasn't a problem. Four miles into the day, we came across a man in his yard, who wanted to talk. We conversed for a good forty-five minutes before again heading west. Heat was the usual issue, so at midday, six miles along, we stopped under some very large roadside cottonwoods, next to an old homestead. From the looks of the buildings and the size of the trees, it was one of the area's original homes. As usual on the longer breaks, I stripped the gear from the burros.

A short way up the road was a large dairy operation. Some of the workers lived in the old farm houses, which were a part of it. Several of them stopped to talk about our trip. They told me about working on the dairy. They found it a decent life, working for the same employer for many years. Housing was part of their pay, which kept their expenses low, but they'd missed out on the big real estate boom, not owning their homes.

A lady pulled up, as I lounged in the roadside shade. She was the daughter of the man I'd talked to earlier in the day. He had called her, thinking that she might find us interesting and useful, since she was a part-time reporter for a

Twin Falls newspaper. Her dad and I had discussed my best route, so she had an idea where to find us. She interviewed me about my history, and how and why I started burro packing. She photographed the crew, and threw the stick for the insistent Lucy. The article would be in the paper soon.

I wanted to reach the town of Filer, still nine miles away, so I packed up and headed into the hot, late day sun. We zigzagged through the grid, once having to skip a road I wanted to take because it was graveled with large stones. The burros weren't wearing their boots today, so we stayed on smoother surfaces, even though it meant a half-mile on a busy highway, tolerable because of a good wide shoulder.

I became very fatigued, and was really struggling over the final three miles. I would've stopped earlier, but I didn’t find a place to camp. Near the end of the day, when I was really toiling, a woman stopped and gave me some fresh tomatoes and bread. She'd just made the bread, baked with wheat from her own fields. I hungrily gobbled up a big chunk of the delicious, fresh loaf and a couple of the juicy red tomatoes. That boosted my energy for the last couple miles of walking into Filer.

US 30, four lanes wide, ran through the center of town. I had to wait a few minutes for a gap long enough, in all of the lanes at once, for us to get across. From me to Beanie's rear end was a long stretch, and there was no hurrying the burros. If I tried to pull the burros faster, they'd go slower, thinking something was wrong. Several restaurants, a convenience store, and a decent sized grocery store made up most of the Filer business district. The one big thing that Filer had was the county fairground, for the Twin Falls area. I'd been told that we might be able to camp at the fairgrounds. It was our best hope for camping in town, since everything else was divided into small residential lots. I was hoping to find a place to camp in town. I needed supplies from the grocery store.

We pulled into the fairgrounds right about sunset. A youth rodeo was in full swing. There were crowds of people and cars near the stadium. I tied the burros to a tall chain link fence surrounding the fairgrounds, where no one had parked. I asked at the fairgrounds, if it would be o.k. for us to camp, but it was late Saturday, and nobody who worked for the fairgrounds was around to say either way. The people in charge of the youth rodeo didn't think it would be a problem for us to camp in the overflow parking area, away from the rodeo. The thick green grass hadn't been cut for awhile, so it would work for grazing. I tied Lucy to my gear, and went to the arena to watch some of the last events of the day. There was quite a milling around of people, and someone who had seen me with the burros, praised what I was doing, and gave me twenty dollars to help us on our way.

The next morning, I went over to the far side of the fairgrounds where there was an organized campground, full of youth rodeo people. The campground had hot showers, and people told me that no one would mind if I took one. It'd been a while since I'd been completely clean, though I was in the habit of some spot cleaning.

The rodeo events started early and went on all day. It was great fun to see the youngsters, with all of their youthful enthusiasm, trying so hard and having so much fun. The stands were clustered with parents and other relatives, there to watch their youngsters. All of the contestants got much praise for their effort, no matter what the results. It was a good scene for sure, and kept me quite entertained for most of the morning.

I went to the grocery store for supplies in the afternoon, before heading back to the rodeo for most of the rest of the day. I'd had breakfast at the 4-H concession in the stands. After the people at the food counter saw my gear and burros, and heard what I was doing, they gave me lunch. Several of the young kids asked about my journey. One young boy was particularly interested in what I was doing. He had horse packed in the mountains with his dad, and said that someday he wanted to do something similar to what I was doing. I told him that many men came up to me and said that they wished they could also do what I was doing, but couldn't, because of their obligations to families, jobs, etc. The confessions were usually made when their wives weren't nearby. I told the boy to go on his adventure before he settled down with a career and family, or he might never get the chance. He promised me that he'd go on an adventure, as soon as he was old enough to go. I almost never recommended that people go adventuring with burros or other pack animals. I understood how difficult and dangerous it was, and that most people wouldn't enjoy the entire package of hardships. It was just the perfect thing to for me to do because of my unusual attributes and loves. It wasn't walking the burros that was the lesson of the journey, it was the joy created by following my own path. The stay in Filer had been wonderful, and I was glad that we hadn't found a place to camp earlier, or we would have missed the good entertainment of the youth rodeo.

Chapter 11
All Kinds of Friends
August 15 - August 21

August 15.

Filer was the last suburb of the Twin Falls area, on our route. I figured we could camp about ten miles ahead, down by the Snake River. We took a leisurely morning leaving the fairgrounds. There were a couple of miles of houses before we rejoined the farmlands. At one of the last houses in town, I met a man inspecting the construction of his new home. We made an interesting enough sight that he came over to the road to talk. He said the new house was going to be his retirement home. He'd been living in Twin Falls. I congratulated him on being done with work and building his dream home. He said that the modest home was too small to be his dream home. I congratulated him on not building a large mansion, telling him how wasted resources disgusted me.

He liked my journey; so we talked about it for quite awhile, before he wished us well, and we were on our way again. We rejoined the grid, zigzagging to go northwest to our next destination. A road shown on the map didn't exist, but the error had no negative impact, since we could just take the next road on the grid and get there. The countryside was virtually flat with only gentle rolls. Nothing betrayed the hidden surprise lying just ahead, until we were right upon the mighty Snake River Canyon. The rolling farmlands dropped abruptly straight down 500 foot sheer, black lava cliffs, with a rubble of boulders at the bottom, and the wide Snake River winding through the middle. I'd waited for this landmark occasion for many miles, and there it was, spectacular before us. I was truly impressed. We dallied on top for a short while, taking in the view with a few photos. The deep, rugged canyon was such a contrast to the surrounding gentle landscape.

The road into the deep canyon was a steep, gravel track. The narrow winding road was cut into the steep sides of the rocky canyon face, and did a sharp switchback part way to the bottom. The road was covered with loose volcanic cinders, which on the firm surface beneath, was like walking on ball bearings. Even the sure footed burros slipped occasionally. I kept searching out the best footing for the girls, either spots without loose gravel, or places where the gravel was so thick that they wouldn't slip. We slowly made our way down into the magnificent canyon. The slow pace was o.k. with me, since it gave me more time to absorb the spectacular and significant event.

There were scattered houses below, with green farm fields where the bottom was wide enough to support them. The canyon was a separate world, a lost Shangri-La. The valley was lush by the mighty river, a couple hundred yards wide, trimmed with a row of thick green trees and underbrush along its shores. Even the burros wanted to stop and look out at the expansive canyon view opening downstream for miles. Large springs, some the size of streams, escaped from the cliff sides on the far side of the gorge. Water tumbled out of the sheer rocks in a foaming torrent. Beneath them were fish farms, long narrow concrete troughs covered with nets to stop birds. The narrow troughs were set up like steps with small waterfalls between each level to aerate the water. The consistent cold water temperature made it perfect for raising trout for the dinner table.

As we reached the valley floor, the man who was building his retirement home in Filer drove up with his wife. They'd come searching for us so that she could see the unusual sight we made. We had discussed my likely route, so they'd entered the canyon farther downriver, and come up the road looking for us. We talked about the adventure, and again got an encouraging farewell.

A short mile or so after reaching the bottom, we came to a house with the owner in the yard. We waved to each other. She had a small dog that didn't like us in its world, and yapped intensely as we slowly passed the house and yard. We'd walked another 100 yards, when I looked back to see the lady running after us. Her little dog had decided to follow us down the road. I stopped, and when she caught up, we had a good laugh about her little dog wanting to take off on an adventure. I was glad that she'd been in the yard when we passed by, or I might not have noticed the little dog following us, and it might have been squished or lost. We backtracked to her house where I filled my drinking-water sack. She told me about a spot a short distance ahead that might work for our camp.

The spot, a bit off the road, was a small parking area, outhouse and boat ramp amidst the trees and thick underbrush along the river. A short distance up a trail from the parking lot was a flat spot, with a campfire ring, right on the banks of the wide and beautiful Snake River. Large spreading trees overhung the entire area for shade, wonderful shade. The canyon was even hotter than the flats on top, so shade was surely necessary. It was a perfect place for my tent, nestled in the trees, with an outstanding river view. I knew at first glance that we'd have to stay at least one day in the riverside paradise.

I surveyed the rest of the area for grazing. There wasn't much, just a little grassy spot here and there, amongst the thick trees and shrubs, and around the edges of the parking lot. There was also some grazing along the sides of the main road, 100 yards away where I could stake the burros, if necessary. It would work.

I unloaded the burros and staked them out. As I was doing that, I heard a car pull into the parking lot. I took my hatchet back to my gear and went over to investigate. A man in his twenties had parked his small pickup on the boat ramp, facing the river. As I got to the back of his truck, I yelled to announce my arrival. He nearly jumped through the roof! I'd caught him totally by surprise. He'd thought he was alone in the fairly isolated spot. We both laughed at his surprise. When he heard about my enterprise, he came over to see my camp and meet the burros.

As we stood talking, Lucy came over, dropped a stick on his feet, backed up a couple of steps, got into her one-paw-up-ready-to-go crouch, and gave him "The Look." Lucy had developed this approach with most people we met along the way. She could almost always find a stick for a visitor to throw, and with her intense stare and pose, she usually conned the person into participating in her favorite game. He picked up the thick stick, and threw it out into the large river. She dove in and swam hard to retrieve it. She was a pro at this game. Arriving back on shore, she moved away and shook without soaking us, and then dropped the stick at his feet. Again, she backed away, crouched, and gave "The Look." He was impressed and flung it further out. She responded with her usual zeal. The next time, the strong young man wound up and threw the long stout stick as far as he could, into the center of the powerful river. Lucy was undaunted, diving in, and swimming hard. They kept up the game, and she dove time after time into the fast-flowing current to retrieve her prize. Occasionally, she would rest in the bushes for a while, to recover from the strenuous exercise. The young man and I got along very well, and he said he'd come back the next day, after work, to bring me some treats.

I was extremely tired and spent the rest of the day laying on a burro pad, admiring the beauty of the Snake River Canyon, in the last light of the day. I fell asleep there, curled up with Lucy. I woke up later, sometime in the night, and retired to the inside of my tent. In the morning, I made an awful discovery. I wasn't immune to these mosquitoes! I'd fallen asleep with my left arm and part of my back exposed, and had hundreds of itchy welts on my arm, and a solid line of swelling where my shirt had pulled up to expose my back. The itching was bad enough, but I might have a larger problem. There had been radio reports about an outbreak of West Nile virus along the Snake River, which was spread by mosquitoes. With that many bites, if there was West Nile virus here, I had it.

I'd been in places where West Nile virus had been reported in previous years. I figured there was a good chance that the burros and I had all been exposed to it, and were immune. I'd talked to a vet in the past about the possibilities of the burros getting the virus. He thought that the burros were probably less likely to get it than horses. I believed in having a robust immune system rather than trying to stay sanitary. I believed that the immune system was like any other part of the body, doing better with a bit of a workout. I was habitually unsanitary to keep my immune system in shape. Before leaving on the journey, I cut my hand and let it get a bit infected to build immunity. I hoped that would lessen the chance of an infection on the adventure, when I couldn't afford one.

I surely couldn't afford to fear the many mosquitoes I'd encounter during the long outdoor summer. Years ago, I decided not to worry about every last mosquito, and hoped that, if I did get the virus, it would be just a mild case. I'd heard that most people had very mild symptoms, and then became immune. I'd counted on that in the past, and now I'd test the theory to the extreme.

I sat by the roiling river watching it flow by. There were no rapids here, but the water boiled and churned powerfully, swiftly. Waterfowl provided entertainment. Ducks, cormorants, geese, pelicans, blue herons, and egrets moved constantly up and down the river. The tall, statuesque blue herons, and the beautiful, pure white egrets were my favorites. They'd land on logs or in the shallows on the far side of the river and stalk their lunch, while I spied on them with binoculars.

I'd been exhausted. One day off turned into four, and I slept much of the time. The only real chore I had was moving the burros to different grazing spots. Our camp was far enough from the main road that I felt comfortable letting one of the burros wander free. This worked well for the first couple of days, but as the burros became bolder and more curious about their surroundings, the loose burro sometimes wandered near the main road. Libby was so full of herself once that she had to go on a gallop up the road when I went to retrieve her. She wouldn't let me get close, no matter how much I called. She decided it was more fun to play a game of keep-away, than be bribed by a treat. Luckily, no cars came down the road. She stopped when she got too far away from Beanie, her burro buddy, to feel comfortable.

They both enjoyed this game, consequently, I had to bribe them with a little grain when I made my burro call, "Fanny Lou". That was the name of my beloved burro who'd been killed in the fall down the mountain. All throughout her life, when I wanted to catch her, I would call out her name and give her some grain. It then became the call for the other burros. I kept using her name so that Beanie, trained to that sound, would still respond. I made the call every time for the new burro, Libby, so that she too would come to me. The call was an important part of their training, and I used it many times to catch them. I could bluff them once in a while, calling without grain, but couldn't come up dry too many times, or they'd begin to ignore me.

I had to use the roadside grazing after the second day. I staked both of them along the road, and spent most of that time sitting under a nearby tree, keeping an eye on them. When I wasn't doing that, I just sat by magnificent Snake River, under the grand trees, below the soaring volcanic cliffs, smiling within myself, watching the birds.

I'd been hearing along the way, that Bend, Oregon, our theoretical goal, was sprawling with new growth. Everyone said that it had totally changed, and that they no longer liked the once quiet town. After years in Colorado, where I didn't like the hyper-big-growth, I started thinking of other places for us to move, at least for the coming winter. Maybe somewhere along the Snake River would be better, since I was having such a good time here. I was told that the weather along the river, down to Boise, was much warmer than elsewhere in the region. The zone along the river, being low, got hardly any snow. A warmer climate was sounding good, after the cold Colorado winters. I was still minded to go to

Oregon, and searched the map for a likely new target. Nyssa popped out at me, a little town along the Snake River on the Oregon side. It sure was an odd name and, because of my forwards and backwards writing, I saw that Nyssa was assy N backward. It made a kind of sense, that the destination of a walk with burros would be a town spelled ASSY backwards. I'd check it out anyway, and if it wasn't right, somewhere else on the eastern side of Oregon was starting to feel like the place to spend the winter.

The young man I'd met when we arrived at the river came to visit each evening. Lucy would get very excited by the master stick-thrower's arrival. He didn't disappoint her. He brought along friends to visit. They all had criminal records, most had done jail time. Perhaps I should have been afraid of them. I was such a sitting duck for anyone who wanted to mess with me. The "hoodlums" were as friendly and helpful as anyone I met along the way. I trusted them entirely, and they all brought gifts of food and offers of help. One even brought me the ingredients for the classic s'mores. As usual, I was very hungry, and just couldn't wait for a campfire to follow the official s'mores recipe. I just took the graham crackers, spread some peanut butter on top, and added chunks of the chocolate. It was a gourmet delight, full of wonderful calories! I ate until all I had left were two bags of marshmallows. The night before I left, I toasted several over the fire by the glorious river. I was very happy for the helpful friendship of my river buddy, who came by each day to visit. The days at the beautiful river sanctuary had been some of the best of the trip so far.

August 20.

I finally left my wonderful home after four healing days on the magical riverbank. I'd learned over the years that, if I stayed even a couple of days in one spot, I developed an emotional attachment to the place. The higher spiritual intensity on pack trips, combined with the general good times, made any place I stayed even a couple of days a bit of a "Happy Home." It was sometimes hard to leave a spot; like tearing up roots again.

The mountain trips through Colorado and Utah were designed with this in mind. I would get to a lake, or high mountain basin, and stay for up to seven days in one location. This very leisurely travel gave me time to really explore an area, to really let a place soak into me. Maintained trails were like super highways, handy for getting into the wilderness; though the real fun was going off trail. I would tour the area several miles in every direction, getting to know the intimate details of my surroundings. The quest wasn't to see how fast we could get through an area, but how slow we could go. I loved getting to know an area well, finding intelligent routes through the terrain. This year's walk to Oregon was different. It was a moving year, and it was time to move on.

Through the canyon we did flow, past orchards of peaches and plums. I'd already tasted some of the local fruit. The fresh ripe peaches were the best I'd ever eaten. Needing fresh food made them as delectable as could be. The road was narrow and winding, though not very traveled, so we sauntered along without worrying about traffic. I was exuberant and bouncy after four days of rest.

We came to a field with horses and a couple of very large mules. They all got very excited at the sight and smell of the burro-girls. The large beasts stomped and galloped about in frenzy. The mules were particularly rowdy, and one of them jumped through a weak spot in the fence, and came running up behind us, spooking the burros. I knew that this was a bad situation, so I spun us around in a tight circle, hollering at the mule, trying to keep him away from the burro's rumps. Stubborn as a mule, he stuck with us. I picked up a handy stick and threw it at him. He wasn't deterred. The girls were nearly uncontrollable with fear of the aggressive beast on their tails. I was about to lose goofed-out Libby. Luckily, there was a sign right there on the roadside. I LUNGED toward it … barely getting my lead-rope around the post and tied. Despite the continued attentions of the mule, I managed to untie Beanie from Libby, and secure her to a nearby tree. PHEW! I'd barely dodged a bullet that could have done some real harm. If the burros had gotten away, the mule would have chased them to who knows where. A panicked chase, when the burros were loaded, could have easily injured them. The gear would likely have fallen off and tangled in their legs.

I was able to loop a rope around the big mule's neck and lead him back to the pasture. The owner had seen what happened, and was grateful that I was able to catch the mule and bring it back. I helped fix the fence, where the mule had gone through, so there'd be no repeat of the hazardous situation. Having something chase the burros to where I couldn't find them was one of the worst situations I could have. If they spooked and ran away from me in most other situations, they'd eventually stop, and I could catch them.

During my pack trip in the High Uintas, we were traveling above timberline, through a huge, high-basin meadow several miles across. The tremendous meadow was surrounded on three sides by a steep high-mountain cirque. The open end of the meadow went down into a forest.

Shepherds had a camp in the area. Usually, they had their horses hobbled in the mountains, to keep them around; but this particular camp just let their five horses run loose. The amazingly large, lush meadow was just such a natural spot for the horses that they wouldn't go anywhere else. We were walking through the middle of the basin, on our way to the next drainage. The frisky horses came to see what was up. In that huge basin, if the burros broke loose, and were chased around the wide open mountain cirque, it would have been pure disaster. The burros might have been badly injured or lost, and I couldn't afford to lose my precious gear in the middle of the high mountains. There was nowhere to tie the burros in the midst of the huge meadow, so to avoid a catastrophe, I grabbed some rocks and gently threw one toward the approaching horses. That scared them off for a short moment, but soon they came back for more. I threw another rock, a bit harder in their direction, and again they temporarily moved away. Several more times, they regained their courage. Each time, I threw a rock a bit harder. I finally tired of the dangerous game, and threw a fair sized rock as hard as I could. It clunked loudly off the biggest horse's head. That startled the big brute, and they finally ran off for good.

We followed the Snake River, eventually getting to a more built up area, new growth, a golf course, and a busier road. Heat was quickly building in the canyon, and shade was necessary. Some people in a pickup stopped to talk. The white haired gentleman said that he lived up the road a few miles, and that we could stay in his orchard if we wanted.

I found the place, with his directions, but he wasn't home yet from his errands. We gladly stopped there to get out of the sun, after only an 8-mile day. The orchard had big old apple trees with lush, green grass underneath them for the burros. The owner was an old-time preacher. When he got back, he and some of his followers came out to visit. They were all very friendly. Some of the youngsters threw the stick for Lucy and petted the soft furry burros. I was amused by the contrast between hanging out with the hoodlum-boys and a fundamentalist preacher on the same day. It demonstrated the great, wide-ranging appeal of walking the west with burros.

August 21.

Three months on the journey! I visited with the preacher in the morning. He was a farmer by birth, and had a several-acre organic vegetable farm to support his lifestyle. He was up early working with his plants in a large greenhouse. Most of his crops he sold to expensive resort restaurants. He had work to do in the garden, so while we talked, he continued to move gracefully, like a monkey at home in the jungle, amongst the many plants. He picked the ripe fruits of his and God's labor, dancing carefully through the plants, so not to destroy even a single leaf of his beloved plants. He believed strongly in his hard work, clean living and good food. His way had done well by him; for he sparkled and was spry as a child. He heaped me with fresh vegetables for my journey.

Visiting made us start late, so it was already hot when, a few miles into the day, we joined US 30. It was very busy, but had a good shoulder, so traffic wasn't terrible. Miles later, we stood, looking at an uncomfortable obstacle: a bridge across the Snake River. The span was several hundred yards long, narrow, with low guard rails on both sides and no shoulder. It was the situation I dreaded, but unless we swam the river, we had no choice. I took a deep breath and headed across. The bridge was straight, flat, and we were wearing orange, so people in vehicles could see us easily. If a fast moving car didn't seem to see us, I gave them a warning wave with an extra piece of orange cloth. All of the passing vehicles slowed and gave us space. A few had to stop completely when vehicles came from both directions at the same time, leaving them no room to pass us safely. I appreciated their consideration, and was thankful to cross the bridge without mishap.

We came to a similar situation a short distance further; guard rails on both sides of the road and no shoulder, but this section had an outer gravel shoulder that looked wide enough for us. The edge of the shoulder was a short, steep bank dropping into a swamp. I paused, and considered the options: stay on the road with the traffic, or stay outside, where it would be difficult to turn back if there was a problem. I remembered an experience years before when I'd learned not to travel outside guardrails.

We were following the Continental Divide Trail north from New Mexico, in the first stage of the Oregon odyssey, approaching Wolf Creek Pass in the majestic San Juan Mountains. There was a ski area on top of the pass where the trail crossed. I needed to make some phone calls, so we cut off the main trail onto some old logging roads, down to the ski area. The ski area had no phones available at that time of year; so I had to make my calls with the help of a road department employee, working across the road.

The next day we headed up the busy highway a couple of miles, to rejoin the Continental Divide Trail. That section of highway had curves with guard rails on both sides. So that we wouldn't be trapped on the road with the traffic, I took the burros outside the guardrails, along a steep embankment. The guardrails were fastened to the wooden posts with large bolts. The ends of the bolts stuck out several inches from the posts, into our travel zone. Beanie snagged one of her panniers on a protruding bolt firmly enough to stop her progress, Fanny, the lead burro, kept trying to pull Beanie along, until the pannier finally tore off. I had a terrible time getting the panicked burros calmed down and past the rest of the long section of guardrail. I was lucky the worst hadn't happened. It took over an hour to get the burros past the section, then repair and repack the gear.

I looked at the situation now, near the Snake River. It was a different guardrail, without bolts sticking out of the posts. I chuckled to myself, "no bolts", ignored my own advice and experience, and took the burros outside the guardrail. Ten feet of steep, loose gravel dropped from the edge of the shoulder. Libby, who didn't have a lot of trail experience, didn't like being right on the edge, and about halfway along the several-hundred-yard section, she shied away from the edge, and brushed the guardrail. That threw her off-balance, so she leaned even more, and caught the pannier solidly against one of the posts. I saw what was happening and tried to stop her, but she kept pulling hard against her snagged pannier, until it tore off. I quickly tied her lead rope to the guard rail, and popped the other pannier off to balance her load. I swore at myself. How could I have ignored my own experience and understanding like that? Beanie, who had much more experience on hillsides, and hated snagging her panniers, walked the rest of the section without a problem. I tied her to the right-of-way fence, and went back for Libby. She made it past the guardrails without her panniers. I tied her next to Beanie, and made two trips back for the panniers. I took out my spare parts and started repairs.

We'd come almost ten miles at that point and since we'd started late, it was blazing hot. I'd planned to take a break at a roadside rest stop, just a few hundred yards ahead. Instead of resting in the shade under tall trees, we baked in the hot sun for an extra forty-five minutes as I retrieved the gear, fixed the pannier, and repacked Libby. The wisdom of listening to my own good advice was literally baked into my brain. I was completely heat thwacked by the time we got going again. I struggled up the road the last little distance, hugely relieved to finally get into the cool, ninety degree shade.

Bathrooms, green lawns and picnic tables. I took the burros to the far end of the park, past the mowed lawn, to tall uncut field grass and shade. The burros preferred the tall grass, and I didn't want to spoil the park. I unpacked the burros, set them out to graze, got water for them from the rest area faucet, and collapsed under a tree. I figured I'd probably camp there. People along the way had suggested it as a good place to stop, but, not long after we arrived, a state worker came by, and was extremely upset to see livestock in the rest area. I pointed out that my animals were off to the side, not on the cut lawn, and that there were no signs saying we couldn't be there, as there usually were if they didn't want horses. The state worker didn't care that it was blazing hot and we were exhausted. The important thing was that the fine, trimmed lawn not have any burro-poop. I didn’t want any problems with government world, so I grudgingly told her we'd move. I didn't hurry, hoping that some rest would help me recoup. I dallied an hour before repacking. The short break wasn't very restful, and I was still extremely fatigued when we headed back down the blistering highway. We needed to find a place to camp, and soon!

Most of the area was intensively farmed, except for a little patch of unused land just inside a roadside gate, less than two miles down the road. There was grazing, and a ditch with water, next to some large trees. I didn't know who owned the land, but I was so desperate to stop, that it'd just have to do for an emergency camp. I opened the gate, and entered. A few small saplings along the roadside fence shielded us a bit, from the close-by traffic, but we were very visible to anyone who was looking. I hoped the property owner would come by, and give us permission to stay, before I unpacked and set up camp. I didn’t want to have to repack if we couldn't stay. I waited until dark. When no one stopped, I set up the tent and stayed the night. It had been a too-hot, 11-mile day.

Chapter 12
Following the Snake
August 22 - August 24

August 22.

We left our roadside resort early, facing another hot day, and not wanting to stay long in an unauthorized camp. Early in the day, we slipped through the little town of Hagerman without stopping. It was way too early for a break, and we needed no supplies. Four miles further, the main road climbed a long hill out of the canyon. We moved onto a gravel road which stayed in the canyon, following the Snake. I was glad to be on a narrow, less traveled road where the cars were slower. We passed some houses set among the lush trees of the river bottom. At one, an old-timer from the area came out to visit, since we'd made such a sight coming down the road. His wife came out to join the conversation. They had several large, old fruit trees in their yard, and they piled me with ripe, juicy goodness. The couple appreciated the entertainment on their usually sleepy road.

We'd gone eleven miles that day, when we got to another bridge across the river. The road we followed crossed back to the south side of the mighty river. After the bridge, the way would come somewhat near the river in places, but be far above it. I couldn't count on water for a long stretch ahead, so we needed to camp somewhere near the bridge. Before we reached the bridge, a little road led to a boat ramp and parking lot. I was hoping to use the public land at the parking area, but there was no shade. I'd been planning to take a day to rest and prepare for the upcoming long, thirsty stretch. We'd need some shade for the burros during that time. There were a few small trees over the fence at the end of the parking area, but the terrain was too uneven around the trees to be workable, and I really didn't want to go through the fence. I quickly scouted the whole area, but nothing was satisfactory, mostly because it was so steep and rocky.

Frustrated, I was about to give up the idea of camping by the river. I'd have to head back up the road disappointed, looking for a place to camp. A government sign, several hundred yards up the fence, caught my attention. Lucy and I walked up the gentle slope to investigate, and found that the land across the fence from the parking area and uphill a way, was public land. I explored, and found a group of large trees at an old homestead. The big trees offered shade but it sure was a long way from the river for water. I searched further, and found a spring close by. Clear cold water flowed at a good rate. It was not only big enough for burro water, but also clean enough for me to drink. Happily, we'd found the perfect place to rest.

I went back for the burros and brought them up to our new home. We'd gone from not being able to find even a lousy spot, to a genuine oasis in the otherwise quite austere landscape. Excellent! I was JUBILANT!! The tremendous trees were particularly impressive. I usually hid my tent in the most wind-protected spot, but after checking those spots, I opted to camp in the open, under the shade of a high canopied tree, hoping to catch a cooling breeze. I figured I could drag my gear fifty yards to a more protected spot if it got too windy. The meadow grass was extremely dry, and I was concerned about the possibility of starting a grass fire, when I used my cook stove. I pulled the dry grass for about ten feet around the front of my tent, and then got several buckets of water and wetted down the area. I kept a bucketful of water as a further precaution.

There was a large, fairly flat area nearby for grazing, but it was nearly all just dry cheat-grass, which is pretty much worthless for feed. Luckily, there were enough shrubs and smaller greenery amongst the dry straw to keep the versatile burros going. The real blessing of the grazing area was that there were enough big trees for the burros to always have some shade, during the heat of the day.

The weather forecast called for two more hot days, followed by a cooling trend. It made sense to stay at this wonderful spot for those two days, before crossing the next daunting stretch of desolation. I was glad to have the sanctuary all to myself. I was very fatigued. The proceeding ten days of 100 degree heat had really thwacked me. The burros didn't show any obvious strain from the heat. Traveling with desert animals was good. I was more than happy to use waiting out the hot spell as a reason to camp for a couple of days at the wonderful oasis. So, even though we'd rested by the river not many days earlier, we settled in for more vacation. Being able to take so many days from traveling helped all of us deal with the rigors of the walk. It gave the burros plenty of grazing time. They didn't look like they'd lost a pound, even after all of the walking.

Weather always called the shots on burro trips. Many times, on past trips, we'd had to wait several days for the weather to change before moving. That was particularly true in the high mountains, where the weather and exposure were the most extreme. It paid to have a good knowledge of the local climate, what the normal weather patterns were, and what was happening when they changed.

The Continental Divide Trail, through the Wimenuche Wilderness Area, was almost always on terrain higher than 12,000 feet. The weather in the awesomely beautiful place was the most demanding that I've ever encountered. Almost every day, there was a huge thunderstorm with lightning, rain, hail, and temperatures dropping into the low forties. I walked through the extreme mountains, during my first adventure, clueless in general, and knowing even less about the weather ruling the Rocky Mountains. Not understanding the local weather almost did me in. I'd taken cover under trees during the noon bad weather. When the skies began to clear, we headed out again. I was to learn never to go onto the exposed high places any time other than morning. Our biggest problem that time was that the trail went all the way up to 13,000 feet, near the very mountaintops. Just as we neared the top, another wave of bad weather came in, pounding us with torrential rain and hail. We moved down the wide-open mountainside, lightning flashing all around us, followed immediately by terrifyingly loud thunder. At the base of the peak we huddled under some dwarf spruce trees. At least we were out of the brunt of the wind and wet, though lightning still pounded all around. I hunkered there for about an hour, but when the gray-black skies showed no signs of ending, I had to act. The trail stayed on top of the ridge above tree-line. The north side of the ridge was a huge, sheer drop. The south slope was grassy and rolling hundreds of feet down to timberline. I couldn't stay on top all night, so, in a relative break in the weather, I took the animals down the open tundra slope toward the trees.

This was during the second half of my first trip, when I had the horse, Lady, and the burro, Billy. I had Billy tied to the horse's pack with a breakable link of light thin rope, so if one of them fell, they could separate. As we were searching for a place to camp, Billy suddenly stopped, breaking the connection. I looked back hurriedly, and figured that he'd follow us without being tied. Billy had followed along without being tied to the horse before, so it was a good guess that he'd come along. When I looked back a little later, Billy was nowhere in sight. I tied the horse to a tree, and began to search in the pouring rain. I scoured the rolling tundra, and the rugged "slippery when wet" forest below for my lost burro. I thought I saw burro tracks in the mud leading into the forest, so I searched in that direction for hours.

I only stopped searching when it was too dark. I had a hungry, sleepless night, since I was so worried about Billy, and he was carrying the food. In the first light of morning, Lady let out a distressed neigh for her lost companion. Off in the distance, I heard a most wonderful response, the mournful bray of a lost and lonely Billy. A few minutes later he appeared out of the fog clinging to the mountaintop. I was overjoyed to see my burro buddy. I didn't know at the time that a burro would most likely go back in the direction it had come. Billy had apparently gone back to the short spruce trees at the top of the ridge, where we'd stopped to take cover. The tracks I'd seen in the forest were worn elk tracks.

Walking across southern Idaho, sun and heat were the dominant forces. I was glad for the shaded sanctuary, close to the Snake River, where we could wait for cooler temperatures. I had a good view of the wide and wild river, a quarter mile below us. Dry hills on the other side of the river went up several hundred feet. I loved our camp under the spreading trees of the old homestead. One tree was absolutely huge, with a wide circle of pure shade, under which the burros could hide. How great it was to have the wonderful, cold spring so close. I sat in the shade, trying to recuperate as much as possible during our stay. Possibly, I had a mild case of West Nile virus.

Lucy and I took the short walk down to the river several times, for entertainment and exploration. My favorite afternoon seat was under the large bridge, where it shaded some big boulders. I'd park myself on a large rock, and watch the churning river. The bridge crossed the river at a narrows, where the waters pushed between two rocky points. Upriver was a wide, turbulent stretch of rapids. Even in the relatively low waters of mid-summer, the wildly churning big-water was quite a spectacle. I imagined the amazing, boiling tumult of the spring runoff. The wind over the water, combined with the shade, made this the coolest, most entertaining spot around. I sat contemplating the ruckus of waters for many hours.

The second day of rest gave me enough energy to explore further. Lucy and I followed a dirt road on the far side of the river a mile or so downstream, where I found the reason for the road. An irrigation pumping station sat at the end. Four large pumps, on a platform high above the side of the river, lifted water up the steep 100-foot-high river bluff onto the plateau above. The water irrigated several farms on the otherwise parched, desolate landscape. The man tending the irrigation system came by to check on the pumps, while I was there. He was friendly, so I quizzed him about the system. He'd done the job for a long time, and was full of information, not only about the present-day system, but also the history of the original system, built in the days before the big pumps. Then, water had been taken out of the river farther upstream, and snaked down through the steep, rugged hills in concrete flumes. He told me how, in the steepest and deepest ravines, giant siphons had carried the water past the worst places. Some of the old siphons, made during the 1920s, were still in use. The main object was to get the water to Pasadena Valley, fifteen miles downriver. Pasadena Valley was also our destination. The road we'd take followed the old, sometimes defunct water system.

The water-master told me where we could get off our road, and follow the canal service road. Having detailed information on what was ahead was very useful and helpful. I'd been studying the map, wondering all the way across southern Idaho, if we'd get through the desolate, challenging section. There was always a question as to whether a road on the map actually existed. The desert isolation wasn't someplace I could afford a mistake. Usually I was just guessing about upcoming conditions, from what I could see on my not-too-detailed map, or what I could learn from people along the way. To be assured by someone truly knowledgeable, was a great confidence booster, particularly before a challenging test of competence and good fortune.

The pump-master also told me about the town ahead, Glenn's Ferry. He told me where to find the grocery store, and about two interesting brothers, who ran an equine dentistry school there. He thought they'd be interested in my travels, and maybe have some work for me. I only had sixty dollars, and needed supplies, so some work would definitely be handy. The brothers took part in reenacting the treacherous river crossing by the early Oregon Trail pioneers. The spot was a major fork in the trail, and one of their biggest decision points. They either had to cross the wide and turbulent Snake River with their animals and wagons, risking life, limb, and everything they owned, and still have to cross the river again; or take the Southern Route. The risks they took crossing the river were a testament to the difficulties of their other choice. The Southern Route was rougher than the Northern Route, and had little water and less grazing than the Northern Route. Animals nearly starved on the Southern Route. It was also the scene of a large massacre by the Native Americans.

I planned to take the Southern Route, to avoid the perils of the modern Northern Route. We would've had to follow I-84 through the stark landscape, and slog through the tangle of Mountain Home, and the Boise area. I'd been told that it would have been a really ugly way to try to walk through with burros. The Southern Route on the old Oregon Trail was our only real option.

August 24.

Two days of rest and cooler temperatures set us up for a great day walking through the isolated section ahead. I was glad to have learned about the route in advance. It was so helpful to have no doubts about finding a good route. We left our good camp, crossed the raging Snake River on the concrete span, and climbed the steep hill on the other side. The road was pretty rough and dusty, as we picked our way through changing road surfaces to the plateau top.

The farms ahead were in the midst of their spud harvest. As a result, a caravan of empty potato trucks rolled up the road in the morning. The courteous truck drivers all passed us slowly, not kicking up dust and gravel, or spooking the animals. We avoided some of the road by following the irrigation ditch the pump-master had described. The one-lane, dirt service road was a little longer, since it followed the meandering waterway, though walking along the gentle flowing water was much more pleasant.

The service road had several gaps where the ditch and accompanying road came to deep crossing drainages. The builders had two choices in these locations: follow the contours of the land far up into the side drainage, which required a much longer ditch, or build a siphon through the ravine. The large water-tight pipes just needed the exit to be lower than the intake, for the water to flow through the ravine, and into the ditch on the other side. The siphons were fascinating. I marveled at the intake sucking huge volumes of water into the steep, deep pipe. I sure didn't want Lucy to be sucked into one of them, and made sure she didn't swim anywhere near them. I was impressed with the workmanship of the original siphons. The relatively ancient concrete pipes were still in use and had no leaks. The service road would cut back to the main road at the siphons, and then rejoin the ditch farther along the way. Eventually, we had to stop following the ditch when it passed through private land.

A low barren ridge ran along the south side of the large plateau. Farm fields were a very noticeable green in the otherwise brown landscape. Potatoes were being harvested at the last farm. The loaded trucks rumbled slowly past, with the year's harvest. The passing drivers were all smiles and waves.

The plateau ended after the last farm, and the road got much narrower, rougher, clinging to the steep, barren hillsides dropping down the side of the canyon. We were now spectacularly high above the magnificent river. Sometimes roiling rapids, other times great swirling pools, the river's course was visible for miles. A few trees and brush grew along the riverbanks, but most of the landscape was barren rock, and dry cheat-grass. It was a long way to the far canyon wall, so even though we were down in the canyon, we had an expansive view. The burros even had to stop to take in the grand sight spreading before and below us.

The modern ditch had ended at the last farm, but remains of the old concrete flume still existed. Clinging to the sheer side of the canyon, shrubs, even trees grew in the abandoned aqueduct. All of that work crumbling back into the earth. I marveled at the effort the old-timers went through, to bring the water farther down the steep, rugged canyon, to Pasadena Valley. The pump-master had told me that most of the digging for the flume was done with draglines and mule teams. They'd built a small railroad to haul the pre-cast concrete flume sections to where they were placed. Several large side ravines cut into the canyon sides. Through these huge cuts, mighty siphons were built down and back up the rocky cliffside ravines. I had a hard time imagining how all of this terribly difficult work could have been worth the time and effort, just to bring water to a remote flat valley. Such a huge investment to pay back; but without the water, the land was worthless for farming. The irrigation flume served its purpose for six decades, before they stopped trying to maintain the difficult section, and put large pumps downriver, to bring water to Pasadena Valley. I wondered if the original investors made a profit.

The road we traveled couldn't follow the great siphons of the old ditch, so it snaked up into the dry hills and then back, to avoid the deep side drainages. We climbed several hundred feet, with tremendous views of the rugged river valley below. Between the awesome view and the interesting old ditch, it was a great section to walk. Eventually, the rough little road had to go to the top, away from the river, to avoid a sheer wall rising from the Snake River. It wasn't as hot as it had been during the previous weeks, but still warm enough to tamp us down a bit. When we came to some water in a slough, ten miles into the day, we paused for a break. I tied the burros off, and got the buckets, but, surprisingly, the burros didn't drink much. Near the water, some cows were hiding from the sun in the shade of a very steep cut in the hillside. Trees were scarce; the only nearby grazing was dried cheat-grass. I was tired enough, but didn't really consider camping at a muddy water hole, with no grazing. After our recent R&R, we should be able to walk five more miles to Pasadena Valley. There had to be better grazing in the irrigated valley than in the waterless desert. The canyon was still quite hot. We would've had some trouble, if the temperatures hadn't been lower than they'd been just a few days earlier.

I was interested in seeing the valley they'd worked so hard to irrigate. One step after another got us through the next five miles, and to a farm perched on a bench above the river. It was the first irrigated place, but not in the main valley. Eventually, we got around the last barren brown hillside, and came upon the bright green valley. Everything was either green-green, or brown-brown, with nothing between. The contrast made it totally clear what irrigation was all about. Great rows of sprinkler heads spewed sparkling plumes onto the green garden. The main part of Pasadena Valley was several miles across, apparently with more cropland farther down beside the river. The road we would follow ran through the lush green valley, then up onto and over the dry hills to the west. Somewhere in the next couple of miles, in this green valley, we had to find a camp.

A cattle guard without the required gate in the fence, crossed the road. By old-time law, a gate was required, so someone such as I, traveling with animals, would be able to pass. I'd encountered hundreds, maybe thousands, of cattle guards, but this was only the second time in all of those years, that there wasn't a gate in the fence. I checked each side of the gate to see how the wire was attached. I could use my fence-tool to open the fence, bring the burros through, and close the fence. It was relatively rickety; so I could fix it easily. If it'd been a tight fence, rebuilding it to proper tension would've been hard with my tools. I'd built fences before. I knew what I was getting into and what I had to do.

I thought back to the only other time I'd found a cattle guard with no gate in the fence, many years before, on my first pack-animal adventure. We were coming out of the San Juan Mountains, in southern Colorado, just ahead of the winter snows. The isolated forest road descended the mountains, until we came upon a gateless fence at a cattle guard. We'd only been there long enough for me to see the situation, when a couple of cowboys stopped their pickup, to see what someone with pack animals was up to. They liked hearing that we'd come from such a long way away in Utah, to south-central Colorado. When I mentioned that I hadn't found a gate in the fence, they both immediately pulled out fencing-tools, and started opening the end of the fence so we could get through. They assured me that they were experts at barbed-wire-fence construction. Comically, they completely stopped the deconstruction and looked casual when a vehicle passed by. Even though what they were doing was o.k., tampering with someone's fence in the rural west was very taboo. The helping cowboys waited till the vehicle was out of sight to continue saving my ass. I didn't have the tools, or a clue how to fix a fence properly at that time, so it was quite a miracle that the saving cowboys came by when they did.

Here, it would just be a lot of rigmarole, to open the fence and then rebuild it. I could do the job myself, so I didn't need a saving miracle on the fence, but I still had a camping spot "on order". I checked the map. It showed a side-road grid that rejoined the main road before it left the valley. We took the side way up onto a little rise in the eastern part of the valley. The drier uplift wasn't farmland, so there were residences on several-acre lots. Soon after taking the alternate route, I flagged down a passing driver who confirmed that the road went through. We walked past the higher, drier land, back to the main route, without seeing anywhere to camp. I could see that the road went just another half-mile through the lush, green valley, before starting up the brown hills. All of the crops came right to the edge of the pavement, offering nowhere to camp.

An abandoned home site sat at the intersection where the side road rejoined the main road. The yard would be large enough for the night, and I might be able to get water from the nearby sprinkler heads with my 5-gallon buckets. As I studied the situation, a pickup stopped. Amazingly, it was one of the brothers from the equine dentistry school, with one of the teachers. They were very friendly and intrigued by our journey. The dentist lived just a half-mile back down the road, and said we could stay at his place if we wished. I tied the burros carefully to the old corrals, and hopped into the truck with Lucy, so I could see the situation he had for us. The spot was on a patch of ground a short distance from his main house. It had a corral for the burros, water, and hay. Also, right near the corral, was a little cabin in which I could stay. I accepted his offer, and thought myself extra lucky to meet him. He told me about some of the river crossing reenactments he'd done with his old wagon and team of horses.

I retrieved the burros and walked back to the good camping place. I didn't particularly like sleeping in someone else's space, so I slept out in front of the little cabin on my sleeping pad, under the stars. I was glad to have the option to use the cabin if I needed it. My very jocular and animated host told me to make myself at home, and that he'd stop in the morning to see how we were doing. I was happy that I'd connected with the dentistry brothers. Once again: Burro-Magic.

Many years before, on a trip in Colorado, I was in a tight spot, just 100 miles from the end of a ninety-nine day journey. I needed about five dollars worth of supplies, from an upcoming store, to finish the home stretch. I was penniless, and worried about how to find money. It was a beautiful full-moon night, in a mountain meadow by a stream, with everything gleaming in the moonlight, when I realized I couldn't worry about things not working out, after all the miracles that had already kept me going. So many good things had happened to me while on adventure that I had to believe that The Maker loved me packing burros. I had to have faith that things would work out. The concept brought me confidence. I put aside the fear about the money. Two days later, we got to the small convenience store/restaurant. I tied the burros to the fence on the far side of the parking lot, still totally broke. I turned to walk the last fifty yards to the door. On the ground … at my feet … was six dollars!!! I got my supplies, and with a little help from the owners, some lunch. The perfect timing was consistent throughout my burro packing. It was the theme.

Chapter 13
Glenn's (Tooth) Ferry
August 25 - September 4

August 25.

Next morning, the Pasadena valley sky was clear, so the heat was coming. Still, I wasn't in a huge hurry to get going, since it was only six miles into Glenn's Ferry. The burro-girls weren't haltered, because when they were corralled, I took off the halters to keep them from tangling on something. I learned that lesson on my first pack trip, when I didn't have a clue, and did a lot of learning.

During the second half of that adventure, when I had the horse and burro, we'd been invited to stay in a corral behind a house. I slung my hammock under a shed roof, close to the animals. The water trough was a large tank that had been cut in half lengthwise. It was thick steel, about six feet long, and quite heavy. The cutting torch had left jagged and curled edges. While the horse was drinking, her halter hooked on one of the curled edges. She panicked and began throwing her head up and down, bringing the water trough clear over her head, and then smashing it back down onto the ground with a CRASH! I jumped from my hammock and ran to her, as she kept lifting and smashing the solid metal trough to the ground!! Fortunately, she was a good old horse who calmed down when I yelled "WHOA!" She stopped thrashing her head, and after a tense moment, when she could've freaked out again, and hurt both of us with the heavy steel, I was able to work the halter free from the water trough. Luckily, I'd been right there to help her immediately, and she was a relatively calm beast.

Putting the halter on Libby, ready to leave Pasadena Valley, I noticed a golf ball sized lump on the side of her face. When the colorful dentist came by in the morning, he took a quick look at it, and told me to bring her into the Equine Dentistry School, when we got into Glenn's Ferry. I packed the burros, and we headed through the last of the green valley, into the desolate brown hills above. We went several miles through barren hills, getting into a few houses just before crossing the Snake, on the bridge into town. We arrived at the Dentistry School just as a class was ending. The eight students were almost all from other countries; the school being world renowned. They gathered around to hear the tale of our travels.

One of the instructors got out a tool to open Libby's mouth so that he could see inside. Her problem was that her teeth had sharp edges which were cutting the inside of her mouth when she chewed. Her teeth would have to be filed down, or she'd get worse. My heart sank. I didn't have any money. The instructor chuckled. The procedure would be free. The teacher I'd met the evening before took out his tools and went to work on her teeth, even while the packs were still on her. She wasn't too happy about having her teeth filed, but relented under the hands of the expert. He said that the swelling should go down on its own with the irritant removed. He also filed Beanie's teeth, while he was at it.

The other brother came out to meet us, and very much liked our project. He was also quite a jovial character. I'd been having trouble with Beanie's halter rubbing spots on her head, and had been changing the adjustments back and forth to try to minimize the rubbing. He noticed this, and brought her a special halter that he thought would fit better; and just for good measure, got one for Libby too. Their mother, who lived nearby, came over, and they took pictures of the brothers, mother, burros and me for the record.

I was getting so much attention and generosity that I got a bit light headed and disoriented, feeling like I was in some kind of dream. They gave me a tour of the facilities, showing me a classroom filled with all kinds of horse skulls with different tooth problems. They explained how their teeth grew in, and told me how one can tell their age, by which teeth had grown in, and their condition. At another building, they showed me where horses are brought to have dental work, the operating room, and other classrooms. It was very impressive! All of the students raved about what a great institution it was, saying it was the first and best equine dentistry school in the world. The school even made its own line of dentistry equipment. The brothers were obviously very special people, to have such enthusiastic students; a first class operation, to be sure.

Classes were ending, and there'd be no students around for a while, so I could stay in one of the student apartments in Glenn's Ferry. I was amazed, not only at all the fine gifts and place to stay, but at the miracle of coming into the equine dentistry school on the very day I needed help with the burro's teeth. Anywhere else along the way, I'd have had a hard time finding someone who could do the dentistry, and I wouldn't have been able to pay for it. Whenever I really required a hand on burro trips, it was given. All the small miracles could've just been coincidence, but the frequency and the amazing timing, had me convinced that larger forces were actively at hand. My confidence was sky-high; how could I worry about bad things happening, if the Maker wanted me to continue, and would actively help when we needed it?

The apartment kitchen gave me a rare opportunity to really clean my cook pots. The shower was pleasurable, but was something I missed less than one would think. Being dirty was just the norm on burro trips, so I got used to it.

There was also a laundry room in the complex. I washed my clothes, so I was unusually clean for a burro trip. I bought something other than my usual austere diet at a nearby grocery store, and did something very uncharacteristic. I threw away food. The marshmallows I'd been given on the Snake River had coagulated in the heat into one large glob of sticky goo. The lump of welded sugar had no appeal, so I tossed it away. There was, of course, a bed in the apartment. I slept on it the first night, but found it uncomfortable. I tossed and turned all night. After that, I slept on the floor, on my inflatable sleeping pad. How odd it felt to live in a building. I was a bit confused and disoriented, in this unusual situation.

I had the burros staked-out in some grass near the apartment. The rail yards, with a regular flow of rumbling freights, were nearby. The burros would stop eating, trying to figure out what the huge noisy beasts were all about. I was glad to have the burros experience trains coming so close, because I'd had burros spook at the thundering commotion of a passing train.

My first burro trip went through the extremely dry, desolate area northwest of Green River, Utah. We were traveling along the railroad service road that ran through the barren desert. There were no trees in the powder-dry valley; hence the only shade was under the railroad trestles that crossed the numerous dry washes. The sun was burning, and we needed shade, so we pulled up under a trestle to take a break. I tied Broguey the burro in the shade, and was about to tie Billy, when I heard the rumble of an approaching train. I could have tied him to the trestle, but decided to lead him away from the tracks . . . too late! We were only twenty feet from the tracks, when the speeding train blew by. Billy broke away in a panic, and ran up the service road along the tracks, in the same direction as the train; with me behind him in desperate pursuit. Luckily, it was only a short passenger train that was soon past, instead of a long, slow freight that would have taken a long time to pass. Billy stopped and watched the fast train rumble into the distance; so I caught him easily. I imagined an amusing scene of someone in the train looking out the window at the desolate landscape in the middle of nowhere, when suddenly … a burro and man were running beside the train. The astounded observer turning to the person in the next seat, "Did you see that … a man and a burro running through the desert!", and getting a very skeptical look.

The first day of our three-day vacation in Glenn's Ferry, I staked the burros in the grassy area, and Lucy and I took the three-mile walk down to Three Island Crossing, where the Oregon Trail crossed the Snake River. A picnic park with green grass and large trees was a short distance upriver. We bypassed the park, and went over to the visitor center, with its Oregon Trail museum devoted to the pioneers and the nearby area. I tied Lucy outside, under some small trees by the building. Whenever I left her alone, I always left my little backpack with her so she could be with a piece of me. I always carried my pack so that I had a snack, water, flashlight, or a jacket if I needed it.

I was very interested in the exhibits and artifacts in the museum, since my adventures gave me such a bond with the early travelers. I loved the pioneer equipment. Particularly interesting were the remnants of steel-soled shoes worn by some of the early travelers. How brutal it must have been to wear the cumbersome footwear. I imagined that most of their shoes were leather soled, slippery when wet, and wore out easily. Cobblers were handy people to have in your wagon train. I'd read accounts of the early travelers going barefoot after their boots wore out. I marveled at how things had changed in just 150 years; even the footwear was much more advanced. Comfortable shoes with good traction rubber soles would have been worth a fortune to those people. The lady working the information desk said that she had seen the article about my burro packing travels in the Twin Falls paper.

Lucy and I ambled down the last quarter mile to the river, to the actual crossing. They'd picked the shallowest spot in the river, where there were a few little islands. They went from island to island, and cut across the wide river at an angle, staying on a rock bar with the shallowest water. The river riffled quickly over the shallows, and would have pulled at their animals and wagons, tugging them toward deeper, drowning waters. I sat on the riverbank, contemplating their amazing feat in crossing the wide river. It surely confirmed how lousy the Southern route was. That was a bit ominous for us, since we'd be going that way. Luckily for us, things had changed a lot. There'd be more water, and, even more important, we wouldn't have to compete for grazing, like the old-timers. Lucy naturally got to chase the stick into the river.

During the walk back to town, we came across an interesting building, an old high-school that had been turned into a museum. I tied Lucy in the shade of a tree, and went inside to investigate. Several rooms had different kinds of displays. An older gentleman came over to see if I needed help. I was going to ask about the Oregon Trail, but I noticed his railroad hat and blue coveralls. We were in the railroad part of the museum, so I inquired about that. His eyes lit up. He'd worked on the railroad, starting at a very young age, and had continued the career all of his working life. He'd been retired for quite a long time, but his love for the trains was still very alive, and he happily poured out his knowledge. He pointed out pictures of the different kinds of trains he'd worked on, and told me stories of the old days. He explained that, in the days before radios, they had to send messages by hand signals. He went through a very animated demonstration of the hand signals, showing me the official ones, and a couple of the unofficial ones, like when the boss was coming. It was a most enjoyable and informative talk, which could only have been told by someone who had really lived the life and loved it.

I spent the next couple of days resting and wandering around Glenn's Ferry. I planned to ask the dentists if they might have some work for me, but even though I'd rested ten of the previous sixteen days, I was so tired I just recuperated. During the last day of our stay, the second brother took me out to his house, to show me around. While there, he offered me a place to live in a room off the garage. He also said that he had enough work to keep me going through the winter. It was an extremely enticing offer; with an opportunity to learn so much, and be associated with these wonderful people. I ran it through my mind several times, but the same answer kept coming up; keep going to Oregon. It was just too early in the year to stop. I figured I could use Glenn's Ferry as a backup, if things didn't work out farther up the road. I just had the very strong inclination to keep on going to Oregon.

August 29.

My vacation had my gear disorganized. I'd packed as much as possible the night before, so we'd be able to leave early. We took the secondary highway between I-84 on one side and the railroad tracks on the other. I was glad that the burros had gotten used to the rumbling trains in Glenn's Ferry, because one of the huge masses of steel and noise rumbled by, and there was nowhere to get away. The burros just watched it roll by. The road was sandwiched between the tracks and the freeway for about seven miles, before they turned northwest, away from our route. I was glad to be away from the noise and commotion that always accompany major commercial travel routes. We continued west through the few businesses and scattered houses that made up the small town of Hammett, where we got onto Route 78.

I'd gotten supplies in Glenn's Ferry, spending all but ten dollars of my money. During decades of poverty, having so little money was very familiar. I was so poor for a while that, if I had as much as ten dollars, I felt comfortable. I had a good chuckle looking into my billfold, as we walked along the rural highway, and seeing the lone ten-dollar bill. I remarked to myself, "plenty of money", remembering my old wealth benchmark.

I felt better than I had for a while. The rest had finally helped me get over my general fatigue. It was good that I'd spread out the ten days of rest into small chunks. In the past, when I'd stopped for ten days at a time, I started to get out of shape. I didn't want to lose the conditioning I'd gained during the months of travel. After Hammett, the road was much less traveled. A pickup stopped and a Mexican man poked his head out the window, pointed at the burros, and said, "A burro was my first car." We both laughed. He'd emigrated from Mexico thirty-six years before, and had worked on the same ranch, for all of those years. He was very friendly and gave me five dollars.

We'd walked fourteen miles, when we came to another bridge. We were tired enough to stop. After we crossed the river, I didn't know about any water in that section of the Southern Route. Fortunately, there was a usable place to camp by the bridge, where the old road had come through. This gave us a good wide swath of land to camp between the river and the new highway. A few Russian olive trees grew along the edge of the relentlessly flowing river. I used one to hide my tent from the steady breeze that could turn into a too-strong wind. With the road so near, I kept both burros staked. There were a few small trees where they could find some shade, but they mostly chose grazing instead. The grazing wasn't great, because there was only worthless dry cheat-grass and weeds.

Lucy and I moved under the nearby bridge to hide from the sun. She cajoled me into throwing the stick into the river. She'd fling herself from a boulder with a large splash, and churn ferociously out into the slow-moving river after her quarry. She'd shake-off a few yards away from me before dropping the stick at my feet and giving me "The Look." Her exuberant passion made her hard to resist, and brought me much joy and laughter.

The Mexican man I'd met earlier came visiting with a couple of fellow immigrants. They didn't believe his story of an American traveling the countryside with burros. One gave me a beverage, and the other five dollars. I'd doubled my money in one day, bringing my bankroll up to twenty dollars. As I'd believed, having only ten dollars wasn't a problem. He came back to visit twice more, once with a very helpful bale of hay for the burros, and another time with food and sodas. These gifts once more confirmed the wonder of crossing the land with the burros. It was good to be on the road again. Being in town had disoriented me somewhat. I sat by the riverside, watching the flow, and contemplating the upcoming dry stretch. We'd probably walk some long days to reach water. The evening brought a glowing pink sky.

August 30.

After we crossed the river, a few miles of winding road took us to a paved, four mile straight stretch. We plugged along at our usual two-and-a-half-mph pace. This included occasional short pauses for one thing or another. There was only sporadic local traffic. I'd developed a routine for traveling wide open roads without shoulders. We took up about half the lane, so when I saw a car heading toward us, I looked to see if a car coming from behind would reach us at the same time. If they were going to reach us at about the same time, I would, if possible, pull the burros into the ditch. I would also get off the road if a vehicle coming up behind us didn't have enough visibility to pass us safely. I stayed on the road if there was only one car coming from either direction, and they could safely pass. The other situation I had to watch for was a straight stretch with a line of cars passing each other. On the whole trip, only a few cars passed us close and fast, everyone else slowed down, and gave us as much room as possible.

The beginning of this stretch of road wasn't as desolate as I thought it would be, having a few farms along the way. Cooler temperatures also helped. We climbed a hill with a good view of the Bruneau Sand Dunes lying a few miles to the south. The great sand hills rose several hundred feet above a lake, of all things, visible even from miles away. There must have been some very interesting winds in the area, to build the large sand dunes, but I never heard the story. Shortly after we passed the road to the dunes, a man and a woman stopped to talk. They'd seen us earlier, on their way into Glenn's Ferry, and were curious enough to stop to hear our story on their way home. They liked what they heard, and said that, if we got to Bruneau, six miles ahead, I could have a home-cooked meal and a shower. I didn't know if we could make it all the way that day, since we'd already come twelve miles. I got directions to their house, and thanked them for the offer.

A couple of miles farther, we connected with the much busier and faster Route 51. The two roads stayed together a little way past Bruneau. Luckily, the road was wide open and fairly straight so that, even with the seventy-five mph speed limit, everyone could see us, and kindly gave us plenty of room. We came to a rest area with trees and great grazing, for this area, but there was no water, unless I could get some from a house, several hundred yards away. The wind was really blowing; enough to make camping difficult. My tired legs wanted to stop. Instead, we just paused to rest, before heading on to Bruneau. The draw of visiting with the friendly couple, and having a good meal, kept me going. We had a hard uphill climb on tired legs, and I was very glad to crest the hill. We had a fine view of the wonderful green swath that was the Bruneau valley.

Our weariness was eased by the final, downhill stretch of road into town. I found the friendly couple's house easily. They were very happy that we'd put in such a long day to get to their home. I dropped my gear in a corner of their property, and staked out the burros in the small yard. The lady was very animated and excited at having such an unusual visitor. I took a shower before being fed a big delicious meal. It was fun to have conversation and be treated so royally by the good couple. I was offered the couch to sleep on, but I slept in my tent, as I preferred.

August 31.

Early in the morning, I was given a big breakfast. We parted good friends, and I promised to visit, if I ever came through the area again. We followed the road out of the lush, green valley, to where the brown hills began, at the split between Route 51 to the south, and Highway 78 to the northwest. The rolling hills had an occasional farm, so the way wasn't too desolate. A cloud of gnats followed us up the road, bugging us all greatly. I wished for some wind, to relieve the torment, but it didn't happen. There were markers along the roadside showing the exact path of the Oregon Trail, where traces still existed.

Just below a large dam on the Snake River, we left the highway, and followed the river road beside the rolling waters. I was hoping for a camp when we got to the river, about twelve miles into the day, but saw nothing suitable. We took the pretty winding road all the way into the small town of Grand View, for an 18-mile day. I still couldn't find a good spot to camp, finally settling on a questionable spot at a boat-ramp. It was adequate, mostly because of my sore legs, and the need to stop. There was enough grazing around the parking area for the burros, to make do for the night. I set the tent under a tree about ten feet from the road. In the evening, I sat out on a small jetty of large rocks that protected the boat ramp from the forceful river current. The river was too fast and churning for Lucy to play stick, so she was disappointed.

September 1.

A business across the road let me use their facilities before I packed up and headed down the road. We were able to keep to side roads for a few miles, before rejoining the highway. The day's entertainment was a back-and-forth flow of county dump trucks, passing us numerous times with load after load of gravel, for an unknown project. We waved at each other many times as they drove by. I imagined their speculation about our journey. I was sure we gave the drivers something to talk about on their radios. We left the farmlands after about seven miles, and followed the road into dry hills. We passed the side road to the gravel pit, and stopped seeing the orange trucks.

We crowned a hill that gave us a bit of a climb, and got a good view of the Owyhee Mountains to the west. The steep-sided, sculpted peaks were 4,000 feet higher than us, an impressive sight rising out of the desert below. Despite their height, they were still barren, except for a few trees in the highest north-facing folds. I was tired most of the day. The valley below had a stream. After that everything was dry-dry, so we had to find some kind of camp. Several ranches were spread along the water. When we got to one driveway, a lady came out to meet us on an ATV. She'd seen us coming down the highway from her house, and had to see what we were about. Several years before, she'd helped people traveling by horse and wagon, so she was inclined to help weary old-style travelers. She offered the use of forty fenced acres, across the road from her home. If we needed the rest, we could stay longer than just the night. We were ready for a rest. After walking thirteen miles that day, combined with what we'd traveled the previous three days, we'd walked sixty miles in the last four days.

I made camp on the fenced parcel of land, and turned both burros loose. I had to keep an eye on them if I left my tent site, or they might ransack my gear. The mischievous burros would chew on my gear, just for the fun of it, if they had a chance. Whenever they came close to my camp I'd drive them off. This worked during the day, when they were grazing, but that evening they became such a nuisance that I had to tie them out.

The next day, we took a very lazy day off. There were trees under which the burros could find a little shade, but there weren't any trees where I could set up the tent. I stretched my tarp outside the front of the tent, with my extra tent poles. The tarp worked pretty well until the true heat of the day, when there wasn't enough breeze to stay cool under the nylon. Lucy and I resorted to the usual best, coolest place to escape the heat, under the bridge across the little stream. Since the ground under bridges was never heated by direct sunshine, it was cool, like going into a cave. Bridges with water under them were the best escape, for coolness and entertainment. Waiting out weather had left me sitting many hours in a wide variety of places, without much to do other than just look around. Lucy, the fetchaholic wonder-dog, helped pass the time. I tossed the stick into the little trickle of water to help her stay cool, and give us some fun. The bridge was pretty rickety and really shook whenever a large vehicle went flying over, at wide-open country speeds. My sore, stiff legs relished the rest.

I thought the lady was very brave to invite me into her home, when she was by alone on the ranch. She was very friendly and helpful, giving me fresh vegetables from her garden, and eventually offering us a place to live in an empty trailer on the property. The ranch was relatively isolated, and there was no car, I thought I'd feel trapped fairly quickly. I still had a very strong urge to get to Oregon, so I thanked her for the offer and all of her help. I'd be in touch if my plans changed.

September 3.

We headed into The Dry. The lonely road through the austere landscape had long straight stretches with occasional ups and downs. There were no farms after we left the valley. I noticed that fewer people waved to us than usual, and thought it might be because it was Labor Day weekend, with more tourists out than usual. The road passed through very dry country, with nothing but sagebrush, cheat-grass, low hills, and an occasional fast-moving car. No shade to hide under, or grass for the burros. We kept moving most of the day, taking only short pauses along the way. I sucked hard candies, keeping my energy up and my throat from parching.

Fourteen miles into the day, we crossed a rough rocky ravine with flowing water. A posted side road went into the drainage. The next water was six miles away in Murphy. Twenty miles was too far in the heat, so we'd have to enter the private land, at least for water and rest. We descended to the flat ravine bottom. Trees grew next to the small stream. I pulled the gear from the burros in a group of trees behind a huge "No Trespassing" sign. The sign also stated that, with permission, one could be on the land, so I figured our being there wasn't too deadly. I was invoking my "rights", as a traveler across dry country with animals, to stop for water. People in ranch country were more helpful to people with animals, than to people alone. The burros opened up opportunities that a person alone wouldn't have.

I staked the burros in the canyon bottom to graze. I was beginning to realize why the old-timers crossed the Snake River to avoid this section. Water was available at long intervals, but the grazing was just terrible. On the old Oregon Trail, with all of the animals coming through, there would have been no grazing at all. Even along the stream, there were only weeds and brush for the versatile burros to graze. We'd walked the long journey slowly enough, and had taken so many rest stops, that the burros still hadn't lost a pound. Actually, I was hoping they'd lose a little weight. Horses required far more food than burros. If I'd been traveling with horses, it would've been hard to keep them healthy.

A car showed up, with the occupants hoping for permission to use the property. I asked them to mention me and my situation when they saw the owner. A little later, they came back down the road, saying that no one was home. Later, a few more cars came by with people who lived on the large property. Even though they couldn't officially give us permission, they said it would probably be o.k. I waited until dark to pitch my tent, in case we had to leave. I was beginning to be really excited. We were so close to the long awaited and worked-for goal of Oregon, now less than sixty miles away. Soon, I could really start looking for a place to spend the winter.

September 4.

We rejoined the main road and continued northwest out of the small rocky canyon and across dry, open ground into Murphy. One person stopped to talk, and gave me a couple of bucks. We stopped for an hour-long break to water the animals and get a snack, before heading down the road again. The busy highway led through rolling terrain. I had to keep on my toes with the traffic. I was in a bad mood, and again noticed fewer waves and smiling faces. I forced myself to change my outlook, or risk creating a sour experience for myself. I didn't want any of the bad luck that came with a bad attitude. Shortly after I consciously changed my attitude, a lady stopped and came over to visit. She and her husband had burros and a small covered wagon, with which they took trips. She was anxious to meet us and help if possible. A friend had seen us near Murphy, and called to tell her about the burro train coming across the countryside. She showed me pictures of her burro trips, to prove she was genuine. The fellow burro-lover gave me some food, and then drove ahead to scout out a place for us to camp. The friendly reception was a great boost. She soon returned to describe a spot where we could camp by the river, and said that she would return with her husband, hay, and supplies.

After a 13-mile day, I found the spot she'd described, on the banks of the Snake River. It was BLM land, amidst private property, so anyone could use it. From the trash, it was obvious that many people used the riverside property. The gift-bearing burro people arrived shortly after we did. The hay was very appreciated, since the area was nearly barren, even though it was near the river. They also brought canned food, and a large container of apple juice. I immediately gulped down much of the delicious cold juice to help dissipate my heat.

We compared our burro trips. I was glad to meet someone who used burros for journeys, since I'd never met anyone else who'd done it. Once in a while, I'd met people using horses or mules. All of them either rode or used wagons. No one I had ever met used animals and walked, except people using lamas or goats. For years, I'd been interested in the possibilities of using wagons, particularly in the desert. I could bring more water, and supplies; though using a wagon restricted where we could go. We couldn't take trails, and a wagon would always be in traffic on roads. I'd also noticed that gates at cattle guards were not always passable for wagons, so I'd stayed with panniers.

The burro-lady's husband was a logger in the mountains, and was away from home a lot. They said they'd give me fence-building work, and a place to stay a while if I wanted it. I took directions to their place, thanked them for all the help, and told them I might take them up on the offer. The river current was slow here, so I sat by the river in the evening, throwing the stick for Lucy. I thought about resting the next day beside the river.

Chapter 14
Almost Home
September 5 - September 22

September 5.

We awoke to a terrible swarm of gnats, some on Lucy and me, and a huge cloud on each burro. I sprayed the burros with insect repellent. That helped, but it was still miserable. The combination of bugs, no shade for the burros, and all the trash had me quickly packing. I thought of crossing the river to the burro people's place. It would be twelve miles out of our way and, despite having only eighteen dollars, passed the opportunity, I had the urge to stay on Route 78 on the south side of the river. Givens Hot Springs, thirteen miles ahead, had popped out from the map as a place I wanted to visit since I'd first considered this route.

It was another hot day, and I was supremely glad to see the large trees and green grass of the hot springs oasis getting closer with each step of our slow but persistent pace. We'd come about 100 miles in the last eight days. I was surely ready for a rest, and hoped the hot springs would be the place. A man moving sprinklers around the large green lawn came over to see what we were doing when we pulled up to the fence in front of the property. I must have looked as tired as I felt, because he immediately asked if we needed some shade to rest in for a while. I told him that what we really needed was a place to rest for that day and the next, if possible. He unhesitatingly accepted the idea, and showed us to a building behind the lawn and parking area.

There was a large tree for my tent, and other close-by trees with grazing for the burros. The nearby building had two open sides with picnic tables inside; a perfect place to set up my kitchen, and a good shady spot to relax, a great situation for us. I thanked the man, who turned out to be the fourth-generation owner of the hot springs. Ownership had been out of the family for only a short period in the 125 years the hot springs had been in operation. They'd have their 125th year anniversary celebration in four days. The theme of the celebration was going to be "From Wagons to Wings", highlighting the huge changes that had happened in the world during the time the family had run the fantastic property. He thought the burros and I would fit right in with the festivities, as an example of the old-time ways, and asked me if we would stay long enough to participate. He also offered me some work, and meals with the family while we were there, and I'd be able to use the hot springs. How could I refuse? I accepted the generous offer of the great place to rest, and the opportunity to gather some much needed money. I set up my home under the tree, and put the rest of the gear in the covered picnic pavilion. The pull to reach Oregon, now only about thirty miles away, was strong; but I wasn't in any real hurry. I wouldn't have been walking burros if speed was important. The 100 miles of extreme effort and discomfort over the preceding eight days could've been easily covered in an hour and a half driving a comfortable air-conditioned car.

It'd only been eight days of hard effort in sweltering heat since my last shower, so, by the standards of the trip, I was hardly ready to get clean. Even so, I couldn't resist going directly to the hot springs. There was a large indoor pool with 100 degree water, and smaller, hotter, individual tubs along the side. The warm silky water of the main pool sure felt good. I paddled around in the wonderful warm water until I was good and wrinkled. While in the pool, I had a good long conversation with an older gentleman and his grown son. The elder was trying to recover from shoulder surgery in the soothing waters. When they left, the owner came over and told me that the unassuming gentleman in the pool had been one of the most powerful men in Idaho state politics. I'd thought he was a farmer. After the swim, the pretty young girl who worked at the hot springs made me a pizza for lunch, and threw the stick for Lucy.

That evening, some long-lost friends of the owner's wife came to visit from Utah. Recently, they'd been reunited after not seeing each other for over forty years. They'd come to see their long-time friend, and be at the anniversary party. The couple had just retired and was looking forward to traveling the world. He was a total romantic; having taken out his wife for lunch every day throughout their working careers. They were amused by my story. I was honored that, even though we'd barely met, the owners invited me in for a great dinner with their guests.

The first day, I slept most of the morning, took a swim, and had another pizza. I worked in the afternoon scraping paint from one of the guest-cabins. A nearby neighbor brought hay for the burros, since the grazing wasn't adequate. I again had dinner with the owners, and enjoyed the conversation and excellent home-cooking. The next two days, I painted part of the guest-cabin, swam in the wonderful hot springs, and enjoyed socializing. I felt very privileged to receive such fine care and be fed so well every night I was there. Each day, I worked at painting the guest-cabin.

Saturday, the party started at noon. People who were exhibiting showed up a couple of hours in advance, so they could set up in time for the party. It was quite a production. A couple of covered wagons, a fancy stagecoach, gold panning lessons, a blacksmith, antique cars, and food. Much to my wonder, a Blackhawk helicopter flew in, and landed in the parking lot. I'd thought the owner was kidding, when he told me a Blackhawk helicopter was coming to the party. It was part of a nearby National Guard troop and often gave demonstrations at local events.

I put the mostly empty panniers on the burros and joined the party. I had to leave Lucy tied up at camp, so I wouldn't have too much to handle. First, I headed over to the large, menacing-looking Blackhawk helicopter. The pack burros and I, with my thick beard and grass hat, alongside the hi-tech helicopter, made an interesting contrast. The pilots were amused. Many people arrived for the celebration, and I spent the next four hours walking around the park amongst the visitors. Many people who came were part of the owners' extended family. I had many good conversations. Most people were surprised to learn about our journey. Hearing that it was my lifestyle, and not just a one year adventure, impressed many of them. Some people thought I was an actor, not believing that anyone actually traveled in such a manner anymore. Libby was all full of herself after lounging about for the previous three days. I had a hard time getting her to stand still while I talked to the visitors. She pulled me all over the place, so I had to keep spinning her around in tight circles to control her. Everyone took pictures, and I had an all-around great time being part of the show. I met a man who lived in a town we'd pass through once we were in Oregon. He gave me his phone number and directions to his home, and hoped we'd stop by when we got there.

Givens Hot Springs was one of the highlights of the adventure so far. My reception at the anniversary celebration was very encouraging. It helped to be appreciated, after all the effort of the journey. I was glad I hadn't taken the option of working for the people with the burro wagon. It wouldn't have been bad, but it would've been hard to beat the celebration at the hot springs. The owners made me feel like family during our 4-day stay. Their trust and help was admirable. I was very warmed by the entire event.

September 10.

After one last swim, loading my gear (well scattered after four days of leisure), and a last visit with my new friends, we finally resumed our trek. It was hard to leave the good times at the hot springs. I thanked the owners, left the righteous place, and headed up the highway toward Marsing.

The road was somewhat hilly, making walking a little hard. My legs had tightened up during my vacation. Along the way, we met another male burro. Again, I had a hard time getting the girls to pass a boy without visiting. A passing motorist gave me some money, so, when we got into Marsing, I stopped at a local diner for a quick bite. There wasn't a suitable spot for the burros to graze, so I just tied them to posts, left them loaded, and gulped down my food. I was very tired, even though we'd only gone eleven miles. The meal gave me some energy.

We left the main road just outside town. My map showed a road grid we could use for a while, so we started to work our way through. People told me that, in another couple of miles, we'd come to open space and ponds where we could camp. I was so disappointed when I found signs saying, "No public entry." It was a wildlife refuge. Luckily, there was an unused wedge of land outside the fence, where the road used to go. It was kind of a weird spot to camp, since the area was otherwise covered with houses and farms. But there was water, grazing, and I was tired and had no idea where else we might camp. Therefore, we made do with what we had. I had to climb the barbed wire fence and ease down a steep little embankment to get water for the burros. Climbing back up the hill, with a bucket full of water, was barely doable, particularly when I was so tired. I rested an hour, which helped. At the end of the day, I took a several hundred yard walk to a closed church, and filled my drinking-water sack from an outdoor faucet.

September 11.

I awoke to a morning talk-radio station reliving the infamous World Trade Center destruction. I remembered where I'd been on that day: in the Flat Top Wilderness area, walking from southern to northern Colorado. Usually, in the mountains, I could only get nighttime AM radio reception, but that historic morning, I happened to be camped where I could get a Denver station all day. I was enjoying my breakfast, lolling a bit, waiting for the warm sunlight to hit my campsite, before going out for the day. The news-radio station announced that the first tower had been hit by an airplane. I listened in disbelief as the second tower, and then the Pentagon was hit.

The idea of the World Trade Center collapsing was totally mind-boggling. Years before, I stood under the towers, looking up, imagining how amazingly destructive it would be if the taller-than-tall towers fell like great trees. Hearing that the towers had actually fallen was like Orson Welles' "War of the Worlds" radio drama, but it was actually happening. I spent the rest of the day listening intently to the tragedy that gripped the nation. I could hear the fear. No one was quite sure how widespread the attack would be. People usually think that wandering the high mountain wilds alone is dangerous. At the moment, I felt like one of the safest people in the country. Terrorists weren't going to bomb some guy traveling with burros in the middle of nowhere. The next day I packed up and moved on. I came upon some backpackers who didn't have a radio. They were in shock and disbelief when I told them that "Pearl Harbor Two" had happened, and described what I'd heard. It was almost a month before I left the mountains and finally saw the footage of the planes smashing into the World Trade Center towers, and saw them falling. Seeing it happening was much more profound than hearing about it.

Five years later, I packed up, and we headed up the road. Oregon was tantalizingly close. We kept to back roads, near the Snake River, but since the roads were a grid, we had to jog west, then north, then west, etc., to keep on our northwesterly direction. We made it into Homedale, looking for a place to stop for a lunch/rest break. There was no likely spot downtown to park the burros for the short stop. Someone told me I might find a place for the burros at a park near the river. I followed the directions, through a residential neighborhood, a few blocks to the park. A nice tree in the middle of a field made a good place to unpack, rest, and graze the girls out of the sun. I ran quickly back to town, got a few items, and went back to my gear and girls. I took a seat by the river, and watched it roll by for a while. I wasn't in the mood to load the burros and look for another place to camp, even though we'd only gone eight miles. Motivation appeared in the form of a town worker, telling me the poop-making burros weren't really welcome in the park. I understood the problem. We probably shouldn't have been there at all.

Again, I got it together and moved on. We had to go back through town to the road we needed. I was still hungry; so I tied the burros to an alley fence and went over to a nearby drive-in for a quick bite.

Straight up the main highway, Oregon was just five miles away; but that way was pretty busy with traffic, so we cut off on a side road. It would be farther to the Oregon border, but about the same distance overall. Also, the side road would probably be better for finding a camping spot. It was tempting to try to get to Oregon that day, but I was tired and needed to camp before then.

Shortly after that, an older rancher gentleman pulled up to find out our story. He was very friendly and helpful, offering us a place to camp on his ranch. He drove his truck slowly up the road to the gate into his land. We followed him to his private road, and took it to some old ranch buildings, near a small creek. Large old trees gave cooling shade and protection from the wind. He grabbed some hay from his stack, to help the burros graze. We'd come only ten miles, but I was exhausted. I still wondered if I'd caught a mild case of West Nile virus. The rancher said that there were a lot of cases in the area. Some people he knew had been very ill. He said that he used to have a lot of Magpies at the ranch, but they'd all died, probably from the virus. Magpies are large black and white birds, related to crows, which apparently get the disease relatively easily. I felt sure that, by that point in the journey, we all had been exposed to the virus, by the many mosquitoes that had chewed us. Also, most of the mosquito population was already dead, this late in the summer, so I didn't worry about it too much.

Treasure Valley along the Snake River was a garden-paradise, compared to where I'd lived in Colorado and northern New Mexico. Corn wouldn't even grow there, much less tomatoes. The rancher brought me fresh vegetables from the nearby garden, including some delicious grapes from his yard. No wonder they called it Treasure Valley!

He was a very kind, good man and a hard-worker for sure. Even though he was in his mid-seventies, he was looking to buy more land so that he could expand his herd, and take on more work. The next morning, he took me into town for coffee and conversation. Instead of going to a coffee shop, we went to the local feed and hardware store. It was his usual spot. He even had his own coffee cup there. We had a good talk with the friendly people working there. I went to the grocery store for supplies while we were in town, and because I was with the welcome rancher, was also treated well there. By the way he was received by the people in town, he was obviously a first-rate man. He knew an older couple who might need a ranch hand for the winter. They lived in Jordan Valley, a very isolated area in southeastern Oregon. He worried about the couple being by themselves so far from everyone, and left a message on their phone about me looking for a place to live. I was extremely tired, slept a lot of the day, and finally felt better late in the afternoon.

Homedale was a good place to rest, and because of my good host, I decided to take another day off. Being so close to Oregon made me anxious to get there, but as slow as we'd been traveling all summer, it was no time to get into a hurry. I helped the rancher by picking up irrigation pipe along a ditch, so it could be put away for the winter. He was going into town to do some errands, so Lucy and I hitched a ride with him, getting dropped off in the middle of town. We wandered around the small town for a couple of hours, for the entertainment. I splurged on lunch at a hot dog stand. We walked back a couple of miles to the ranch. The Jordan Valley couple hadn't called back, so I planned to leave the next day. The weather forecast said it was going to be twenty degrees cooler than it had been, and I wanted to take advantage of any cooler weather. Even though the heart of the summer was over, we'd still been suffering some from the heat. People all along the way had mentioned what a hot summer it had been. It had only rained, briefly, a couple of times all summer.

September 14.

It was finally time to get to Oregon! I said my thanks and goodbyes to the good-hearted rancher and walked up the back roads toward our long awaited goal. We were still on a road grid, so we went this way and that, working our way northwest. We were basically following the course of the Snake River, which took a big swooping curl to the west. It was the only place that the Snake River went entirely into Oregon. Farther downriver, it is the border between Idaho and Oregon. We came by a dairy farm, and, as had happened several other times on the trip, curious cows stampeded over to the fence to see the strange sight on the road. The unusual burros were probably what interested the cows most. Dairy cows were more intrigued with us than beef cattle, possibly because they were all together in a more contained corral than beef cattle, or maybe because they were handled more by humans. Several times during the summer, a rush of dairy cows had spooked the burros. I held on tight, and moved to the far side of the road, trying not to lose the burros because of a bunch of charging dairy cows.Beef cattle weren't totally uninterested in us. Several times while walking through land with range cattle, we'd had a large herd of them following us. During my first burro trip, I was sleeping on the ground without a tent, and awoke to a ring of cattle surrounding me, shoulder to shoulder, thirty feet away, all staring intently at me: the alien in their pasture.

It was about six miles to the Oregon border, and with each step my excitement mounted. I wasn't sure exactly how far we had to go, so, as we came past scattered houses, I checked the license plates on cars in the driveways, to see if they were Idaho or Oregon. They kept being Idaho plates for longer than I thought they should, but … FINALLY … at the side of the rural road, was a small sign with some extraordinarily exciting news: "Oregon Border." I tied the burros to the sign so I could get a picture of the great occasion. I did a little dance, hoot, and holler to celebrate the hard-won goal. We paused there for about ten minutes to "take in the moment" and then continued up the side road.

Three miles farther, we rejoined the main highway and headed north. Traffic was minimal. We walked past farms, some with onions, a crop I'd been seeing more of recently. Oregon had a different feel to it. Idaho, along the Snake River, was in the throes of hyper-growth. I'd seen some of it, and had heard from people how much the Boise area had been exploding with growth. People liked the relatively mild climate along the Snake River. The elevation was comparatively low, and water was available from the river to make it green. Oregon had stricter zoning laws about cutting up farms and ranches for development, so I immediately noticed much less growth after we crossed the border.

We'd put in a full day of fourteen miles when we entered the tiny town of Adrian. The main road, in the middle of town, had a couple of businesses and an onion-packing plant. The man I'd met at Givens Hot Springs, who wanted me to stop at his place, lived near town. I tied the burros and Lucy on the main street, and entered the country grocery store. They let me use their phone to call him, but all I got was an answering machine message. The store's owner made it clear to me that he lived just a mile away.

I found his house, but he wasn't home. He'd been insistent, when I talked to him at the hot springs, that we come and stay at his place, so I unloaded the burros in his back yard and tied them out in the unused lot next to the house. There was enough grass at the edge of the nearby corn field for them to graze for a while. I had to be careful not to stake them too close to the corn, so they wouldn't mess with the crop. More important, corn had too much protein for the burros, and would be harmful if they ate too much.

He got home just as it was getting dark, and was surprised and happy to see us in his yard. He was very hospitable, cooked me some dinner, and made me feel very welcome in his home. We had a good talk that night, and the next day he surprised me by offering me a place to live for the winter. He owned thirty acres, on which, besides the house, was a large double-wide trailer. The renters who lived in the trailer would soon move out. He was going to move into the trailer, and rent the house. He offered me one of the rooms in the trailer, and said that, once the corn was harvested, a corral could be built for the burros. I was in shock at finding a place to live my first day in Oregon. I told him I'd probably take him up on his offer, but would have to mull it over before deciding. I met some of his friends. One owned an onion farm, and said I could get some work when the harvest began.

My host had young kids from a past marriage, who came to visit on the weekend. They loved the soft, friendly burros hanging out in their yard. Kids in the neighborhood where I used to live in Steamboat, Colorado called the burros big teddy bears because of their docile friendliness. We took a tour of the local sights, including a nearby recreation area, which had a reservoir and little hot springs amidst the barren rocky hills. Adrian, close to the Snake River, had a relatively warm and dry climate, rather desert-like anywhere there wasn't irrigation. The only trees grew where people had planted and watered them, or right next to water sources.

There was an unused corral across the road from the house. I got permission to use it for the time being, and found a few bales of hay to keep the burros going. He had another house in the Boise area, which he was selling, and had to go move his stuff out in the coming week. I could help him out by taking care of his old dog and a newly acquired hyper-puppy while he was away.

He took his kids back to Boise on Monday morning, and left me in charge of his house and dogs, until his return later in the week. It was amazing that he trusted me enough to leave me alone with all of his possessions, but it wasn't like I could strap a TV to the burros and walk away.

While he was gone, I took the mile walk into Adrian, once a day, for something to do. Right away, I got some notebook paper, planning to start writing a book about my adventure: walking from Colorado to Oregon with burros. I realized that writing a book was essential, when the adventure had turned into such a unique journey. Most of my trips had been just going from one beautiful place to another, and immersing myself in nature's glory. This walk was an adventure in faith. I started the improbable journey with little money, counting on help along the way, and as predicted, awesome things happened just when we needed them. The walk was such a departure from the usual attitude of the times: being afraid to trust. The saga of meeting and being helped by all of the perfectly wonderful people seemed a story worth telling.

I was very lethargic in body and mind. The house had a satellite TV system with about 200 channels. I got sucked into TV world. I'd seen hardly any TV in over a year, so I was mesmerized; cruising the news channels first, to see what was going on in the world, and then scrolled several times through all of the rest of it, searching for something interesting. Even though I didn't really find anything in all of those channels that I really wanted to watch, I left it on, filling some need caused by my isolation from the rest of the world. I became depressed and much disoriented. I was half in a dream world. Nothing seemed real.

Lucy and I walked to the hill rising above town. Near the top of the bare hill was the town letter, a large capital A, made with painted white rocks. It was very common in the rural west to anoint a close-by, open hillside with the town's letter. We followed roads through a few miles of fields before reaching the base of the hill. We crossed the irrigation ditch at the bottom of the hill, using a plank left for that purpose. The hillside was bare, except for grass, so I had easy access up the steep hill by zigzagging across the face. We were rewarded with a fine view in all directions from the top of the solitary summit. Treasure Valley lay to the east, along the Snake River. West, the dusty, desolate, rocky hills and great wide-opens, literally went on for hundreds of miles. Both views blended on the north and south, depending on irrigation. I realized that the hill would be a frequented spot if I stayed in Adrian for the winter. I would always find a piece of nature where I could escape town life, wherever I lived. The little, bare hill was the closest wild spot. I sat on top and meditated upon my situation.

I plinked along for several days in disoriented depression, taking my daily stroll to the store, but watching TV more than anything. I wasn't up for starting to write the book. It just came to me, that this wasn't the place we were supposed to spend the winter. I didn't see how I could support myself financially, after the short harvest season. I didn't really have a clue about farming, and in the winter, there wouldn't be much farm work even if I was experienced. Also, it was questionable what kind of spot I'd be able to work out for the burros. I wanted them to have a great place for the winter; after all they'd done for me. They were my pets, my love.

Adrian just didn't feel like the right spot for us to be for the winter. I felt pretty clear that I wanted to get into the mountains for the winter, rather than stay in the flat lowlands. There were mountains farther northwest. We were going to have to continue our journey. I called the owner and told him I needed to go. He was disappointed. He'd be back next day with a load of his stuff, and hoped that I would stay until he got back. He arrived home late the next day, with a moving van following him. The van pulled up next to a storage container on the property, where the movers emptied the contents of the truck. He took me out to dinner that night for a party.

September 21.

Four months on adventure. I helped him move a lot of his belongings out of the house and into the storage container to assist him with his move. I thanked him for all of his help and kindness. He extended his offer of a place to live, if things didn't work out for us ahead.

I didn't get the burros packed up and ready until three in the afternoon. We headed north toward Nyssa. It didn't feel like the place for us to winter anymore, but I still felt obligated to check it out, because of the "assy-N" connection. Thankfully, the weather had cooled during the last week, and even rained a little. It was the first rain we'd seen since halfway across Idaho. The wind was blowing strong from the west, as we made our way north. I was still disoriented and out of sorts, as I took the burros up the fairly busy highway. If I hadn't been interested in going through Nyssa, we could've taken a shortcut northwest across barren landscape, though we would have had questionable water and camping. This route kept us in the fertile green farmlands. We moved onto a side road at the first chance.

I was mentally moving too fast, so when we came upon a good place to take a break, behind a row of trees that hid us from the strong wind, we pulled over for fifteen minutes. I couldn't afford to be frazzled and fast on the road. That frame of mind was dangerous and not much fun. A good attitude was my best ally. I sat down, took some deep breaths, and tried to reorient myself to burro walking. I mentally got my feet back on the ground, and we continued up the road. Nyssa was a couple of miles out of our way to the east. We worked our way through the farmlands on the road grid.

We entered a housing area near town. Along the way, two young boys were playing in their yard. They stopped their game to watch us approach. The sun was in their eyes, so the older of the two young boys shielded the sun's rays with his hand and gave us a good look. He turned to his younger companion and pronounced with great disappointment, "Oh, he's an OLD guy." We came up along their yard, and the boy continued to put me in my place, "What, are you with the CIRCUS or something?" I laughed and admitted the truth in what he said, "Yep, the circus or something. We walked from Colorado. You can look it up on a map." I replied as we passed by.

We crossed the main highway about a mile north of Nyssa. I stopped us at a little store/restaurant for some food, tying off the burros to a fence behind the establishment. The tidy little store was run by Mexican immigrants. I gathered from what I'd seen that immigrants made up a large part of the local population. I ordered two large burritos, made fresh to order. They were some of the best burritos I'd ever had. I gulped down one and a half of them, and saved the last part of the delicious meal for later. The owner/chef came out back to talk with me about the trip. I was glad to have given him my business. The friendly store staff gave me directions to the back roads through the area.

The late start caught up with us a little later up the road. We'd come thirteen miles since 3 p.m., and it was getting dark, too dark to travel up the road with the burros. I paused to get water for the girls, not being sure what kind of camping spot we'd find ahead, when I saw someone at a house. The neighborhood ended at a large onion processing plant. The end of the property had a long, high wall of large onion crates. The crates were each about three feet high by six feet wide, and made a wall about 25 feet high by 300 feet long. Next to the wall-of-crates was an open field with some decent grazing. I didn't see anyone at the processing plant to ask permission to camp on the property. Without any better prospects, and needing a place to camp immediately, we moved in for the night. I tied the burros to the crates while I unloaded the gear and then staked them out to graze. The imposing wall held another benefit; it blocked the strong wind that had been blowing persistently all day. I set up the tent next to the protecting wall.

September 22.

I got up early, so I wouldn't overstay the welcome I wasn't sure I had. The only thing we needed in the morning was a bucket of water for the burros. I saw activity at one of the houses across the street, so I took my bucket across the road and knocked on the door. The lady who answered was surprised to hear I was camped across the road. My tent was hidden from view by the onion crates. She'd seen the burros, and thinking they'd escaped from someone's field, had called the police about the lost animals. She showed a lot of good faith, even though she was alone, when she let scruffy-dirty me into her house to fill my bucket.

I was nearly packed and ready to go, when a police car pulled onto the edge of the field. I walked out to him, worrying what he might say about our blatant trespassing. I quickly told the officer about our journey, and needing to stop somewhere when it got too dark for us to travel. I said I'd looked for someone to ask permission from at the plant, but had found no-one, and that I didn't believe we'd be doing any harm to the empty lot. He agreed that we were o.k., saying that he was only checking out what he'd thought was loose livestock. No one had called about a trespasser, so he wasn't concerned. We talked for a while. He liked our adventure. I was glad he didn't mind us being there.

A short time later we were walking north toward the largest town in the area, Ontario. When we were a couple of miles away, we cut west, to avoid town and the major highway that ran west through the area. Thirteen miles into the day, the country road was close to the busy highway. Just before the junction, we came by an unused field and an irrigation ditch full of water. It made sense to camp there, so we moved in for the rest of the day. We were in full view of the gravel road. I waited before setting up camp, just leaving the gear in a pile, where I'd dropped it from the burros. A short time later, the owner drove by. He was kind enough to let us stay the night.

Chapter 15
Trees, Real Trees
September 23 - October 9

September 23.

A short distance down the side road took us to Route 28-20. The highway was as fast and busy with traffic as any we'd been on the whole trip. Fortunately, there was a shoulder and a good ditch to walk in. Even being able to avoid the dangerous traffic, walking so near to the rush of fast moving vehicles was disturbing. I didn't look at passing cars as I usually did, so I missed the opportunity to wave at passersby. The constant wall of fast-moving cars was just too much to try to connect with. I was glad to finish the busy six mile section, and arrive in Vale, with its tiny park right across from the grocery store. There were signs talking about the Oregon Trail, which had gone through here. It was a good place to unpack and stake out the burros, while I went into the store for supplies. I took a leisurely time snacking and relaxing. Some curious people came over to find out what we were doing.

Vale was the fork in the road for the two different routes across Oregon. Route 26, more heavily used, went straight west. Route 20 went to the northwest. Route 26 was the quickest way to Bend, but there wasn't any pull at the moment for us to go Bend, so we headed up highway 20. I was pleased to be away from Route 26. It had the feel of people trying to get somewhere far away … fast. Route 20 had locals who were just going up the road a way, slower and friendlier.

A couple of miles past town, I stopped to check out a possible camp site. The little chunk of vacant land sat next to the old pioneer cemetery. It was small, and right on the road, but water nearby made it workable. I was considering ending the 11-mile day there, when a man pulled into the driveway across the road. He got out of his big pickup to unlock his gate, and while out of the truck, gave us a look and then a friendly wave. I crossed the road without the burros, which were tied to the fence, to ask if he thought it would be o.k. for us to camp there. He was a semi-retired rancher, who kept a small herd of cows and a saddle horse on the property, with a few more head of cattle on another piece of property, just up the highway. His self-imposed chore was feeding the cattle every day. He liked my old-school adventure, and invited us to camp on his property for a couple of days, if we needed it. We'd been moving three days in a row, and this was a good situation for us, so I accepted the offer. I moved the burros across the road, unpacked, and put them into a corral. He got some hay out of his stack for the girls.

The first day off, I walked back into Vale. I toured the little town, ate lunch at a restaurant, and got a detailed map of the upcoming Baker-La Grande area from the BLM office. The burros were cribbing, chewing the boards of the corral. I didn't want them to harm the well built fence, so I moved them into a larger corral, with his horse and grass. The horse was afraid of the burros, so it didn't chase them, as I'd thought it might. The fresh grazing kept the burros occupied, so they stopped chewing the fences. I toured the pioneer cemetery. It told a harsh story, of a harder time, with a large percentage of the gravestones being for young children.

The next day, I helped the owner put a large tarp over his haystack: protection against the upcoming winter storms. It was the only chore on the property he needed help with at the moment. He took me into town for lunch, as part of my pay, and for the company. He'd always been in the cattle business and had done well, even owning several stock-auction yards over the years. I picked his brain for information about our upcoming route and towns that we'd go through. I was starting to feel that the Baker-La Grande area might be the place to spend the winter. They were somewhat larger towns, of at least 10,000 people each, so there'd probably be enough opportunities for me to scratch out a living. Also, the larger towns had some chance of hosting one of my favorite activities, live music. La Grande seemed the most likely place for music, since there was a college in town. My advisor didn't like La Grande, because it was so windy in winter, but he'd always liked Baker City. It sounded like a pretty area. Both towns were in large farming valleys, with timbered granite peaks rising 5000 feet or more above them. Somewhere in those higher valleys seemed like the place for us. I was told that there were real winters in Baker and La Grande, compared to the warmer climate along the Snake River.

September 26.

Leisurely, we left Vale. The summer heat was mostly past, making life much easier, since I didn't have to get up so early and rush to beat the pounding heat. Afternoon shade was no longer an imperative, as it had been most of the summer. The road went up through a farming valley, about four miles wide, with low barren hills to each side. It was onion-harvest time, so an occasional onion truck filled to the brim would come down the highway. The roadside had many onions on it, dropped by the passing trucks. I picked up several to use in my cooking.

Lucy-dog had for a long time now been a pro at walking up the road. She understood that I wanted her walking on the side of the road like the burros and I. I'd call her name to alert her if we were going to change sides of the road. When she looked, I'd point, with my full arm, in the direction I wanted her to go. She'd understand and go to the other side of the road. She was very smart and aimed to please. If she trespassed into the forbidden zone, I gave a harsh, loud yell. Along many roadsides, off-pavement wasn't very good walking, so I allowed Lucy to be on the pavement, but not over the white line along the edge of the highway. She understood, and went along with the subtlety of being on the pavement, but not in the traffic lane. Also, I usually didn't want her going onto the properties beside the roads. If there was a fence along the road, and private lands on the other side, I tried to keep her on my side of the fence. I allowed her on fenceless land and counted on her desire to be with me to keep her close. The only thing I had to really watch was if she found road kill and got interested in it. I might not notice, and leave her behind. This happened several times when I wasn't paying attention, though it never proved to be a huge problem. She was ideal for my kind of traveling, a great companion, and I'd become very attached to her.

My other new recruit, Libby, was beyond extraordinary for a rookie. She was so willing to go, and just loved walking. If anything, I had to work to get her to stop. She had such a sweet temperament. I was truly blessed to have gotten these two new companions. Beanie was her reliable steady self. In all of the sixteen years we'd been together she'd never hurt me, and had been my good buddy all along the way.

The road was straight and flat, so we made a good twelve miles, before finding a likely place to camp. It was property where the road department stored gravel, for resurfacing the highway. Grass at the edges and back of the parcel would work for grazing, and there were even a couple of small trees where I could hide my tent from the wind and have some privacy from the road. A nearby irrigation ditch held water. After a while, a pickup stopped to see what we were up to. The property owner leased the spot to the state, when they were doing road work. He was happy to have us there. He brought fresh vegetables from his garden, and some drinking water.

September 27.

We had another straightaway day on the back road through the valley. It was a bit hot, particularly on the black asphalt, even though September was almost over. Ten miles into the day, I was ready for a break, when a pickup stopped on the shoulder of the road ahead. The large truck was really jacked up, with jumbo tires, and rebel flag stickers on the back window. Two young guys got out and waited by the side of the truck, as we walked toward them. They lived nearby, and were out for a cruise. Typical stereotyping might anticipate a problem, but I was walking burros, and wasn't typical, anyway. The friendly young men loved the journey we were on, and thought highly of my adventure. They gave me a couple of cold beverages and their friendliness cheered me greatly.

A couple more miles up the road, brought us to the tiny town of Brogan, 12 miles into the day. The retired Rancher who gave us the place to stay in Vale, had told me that the people who ran the store were good folks. He'd told them of our impending arrival, so they were happy to see us. Next to the store was a yard with a couple of cabins. The owners said that we could camp on the lawn. A neighbor brought over a bale of hay to give the burros some easy eating. It was a good place to stay, with easy access to the store, which was the hub of activity for the area. Brogan was very small, but the little store was hopping. Everyone in town seemed to stop at some point for gas, food, or just to visit. I bought some food, and joined the party on the porch. I was impressed by everyone's real friendliness, and by what a good business the cheerful owners ran.

One of the patrons on the porch told me how he and some other men had taken 2600 ounces of gold from a placer mine in the nearby hills. Gold mining had always excited me. In high school, I'd searched out and read every book I could find on the subject. I'd panned several times, through the years in the mountains, finding some, but never putting in enough time or effort to collect very much. I got gold fever, hearing that someone had recently found so much gold.

September 28.

We left the Brogan country store to waves and "good lucks." A short walk later, we turned onto a side road. We took the gravel road through the treeless hills, in a narrow steep-sided canyon. The stream flowing beside the road had lots of poison ivy along its banks, all in brilliant red fall colors. We hadn't been in much hilly terrain, since halfway across Idaho. I relished the rougher, hilly landscape. The uphill walk, through the scenic ravine, made us work more than we had for a while. Piles of river-rock along the canyon bottom were signs of past placer-gold mining. We passed a family in an RV on their mining claim. The prospectors said they'd found some gold, but mostly just did it for recreation and fun, rather than trying to make money. I told them about our journey, and my interest in placer mining. They admired our adventure. Lucy got the son to play stick with her while we talked.

The remote road took us out of the rough, narrow canyon and onto a wide-open basin, surrounded by hills. Sagebrush covered everything, but, on the farther higher mountains, I got a glimpse of a very exciting sight, trees. Large evergreen trees miles away to the north and west! I was like someone who'd been stranded on the ocean, finally seeing land. I let out a "HOORAY, trees ... REAL TREES!!" and did a little dance in the excitement of the moment. It was obvious why living down in the flats and stark brown hills around Adrian hadn't worked as a place to live. Mountains, with trees, were what I was looking for, yearning for. I felt that we were finally close to where we could spend the winter.

Malheur Reservoir lay in the desolate valley ahead. Only a couple of ranches dotted the entire area. A few vehicles passed by on the dusty road, in the stark, but pretty landscape. We'd come fourteen miles, steadily uphill, when we reached the sizeable reservoir, ready to stop walking. A little stream gave us a usable campsite, several hundred yards from the lake. I would rather have camped on the reservoir shore, but grazing was better near the little stream. Grazing was a way higher priority than the view. There were no trees or posts, so I had to tie the burros to sagebrush to unload them. I knew that tying the burros to sagebrush was an unsure thing, and remembered learning that lesson.

It was one of the earliest burro "experiences", at the beginning of my first trip. We were traveling along the highway, and I had tied the burros to some sagebrush during a break. A large truck roared by, spooking the burros, who easily ripped the flimsy sagebrush out of the ground. The panicked burros ran up the road. Luckily, the truck driver had seen what happened, stopped his big rig, jumped out, grabbed the lead-rope, and stopped the frightened beasts. It was a major event in my burro packing career since, if the truck driver hadn't been able to catch and stop the burros, they likely would've run all the way back home. Had that happened: I may have given up on the adventure, and never gotten into burro packing for the (very) long-haul.

September 29.

The next morning, as I packed the gear, a Native American couple stopped to talk. They were amused by my crew, and our adventure. They gave me enough Indian fry-bread and cheese for my breakfast and a later snack. Lucy usually got a piece of the action and wasn't often disappointed.

After we left the reservoir, the road north started a fairly long climb up the sagebrush covered mountains. We passed more placer tailings along the way. Part way up, we came to an old homestead with a couple of trees and a spring. I was surprised at how many springs we saw in the hills. From a distance, the hills looked totally dry, but there were little pockets of moisture here and there. It was hot in the sun, and we were climbing a south facing mountain. I was glad and excited to reach the summit. We were rewarded with a spectacular view. I tied the burros, and took in the magnificent scenery. Behind us, to the south, was the broad valley and Malheur Reservoir. Everything in that direction was burnt brown. The valley to the north was green, and to my huge excitement, even the south facing slope of the next mountain ridge was covered with conifers. We were at a climate transition zone; a change for the better as far as I was concerned. We were making huge progress; all we had to do was cross the next, even higher, mountain ridge, and we'd be in the Baker City area.

First, we had to go down this mountain. The road made a steady, fairly steep descent into the green valley separating the two mountain ridges. At the bottom, I realized that Libby had lost one of her rubber boots. I tied the burros to a fence and scrambled back up the road a half mile, before finding it. I frequently checked their hooves to make sure the important boots were still there, so I wouldn't have too far to go, if they did fall off.

We'd reached the few houses of Bridgeport. I wondered why a small mountain town was named for a port with a bridge. The 14-mile day had me plenty tired, so we stopped at a wide spot between the road and the fence. Water flowed in a nearby ditch. I was disappointed that I hadn't found a better spot, since it would only do for the night. We'd gone four long days in a row and needed a day off, for a real rest. I didn't know when we'd find water next, so I succumbed to fatigue and stopped for the night. Luckily, the road next to camp was very lightly traveled.

September 30.

As soon as we started, I was scouting for a place to rest for a day or two. We went three miles up the pretty green valley, when I found it. The "new" road took a shortcut over a little hill, while the old road stayed on the valley floor. Between was a kind of no-man's land. We stayed on the new road until it rejoined the old road, then cut back up the old road a hundred yards, to a good place to camp. It was a great spot, with a row of trees between us and the road, and water running right by my camp. The only negative was that the grazing was skimpy, but there still was enough grass to make it work.

I needed drinking water so, after I set up camp, I took my water-sack across the road to a ranch house. I was a little tentative about going to the house without the people seeing me with the burros, but I needed water. A dog came into the driveway, but instead of protectively barking at me, it rolled over on its back and begged for a scratch. An older man came out of the house to greet me. I told him my story and my need for water. He called for his wife to come out and meet me. A neighbor, who lived up the road, had seen us walk by and called to tell them about us. They'd been watching for us, but because we'd cut off the road just before them, they wondered what had happened to us. They'd lived in the area for most of their long lives, and were happy to see someone traveling with pack animals. I told them we were going to take the paved, twisting, narrow road over the next mountain ridge. They said we could take a small rugged road that went from their house to the top, instead. It wasn't on my map, but they assured me it went to the top of Dooley summit. They'd spent many decades there, grazing cattle on the mountainside, and I trusted their account. The Forest Road would be much better than the narrow, winding, dangerous highway. He was

Basque ... proud, and, despite his advanced age, still rode his horse, herded his cattle, and worked the ranch. We had a very enjoyable conversation. He said my burros could graze in the hay field, across the fence from camp.

I relaxed in the shade of a tree, listened to the radio, and absorbed the pastoral view set in the mountain country. Even though we'd only gone a short way, we took off the next day, to be thoroughly rested, for what would be a long climb up. Lucy and I walked a short way up the dirt road we'd take, just to get into the evergreen trees. I was very excited to be back among friends. I sat against the trunk of one of the largest of the tall silent giants, just to take in their feel. I surely felt more comfortable in trees, than in the open. I guess it was the monkey in me that made me love trees so much.

It was the first day of deer season. The mountain ridge was National Forest, so the area was alive with hunters. Several of them had been going up and down the usually quiet side road. One of them must have neglected to close the gate, because, as I came back down the road from my walk, the rancher's wife was out on the main road, trying to catch two horses, which had escaped their pasture. I ran to my camp and grabbed an extra halter, rope, and some grain. The horses were heading up the main road on which we'd arrived. I knew I could cut them off, if I hurried up the old road. I got in front of them, and with the magic of grain, was able to get a halter and rope on one of them in exchange for a handful of their much loved treat. Horses and burros are whores for a handful of grain, making it possible to get a hold on an otherwise difficult to catch animal. I walked the escapees back to the ranch, glad to help the couple who had helped me.

October 2.

We had one of our biggest climbs of the trip, to the top of Dooley Summit. Thankfully, we had the back road to make the long 2000-vertical-foot climb, instead of having to dodge cars on the highway. What really helped was that it went through trees, which grew close to the road, so that we were in shade all the way. Otherwise, on the south-facing mountain, in the sunshine, it would have been a mighty hot day.

We met a few hunters, who were interested in our trip, and wondered if I'd seen any game. I hadn't. Even though we weren't on a busy road, we wore orange for hunting season. It was a long slog up the hill, and since it was probably our last big climb of the journey, I was anxious to reach the top. I had a very strong feeling that we were close to ending our long journey. We could've taken another dirt road along the top of the ridge and down the far side of the mountain. It would've been a much longer route than the main highway. I would have enjoyed stopping on top, where it was flat and had grazing, but there was no water. I was tired and the day was getting late, so we took the shorter, faster, highway down the mountain. The traffic was light enough to make the narrow winding road not too dangerous. I could hear cars coming far enough away to take evasive action, and kept a piece of orange cloth in my pocket to wave, if it seemed like a vehicle needed help seeing us.

It was a 15-mile day as we neared the bottom. We stopped when we finally came to a workable spot to camp. A side draw, with a small trickle of water, joined the main drainage we'd followed down the mountain. It had enough flat, green, unfenced area for grazing. I felt good about what was happening. We were almost into Baker City's Elkhorn Valley, not far from the Grande Ronde Valley, La Grande, and, hopefully, a good place to live, God willing.

October 3.

A short distance down the drainage, the road intersected with the much busier Route 7. The highway had a lot of curves, which made me really tense, but we eased right through the hard spots. We came into a long, flat, green valley with something we hadn't seen for a long time: good green field-grass. I HAD to stop and let the burro girls graze for a long spell on the roadside, to give them a good fill of the "sweetness". What was amazing was that, after all of the walking and sometimes lousy grazing, the burros were still chubby.

The last stretch of highway into Baker City was tense with traffic on the narrow, winding road. Baker City was a relatively large town of 10,000, so I was wondering how we'd get through it. We pulled into the first gas station, at the edge of town, to get some fuel for my cook stove. I tied the burros at the edge of the busy parking lot, and got a lot of attention from customers. Two men stopped to talk for quite a while about my adventure, and one of them offered his yard for the night. He lived just a short, easy distance away. He was excited to have such unusual guests in his suburban yard, and was very friendly. The other man left on errands, but soon returned with his own offer. His parents lived about ten miles out of town, on a small ranch, and had a bunch of chores to be done. They had a truck and horse trailer, so, if I wanted to go there and work, we could ride there the next day. It seemed like a good plan as long as we could ride back into town, when the work was done. They lived back in the direction we'd just come from, and I didn't want to walk the busy winding road again.

Our host in Baker was very hospitable, and we had a good talk that evening. He took me on a drive around town to show me the sights. Baker was one of the biggest towns we'd been in all summer, with a great downtown area of old, scenic buildings and a strip of newer growth. The old downtown section was filled with buildings from the late 1800s to early 1900s, many of them very ornate and well built. Baker City had been a bustling wealthy hub for the nearby gold fields, farms, ranches, and major highways through the area, including the Oregon Trail. A railroad also went through town. The surrounding valley was very beautiful. The Elkhorn Mountains rose 5,000 feet above the green valley that stretched twenty-five miles to the north, and thirty miles to the east, where the even higher Wallowa Mountains soared. I was very positively impressed with the area, and was excited to be there.

The man had an RV on his property where I could sleep, so I didn't have to set up and take down the tent. The next morning he took me out to breakfast and another tour of the town. I felt pretty comfortable with Baker. There was enough going on that I could probably find some work. The only drawback I could see was that there wasn't any place with my beloved rock-and-roll music for dancing. It wasn't a total deal breaker, but I was still inclined to head on to La Grande. I would see what developed before deciding.

The other man, whom I'd met the day before, came by with the horse trailer in the late afternoon and drove us out to his parents' place. They lived in a side canyon back up the mountain we'd just come down. They had a beautiful piece of property, almost high enough to be in the evergreens, with green fields, and a stream running through it. Aspens grew along the stream. They had horses, cows, sheep and Springer Spaniels, that they raised, trained, and sold to people from all over the nation. I took my gear into one of the fields, a couple hundred yards from the house, and made camp near the pleasant little stream under the aspens. The burros were glad to be free from the ropes, with good grass. Part of the deal we'd worked out was that I would get a good home-cooked meal each night, and I gladly sat with them for good food and friendly conversation. They were a little hesitant at first, but within a couple of days, I felt like part of the family. I did a variety of odd jobs for four days, about five hours a day. I dismantled an old bridge across the stream, and made a few repairs on the house and some of the dog kennels. Conversation in the morning, great meals at night, we really hit it off well, and I had a wonderful time there.

Mornings were getting frosty; with ice on the dog dish, it was surely heading toward winter. I was invited to spend the winter in their RV, if I wanted. I just didn't see how I could make enough money so far from town, without a car, and I still had the inclination to go to La Grande. I thanked them for the offer, work, good food, and friendship. If La Grande didn't work out, I might come back. They hauled me back into town, and gave me more money than we had agreed on.

My first host in Baker was again glad for his unusual guests. He'd bought a Frisbee at a garage sale, for Lucy. She tore after her new toy with her usual intense abandon. He took me to the grocery and health food store, where I finally got my gruel ingredients. I'd been missing my gruel greatly, having only been able to find rice and lentils all summer, after my original gruel stash ran out. My complete gruel was much more complete nutrition than the simple substitute. After buying all of my supplies, I still had $150.

Chapter 16
Home Stretch

October 10 - October 21

October 10.

The ground was white with a hard frost. I took my time getting up, waiting for the sun to heat things a bit. Again, my host generously insisted on taking me out to breakfast. Later, I felt bad that I'd let him pay for the meal, since I had money at the moment. I was in a general state of excitement. We appeared to be close to our goal, even though I wasn't exactly sure where that was.

Once again, we took to the road. We bypassed town as much as possible, but the route was still pretty built up and busy, so I was somewhat tense. When we got past town, we joined the secondary highway north through the pretty farm valley. The road was fairly busy with traffic and not particularly enjoyable. Partway through the day, we left the busy highway for farm roads. The route was longer, but I preferred the lightly traveled back roads. They were so much less stressful than the paved highways, and we'd have a better chance to find somewhere to camp. The roads followed the familiar north-south, east-west grid, so we went one direction, then the other, as we made our way northwest through the scenic countryside. High mountains all around kept me looking at the sights as we slowly moved "one step at a time" closer to what I hoped would be a good place to spend the winter.

Most pressing at the moment was a place to spend the night. A miles-long, straight stretch made a sweeping turn to the left. The fence-lines came together at a right angle. The rounded turn created an undeveloped public land outside the corner, big enough for us to set up camp. The grass hadn't been grazed, so there was plenty for the burros to eat. A water trough, was just over the fence, for that need. There were numerous horses in the field, and the whole herd came over to the fence, to see what was parked next to their home. A sizeable herd of hyper horses so close at hand spooked the burros somewhat. They eventually went back to grazing, when they got used to all of the commotion the jostling horses made. The road had very little traffic, so being next to the road wasn't much bother. I pitched the tent for privacy. We'd walked about ten miles.

October 11.

In the morning, we strolled a few miles to the town of Haines. The small town was bisected by railroad tracks, which had a large freight train rumbling by as we arrived. We had to wait several minutes for the long wall-of-steel to pass. I let the burros graze on some roadside weeds, far enough from the tracks, to keep them from spooking. When the long-rumbling-train had passed, we crossed the tracks, and came into the block-long business district. I tied the burros in the town park for a short break, while I went into the country-store. The friendly owner gave me good cheer and advice on the route ahead. I bought a bag of tortilla chips for a snack. Being hungry, as usual, I greedily ripped open the bag and gobbled several handfuls of the crunchy treats, saving the rest for later.

We rejoined the paved highway, and a short distance out of Haines came to the cemetery. Some vacant land near the front gate looked like a possible place to camp. There was water in the cemetery. I tied the burros to the nearby fence and walked around to scout the prospects, but it wasn't a very good spot, and it was still early in the day, so we continued up the highway. Somewhere, Libby lost one of her rubber boots, but I didn't notice until we'd gone up the road a lot further. I tied the burros and walked back a little way, but figured that the boot probably fell off at the cemetery a couple of miles back. I didn't have much enthusiasm for retracing all of those steps. I felt pretty strongly that the journey was almost over, and that Libby would be OK for the short amount of walking we had left. The boot was just about worn out, so I'd need new boots the following year anyway. The loss wasn't too great, so I gave it up and we continued on.

From a long way away, I could see a man walking up the highway behind us with a large sack over his shoulder, picking up aluminum cans from the roadside. He was walking much faster than we were, so he eventually overtook us, and we had a good talk. He said he took many long walks through the area, prospecting for aluminum. I told him about can-collecting with the burros, and encouraged their use for his walking and collecting. He hadn't seen my burro boot, but told me of a good place to camp at some upcoming fishing ponds.

A sign at the side of the road marked the 45th parallel, halfway between the equator and the North Pole. Since starting the journey at the New Mexico-Colorado border, we'd not only gone a long way west, but also far to the north. Ten miles into the day, and one mile short of the next town, North Powder, we found a place to camp at the fishing ponds a quarter mile off the road. It was a great place to camp, except that, after I'd unpacked most of the gear, I discovered that someone had dumped several dead skunks nearby. There was a strong breeze, and by lugging my gear a hundred yards away, I was able to escape the smell, though it surely tarnished the otherwise good spot for me. I hoped very much that the wind didn't shift during the night.

October 12.

It was calm next morning. Fortunately, the frost had cut the smell of the skunk carcasses. "We left in haste, no time to waste, with dead skunks close upon us." That must be a good old saying somewhere. At least it was mine that morning. We passed under the interstate highway and into North Powder. Several people stopped to talk as we passed through the small town with a couple of businesses and small pretty houses. A few people were concerned about us walking through the narrow, winding, canyon-road that lay ahead on our way to La Grande. I'd already heard we might have a problem in Pyle's Canyon, but unless we walked up I-84, we had no other option. We weren't allowed to walk on interstate highways, and it wouldn't be fun anyway.

We walked a few more miles through pleasant farmland before the road climbed into dry, brown sagebrush-covered hills. I wasn't in a huge hurry, so we stopped for a short lunch break. Even the rolling sagebrush hills and plains were exciting! My level of intensity had gone up a notch with the taste of upcoming winter. Each frosty morning, the change became more noticeable. We definitely needed a winter home. The journey was nearly completed; the realization that, shortly, something wonderful would be over brought sadness. The joy of accomplishment was less sweet than the daily experience. I'd rather have just kept walking, but winter wouldn't allow that.

I habitually expected settling down for the winter to be a survival ordeal, compared to the magic of walking. I just felt SO at home traveling with my beloved burros and dog. The journey had been hard with all of the heat, bugs, distance walked, finding camps, food, etc. The pressure to not screw up and possibly suffer greatly, was always somewhat present. But each day had been my own. I thrived on the complex challenge. I believed that, in town, I'd struggle to make ends meet. The thought of having to get a job and do what I really didn't want to do, hour-after-hour, day-after-day, was just appalling, particularly after being so free for nearly five months. Knowing Freedom doesn't help one be a slave. It would be best if I could maintain my packing faith when I was in town. Unfortunately, I'd separated the two activities into different Universes, as if different laws operated in the two realities. The most devastating thing would be getting trapped in my town survival mode and not doing what seemed most important ... writing a book about the excellent adventure. In my better moments, I realized that my concepts of town were the problem, not town itself.

As we started up the road again, the issue was finding water for the night. My map showed a little drainage, not too far down a side road, near the railroad tracks, that might work. I tied the burros at the corner of the side road, and Lucy and I walked the quarter mile to see if the area might work. The land in the drainage was fenced and posted with no trespassing signs. Also, the possible campsites inside the fence were too close, to the heavily used railroad. We collected the burros, and headed slowly uphill. There was a little rise between the Elkhorn Valley, and the Grande Ronde Valley, which held La Grande. I assumed that the small climb was our last uphill of the trip. I tried to focus as clearly as I could on the passing scene ... soaking up as much as possible of the last steps of the wonderful journey.

The road crossed the railroad line at the top of the divide between the two valleys. The divide was at the butt end of an auspicious landmark, Craig Mountain. The mountain was a seven mile long ridge that went all the way to the Grande Ronde Valley. When I'd gotten the BLM map in Vale, I'd noticed Craig Mountain. The journey had started near Craig, Colorado, my name was Craig, and the journey would end near Craig Mountain. It all made sense. I was feeling very close to the end.

After crossing the tracks, we'd be traveling down the narrow Pyle's Canyon that I'd been warned about. I figured there'd be water down the canyon, but it sure seemed like a better plan to do the dangerous section of road the next day, when we'd be fresh and rested. Also, there might not be an open flat place for us to camp in the canyon. Just before the railroad bridge, a side road led to the half dozen houses of Telocaset, a mile away in a little valley, by the railroad tracks. I thought maybe an antenna on top of a nearby hill gave the town its name. I learned later that Telocaset was an Indian word meaning "top of the world". I could see that any possible camping place near Telocaset would be right beside the train tracks, and impossible. We'd have to camp near the intersection, even though we'd only gone 9 miles. There was a curve in the road just before it crossed the tracks. On the outside was another unused piece of land where we could camp, but no water was in sight. We continued over the railroad bridge. When we got to the other side, I looked back and saw what I was seeking right along the tracks. So close to the bridge that I hadn't been able to see it when we walked across, was a little seep-pond. I could surely get burro-water and water to boil from the little green pond. I immediately turned around, and went back over the bridge to the little piece of land.

I piled my gear near the fence, and staked out the burros. The water ran off the road-corner making a greener than normal spot in the otherwise brown terrain, for the girls. Being on the outside of the curve made us very visible to people coming from either direction. We had to do what we had to do; therefore, I accepted the campsite right next to the highway. I felt very exposed. I hopped the locked gate in the fence three times to get water from the little pond. I got enough to have a full load of water in camp, in case the burros wanted to drink in the morning.

Lucy kept me entertained by playing fetch with her new Frisbee. She dug her now favorite toy out of the gear, on her own accord. I sat in front of the tent, throwing the toy for the zealous Lucy, and watching an occasional passing car. There was a siding, where a train could pull over to let another train pass by, heading the other direction. This made it a busy and entertaining spot for the train-watcher I became for the evening.

October 13.

I didn't need much incentive to leave the exposed, roadside spot. We were on display that morning for anyone who traveled by. It was cold, so I still took time to make a hot drink. The road down the canyon started wide open enough, but soon it was a nervous curvy road. I kept my extra piece of orange cloth close at hand to wave at cars coming toward us. I strained to hear oncoming cars, but the road wound around cliffs here and there, so I couldn't always hear them coming from very far away. The narrow curvy road was fairly dangerous, since we had very few places to get off the road and escape the passing traffic. I just hoped we wouldn't get squished so close to the end, after we'd come so far. It just didn't seem like The Maker would take us through all we'd encountered only to smear us so near the end. Fortunately, everyone who drove by was paying attention.

All along the way, on our left, Craig Mountain rose higher-and-higher, eventually rising 2000 vertical feet above us. The mountain ridge was steep and craggy, mostly barren of trees except on the highest, steep north-facing slopes. I was enamored with my mountain, which otherwise wouldn't have been so special. Suddenly, the narrow constricted canyon broke out into the huge Grand Ronde Valley! A grassy meadow in the foreground opened into the great wide valley. The expansive basin was immediately impressive, about fifteen miles wide and twenty-five miles long, completely surrounded by timbered mountains. It felt like we'd spend the winter here. We made the last mile of the 9-mile day into the little town of Union. I was excited to be so close to the journey's end.

I'd heard of a possible place to camp in town at an old mill-site. We cut down a side street, in the middle of the downtown area, and went the few blocks to the prospective camping area. I wanted to stay in town if possible, so that I'd have easy access to entertainment and supplies. Across the road from the town athletic fields was an entire block of vacant land which was the old lumber-mill site. The mostly open field had a few trees here and there, and a thick row of brush and trees hiding a small stream. The place would work for camping; all I had to do was see if I could get permission to stay there.

As I eyed the situation, a man pulled up in a small pickup, and asked if he could take some pictures. He produced a good old 35mm camera and was obviously very much into photography. He was very friendly and excited to meet someone who had traveled in such a manner. He lived in town, and said he'd be back to visit. The property had one house, and we walked around to the far side of the property toward it. As we approached, a corralled Appaloosa horse next to the house went berserk, neighing, bucking, and desperately trying to get away from the strange burros. I backed down the street until the horse stopped weirding out, and tied the burros to a telephone pole, still in sight of the house, so I'd have proof of our mission. A teenage boy answered the door. I told him our story and of wanting to camp on their property. He called his parents to see if it would be o.k., and shortly reappeared at the front door, to tell me that we had permission to camp. We went to the other side of the land, and set up camp next to the thick undergrowth along the little stream. The trees and brush almost completely hid my tent from the street, even though we were right in the middle of the neighborhood. There was plenty of grazing, the stream was deep enough to get water for the burros, and I could get drinking water across the road at the ball fields.

I walked back the short distance to the center of town. Downtown was an enjoyable couple of blocks of old-style buildings, big trees, and a large clear creek. I got supplies at the rather good small-town grocery store. I liked the feel of the place, but there wasn't much work. Apparently, most people commuted the fifteen miles into La Grande.

That night, Union high school was having its homecoming football game, so I decided to attend the big event. They were playing against Elgin, another small town, about twenty-five miles away. At first, I wasn't sure who to root for, since it was also possible that I could end up living in Elgin. After a while, I decided it would be good for the home team to win, so I cheered for Union. I followed the action up and down the field along the sidelines, and had a good smile at the high-spirited event, even though Union lost.

The next day, the man who'd photographed us earlier came to visit, and gave me a quick tour of that part of the valley. He showed me an alternate route to the busy highway, which we could take toward La Grande. The problem with the side road was that, if we followed it all the way, it would dump us right in the middle of the relatively large town. I liked the looks of La Grande, with enough going on for me to figure out some way to make a living and have some entertainment. He gave me a good tour of the main parts of town so that I could get a feel for the place. I'd surely need to find a place to live on the outskirts of town, because of the burros.

We drove through the countryside a few miles to the east, toward the agricultural heart of the valley. The rural area came right to the edge of town, which was good for my need for a place for the burros, and not having a car to get into town. Many of the farms had RVs parked in their driveways. I imagined I could live in one of them. Since I began journey, I'd thought that an RV on a ranch was one of my best bets for a place to live. It would be inexpensive, and I'd have a place for the burros. I'd prefer my own space, if possible, to a room in someone's house. The biggest thing, other than a workable place for us, was that I didn't want to pay too much for rent. I might get trapped in survival mode, and not write the book, if I had to generate too much money. The way I'd always fallen apart when I worked full time made me believe I wouldn't write the book, if I got sucked into that world. Also, I needed to write the book that winter, while it was fresh in my mind, for the project to succeed. I was willing to live almost anywhere to make it work. During the tour through the valley, my helpful guide got confused about which way to go. We turned onto Wright Road. I remarked that it must be the "Right Road."

I was feeling stressed about finding what I needed soon. During the trip, I told people that I was going to find a place to live by just walking up the road, and meeting the right person ... at the right time ... who had just the right place for us. It had been fun saying that, but now that the day to do it was staring me in the face, I was a bit overwhelmed. I worked at remembering the foundation of my faith, that reality was being purposefully exuded into time and space at each moment, and that I performed best when positively focused in the moment in which I found myself. As in sports, one doesn't make the best play while worrying about failure. It was confidence in success that made athletes perform at their highest level. I had to focus clearly on the tasks at hand. Fear would throw a wrench into the works. Happy go lucky. Be Happy, Get Lucky. It was just the best platform to work from. I visualized the best possible outcome. If a negative scenario started playing in my head. I reminded myself of what brought the best results.

It was raining in the morning on our second day in Union. Weather reports, on the La Grande radio station, predicted stormy weather most of the day, so I decided to stay another day in Union, hoping for better weather the next day. Later in the morning, a policeman came to my camp. One of the neighbors had called us in as trespassers. He was friendly enough, but wanted confirmation from the caretakers that it was o.k. for us to be there. Lucy got him to throw the Frisbee several times. Again, I went over to the caretaker's house and this time met the adults. They said we weren't doing any harm, and it was fine for us to be there.

I walked into town several times during the day, for something to do. The highlight of the day was a long break at the coffee shop, and a visit to the interesting library in the center of town. The more-than-stout brick structure, a gift from Andrew Carnegie in the 1930s, was a miniature "Great Building of Power." I looked up information about the Oregon Trail, having gained huge respect and awe for those who made the long, hard journey. I was mostly looking for diary accounts, but someone had recently checked out those books. I saw and waved down the policeman who'd visited in the morning, and confirmed that we were OK to camp on the old mill-site. Lucy had stayed at the tent, tied in front, so I wouldn't have to figure out what to do with her while I was inside buildings. My very loyal companion preferred to be with my gear if she couldn't be with me. We'd been together almost every moment since I'd found her, and I'd become extremely attached to her. The challenge of finding the place to live loomed in my mind most of the day. I needed some major help from the Maker, and soon.

October 16.

The weather had cleared somewhat, but there were still clouds and bluster in the air. I realized, as I packed my gear that it might be for one of the last times on the adventure. Sometimes, packing the gear in the morning could be a bit of a chore. It used to be my least liked chore on burro trips, but at some point, I realized that, if I was packing the gear, it meant that I was on a pack trip: my Heaven, so it had became a cherished part of the trek. That morning everything was excitement.

We took back roads through the farm/ranch country. Just before joining the road at the base of Craig Mountain, we came to a rail crossing. There were cement pads with metal edges between the rails to make it smoother for cars. There were small gaps between the cement pads and the rails. Libby had crossed similar places several times on the trip, but for some reason, she balked at crossing the tracks this time. Hoofed animals naturally dislike crossing cracks and holes (the reason cattle guards work). So she had some justification for not wanting to cross. I tied her to a nearby road sign, and took the willing Beanie across the tracks and tethered her to a fence. Libby still wouldn't cross the minimal obstacle. I said laughingly and in mock worry, "We've come so far, only to be stymied by this tiny obstacle. Maybe we won't be able to make it." Surely, we could get across this. I performed the classic "full burro pull", leaning forward at a 45 degree angle, for maximum leverage, but Libby kept being a burro; more obstinacy than obstacle, for sure. I quit pulling, and led her off the road, along the tracks, and then, where it was just large

sharp gravel, wooden ties and rails she crossed without hesitating. That surprised me. I didn't think she'd cross that easily. Her stubbornness expressed her preference to cross the rocks rather than the scary looking cracks. Through the years, I always at least considered the burros' opinions, finding them more wise than not.

I was full of adrenalin from the situation of the large and looming need of a place to live before the winter. The road along the base of Craig Mountain ran into the main highway between Union and La Grande at the huge old historic Hot Lake Hotel. The massive brick building was in very rough shape and was under renovation. A long time before, it was a high-class resort. The hot springs had been a famous place since the early pioneers, and the Native Americans before them.

Right after Hot Lake was the important "fork in the road," either the round-about gravel road that the man in Union had suggested or my original choice of the main highway, toward La Grande. There was a wide grassy shoulder along one side of the main road that we'd be able to walk on, to avoid the frequent passing cars. Literally, within two steps of walking down the main highway I got the very strong feeling NOT to go that way. I pulled the burros off the highway, so I could stop and figure out which way we should go at this most important fork in the road. I imagined, as clearly as possible, us going up the main highway and then, the other alternative, going up the gravel road. The side gravel road definitely FELT like the best way to go, instead of my preplanned direction. I took the side road. The other side of the road was Ladd Marsh, a wildlife refuge. I looked at it as a possible place to camp, until I saw signs that the refuge was only open to people during wild fowl hunting season on Wednesday, Saturday and Sunday. It was Tuesday, and I doubted they'd really want us camping there anyway.

We'd come up the gravel road about a mile and a half since Hot Lake, right at the end of Craig Mountain, when a car stopped beside us with a couple and a baby inside. They were interested in what we'd done. In the middle of our conversation, another car came up behind them so that they had to move. I told them that, if they wanted to continue talking, they could pull ahead a little, and let the other car pass, which they did. When the other car pulled alongside, a ranch woman and her elderly mother also stopped to investigate. They really liked hearing about our walk from Colorado. I mentioned that we were looking for a place to live. They were late for an appointment, so they couldn't talk long, but said that they might have a place for us to live. They gave me their phone number and directions to their nearby ranch. They hurried down the road, and I went on to the first car that had stopped, and excitedly told them I might have a place to live. They said that they also had a possible place for us to live. They owned a piece of property back down the road near Hot Lake. All of a sudden we had two possible places to reside!

I decided to backtracked the mile and a half to their property to check that option first, since the other women were busy, and I needed a place to camp for the night anyway. I got to the property they'd described. A large marshy pond stretched before me. The owner came wading across. It was a unique location to be sure, over a hundred acres of land mostly on the steep face of Craig Mountain, but there was a big hitch. The rustic little cabin was almost inaccessible. One either had to hike way up around on the steep slope, or wade across the shallow pond. Also, it was just a summer cabin, with no electricity, running water, or heat, except for a portable kerosene heater. It was also tight to the foot of the steep north-facing mountainside, and after living in a similar situation in cold country before, I knew how very cold a house was in winter, if the sun was blocked by a mountain. The intriguing part of the property, other than being on the side of Craig Mountain, was that it had a hot spring. What an interesting situation, and what a bunch of difficulties all at once.

I stood on the far side of the pond wondering what to do. There was no way my burros were going to let me drag them across the muddy-bottomed pond. Another part of the property was accessible from the road, but had no water. The owner said he could haul over a large container of the pond water for the burros, and had an extra gallon of drinking water for me. They were going back home the next day, so I had to decide quickly. I told them I'd have to sleep on it, and give them my decision in the morning.

So near, and yet so far: a place to live but I couldn't reach it! I was amazed at being offered a piece of Craig Mountain and a hot spring, but the situation just didn't seem possible: Seven miles from town, no vehicle, minimal heat, and no inside plumbing. The lack of plumbing wasn't a huge problem if I had water reasonably near during the winter. The hot springs would supply that. I'd been without indoor plumbing many times over the previous fifteen years, so that would be routine. I spent the evening wondering what to do, with no clear idea which way to go.

October 17.

Morning brought my decision. I hopped up automatically, way before sunrise, and quickly began packing. I felt very clearly that this was not the right spot to stay over the winter. Early in the morning, the owners drove over to our camp, to see what I'd decided. I thanked them for their fine offer, but I didn't see how I'd be able to work out all of the difficulties. They told me to call them if I changed my mind.

I loaded the burros, for what I felt was probably the last time on this trip. We walked back up the road, which we'd started up the day before, to find the people who had the other possible place for us. A mile or so past where we'd turned back the day before, we approached a house close to the road. A large German shepherd in the yard took great exception to us passing his property. The owner came out of the house to see what the commotion was about, and put the dog in the house, to avoid any problems. He liked our story and let me come into his house to call the ranch lady.

Fortunately, they were home, and less than a mile away. We took the gravel road the short distance to their place. The long driveway had a cattle guard, but no gate through the fence anywhere in sight. I tied the animals to the fence and walked the quarter mile up the driveway to the small ranch house. I found the lady I'd met the day before. She thought I might be able to squeeze the burros past the cattle guard, but I didn't want to chance them being hurt. She told me about a gate through the fence, though it was down the road, and would tack another mile onto our journey. I assured her that after walking all the way from Colorado, we didn't mind walking another mile. That last mile was bittersweet. I knew that my wonderful summer odyssey was only a few steps from ending, but I was buoyed by the fact that our journey had been successful, and had most likely reached its rightful conclusion, even though I didn't yet know the particulars of the living situation.

I tried to absorb the moment as much as possible as we walked across the pasture to the ranch house. In the last hundred yards, there was a small stream Libby didn't want to cross. I chuckled at one last obstacle in the final steps of the journey. I followed the script, tied Libby, took Beanie across, tied her on the far side, and with some effort, pulled the reluctant Libby across the last obstacle of the trip.

The lady's husband was in his shop. He was a good mechanic, and a rather jovial fellow. I pulled the gear from the burros, and put it in a garage so that their many dogs and cats wouldn't despoil the pile. The burros went into a nearby pasture, finally free of their ropes.

They told me the situation. Her mom was quite elderly and lived in a new trailer next to the house. Her mom's old ranch house was five miles away, empty, and they wanted someone in it, to keep an eye on the place. Parts of the old house were over a hundred years old. Some of the rooms had things stored in them, but I'd essentially have an entire house to myself. The house sat on more than 300 acres of farmland and pasture, surrounded by large mature trees that had been planted over many decades. The beautiful yard was a treed-oasis surrounded by pastures and cropland. Craig Mountain was very visible, just five miles away. It was seven miles from town, and it would be a challenge to get to town for groceries, etc., but since they were going to let me live there for free, I wouldn't need to generate much money. They had a bicycle I could use, when the strong winds weren't blowing, and they might be able to get an old farm truck running for me. Compared to living in a travel trailer, this was going to be a castle and a great piece of land for all of us.

The house wouldn't be ready to be move into for a few days, so I camped in the shop until it was ready. I got to visit with the good, generous people, who were loaning me their house, and felt very accepted right away. Walking burros from Colorado was a good way to move into a rural area. I doubted that I would find such a perfect place to live by looking in the classified section of a newspaper. Such an outstanding miracle required a lot of BURRO MAGIC! The helpful ranchers took me on tours around town to see the sights. The situation seemed perfect for me to write the book. YAHOO ... It was the perfect ending to the perfect journey. I'd left with $95 and reached the end with $110, more than a 15% profit. Who said there wasn't any money in burro packing?

We were loaded into a trailer, and taken to our new home. Five months on the journey. It sure felt like the Right place, Right off Wright Road. The Right place to Write.

P.S.

10-11-12: Bend, Oregon.

Now, two years since completing the final two legs of the Burro-Adventure to Bend; I had a philosophic realization as important as ALL of my Burro-trips put together: We are SUBJECTS "using" OBJECTS; not OBJECTS with things happening TO us.

37180611R00188

Made in the USA
Charleston, SC
29 December 2014